Food City

Routledge
Taylor & Francis Group

Food City

Dedicated to Leon van Schaik and Martyn Hook

First edition published 2014
by Routledge
711 Third Avenue, New York, NY 10017

Simultaneously published in the UK
by Routledge
2 Park Square, Milton Park, Abingdon, Oxon OX14 4RN

Routledge is an imprint of the Taylor & Francis Group, an informa business

British Library Cataloguing in Publication Data
A catalogue record for this book is available from the British Library

Library of Congress Cataloging-in-Publication Data
Lim, C. J.
Food city / CJ Lim.
pages cm
Includes bibliographical references and index.
1. Food industry and trade--Case studies. 2. Food--Transportation--Case studies. 3. Food service--Case studies. 4. City planning. I. Title.
HD9000.5.L554 2014
338.1'91732--dc23   2013038033

ISBN13: 978-0-415-53926-5 (hbk)
ISBN13: 978-0-415-53927-2 (pbk)
ISBN13: 978-1-315-85256 -0 (ebk)

Typeset in DIN by Studio 8 Architects

Printed and bound in Great Britain by TJ International Ltd, Padstow, Cornwall

Contents

4

Preface

Over the centuries, there has been an undeniable symbiosis between urbanization and agricultural development. The systemization of food production would sustain the birth and maturation of the city, and its importance was such that it would shape the governance, religion, education, transport, health and foreign affairs of urban existence. Food is no less important to the city now as it was then, yet with the advent of industrial and post-industrial economies it has been relegated to the hinterlands, physically and ideologically.

'Food City' reassesses this relationship in an era of unrelenting urbanism and chronic global food shortage, two interdependent phenomena that must reach a rapprochement to prevent an impending catastrophe that is human as much as environmental. A companion to 'Smartcities + Eco-warriors' (Routledge, 2010), 'Food City' explores the same theme of the transformation of cities, but looks at how the creation, storage and distribution of food has been and can again become a construct for the practice of everyday life. The scope of 'Food City' is more ideological and polemic. The book is the result of investigations into the reinstatement of food at the core of national and local governance – how it can be a driver to restructure employment, education, transport, tax, health, communities and the justice system, re-evaluating how the city functions as a political entity. The first section of 'Food City' consists of a series of essays in which the extant political, legal, educational, medical, financial and employment frameworks of the city are reinterpreted through the medium of food and the spatial implications of how the city is governed. Voices of urban residents, stakeholders of varying levels in the city's gastro-economy, permeate through these essays; a reminder that the city is nothing without its inhabitants.

This is followed by a declaration of the policy and aims set out by a notional political party for sustainable living in the United Kingdom, culminating in an ambitious piece of polemic titled the 'Food Parliament', a system of architectonic components that operate as a sustainable stratum over the City of London. The project, described in drawings, is premised on the adoption of food as the local currency standard of London. Given the failures of our debt-based monetary system, the fragility and unsustainable nature of our agricultural practices, and the social exploitation orchestrated by vast unregulated corporations, a reserve currency backed by the tangible asset of food is improbable but not illogical.

The Food Parliament is a provocation; the physical outlandishness of the proposal intended to raise serious questions about the priorities of our governing bodies. Formally unorthodox, the components of the Parliament become metaphors for food immediacy, nutrition, health, job opportunities, green income sources and social cohesion. Each element is designed as an architectural component using spatial relationships to reframe the spaces of food consumption and production, analysed through historical precedent, function and form. Although the Parliament is a fantastical construct, the principles that underlie its premise and the justification for its existence, in some form or other, are both real and urgent.

The book concludes with a look at the earliest civilizations in which life revolved around food practice, bringing the account full circle.

facing page: Makola Market, Accra

The Urban Banquet

14

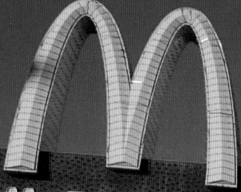

McDonald's

POLO TOWERS

Hawaiian
Marketplace

hollywood

CABLE CENTER
SHOPS

T-SHIRT + | SHOE'S
LEATHER
LUGGAGE

COLD BEER | ONE STOP | COLD WINE

SAVE $$ BOOK TOURS HERE ►

Grand Canyon • Las Vegas • Hoover Dam

OFFICIAL TOUR CENTER

Helicopter

PREMIER

JAQUET DROZ

TOURBILLON
LAS VEGAS

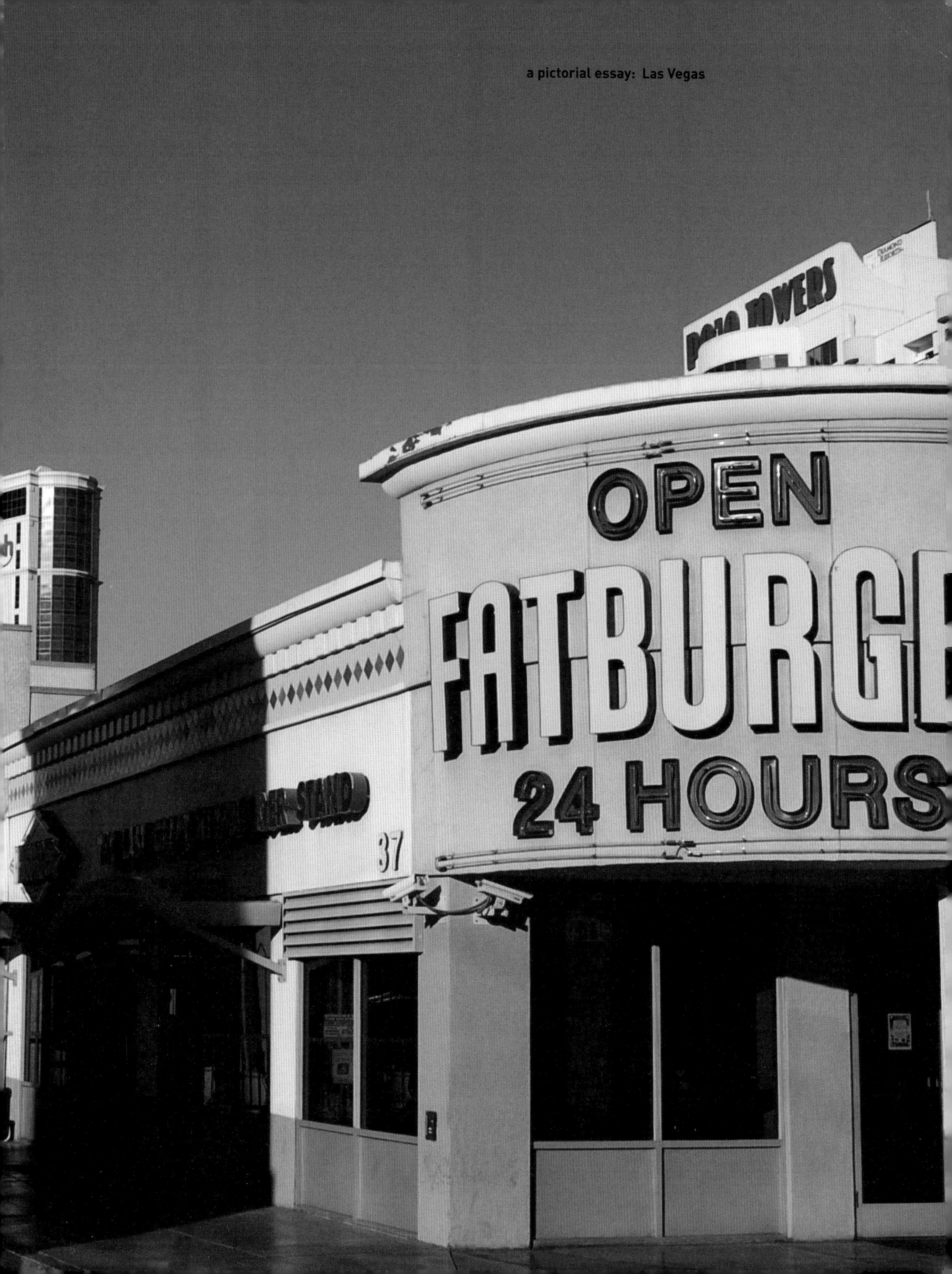
OPEN
FATBURGE
24 HOURS
37
STAND

20

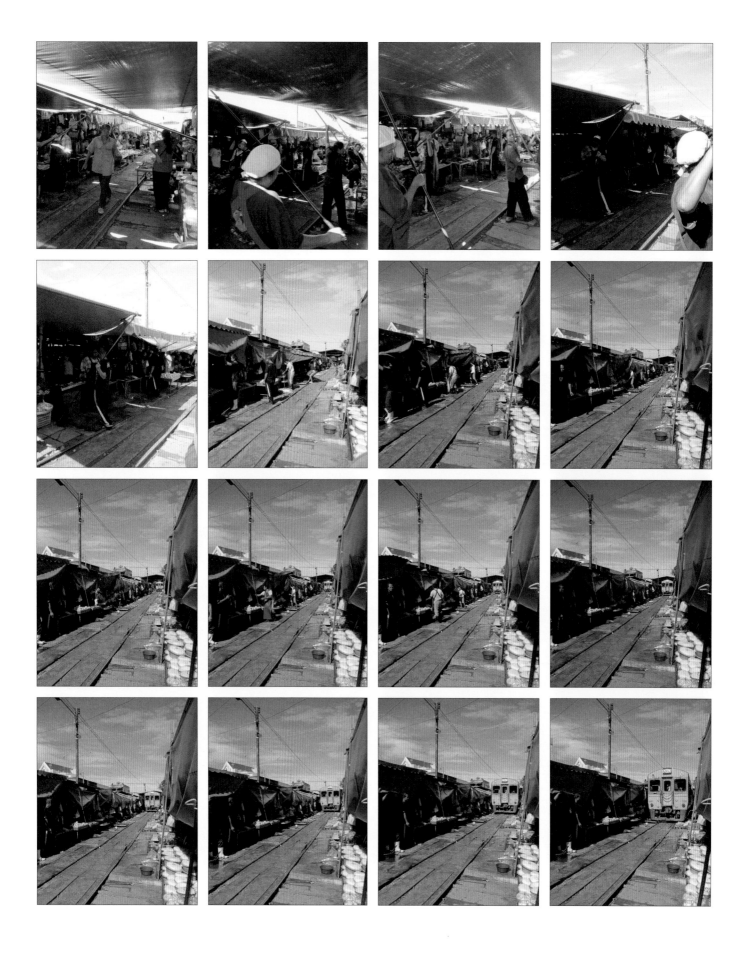

a pictorial essay: Sisimiut and (bottom) Oksboel

30

A Bird in the Hand is Worth Two in the Bush

'There is a serious snag from the foreign visitor's point of view. This is, that you practically don't find good English cooking outside a private house. If you want say, a good, rich slice of Yorkshire pudding you are more likely to get it in the poorest English home than in a restaurant, which is where the visitor necessarily eats most of his meals.'

– George Orwell, 'In Defence of English Cooking', 1945

Power within the food industry is concentrated in the hands of a few. The large multinational corporations, known as 'Big Food', have come to dominate the global trade of food and beverages; in 2005, only 100 retailers controlled 40% of the total global grocery market.[1] Processed food accounts for three-quarters of global food sales and Big Food control a third of this processed market.[2] These monopolies extend beyond the direct trade of food itself; in 2008, the top ten agrochemical corporations were responsible for 90% of the global sale of pesticides and only ten grain corporations controlled 67% of the US$22 billion seed market.[3] On average, people spend 20% of their income on food and the global food market is the domain of a few large companies, gaining increasing control over people's everyday diets and expenses.[4] The influence of these corporations is cited by some as the reason for a visible 'nutrition transition' from simple, traditional, locally sourced meals to highly processed purchased foods.[5]

Often overlooked when analysing the larger systemic inequalities of the global food trade, are the gender inequities inherent in the food system. Women account for 43% of the agricultural workforce, however they are often disenfranchised from the system even at a local level. Despite this, the potential of women is huge and the UN Food and Agriculture Organization (FAO) argues that 'if women had the same access to productive resources as men, they could increase yields on their farms by 20–30%. This could raise total agricultural output in developing countries by 2.5–4%, which could in turn reduce the number of hungry people in the world by 12–17%.'[6]

Around the world, the trade of food has in many cases defined and acted as a catalyst for the traditional roles men and women play in society. In many lower-income countries, women play a larger role than men in the agricultural sector, typically in subsistence production.[7] Trade liberalization, leading to an increase in the production of cash crops, affects men and women differently as a result. Men, predominantly engaged in the farming of cash crops, have seen an increase in income and women, predominantly producing food for local markets and subsistence, have seen a decrease in profits.[8] In India, wages from cultivation are markedly different between the genders; women average 20% of men's wages.[9]

facing page: The Butter Exchange in Cork was central to the urban and social development of the city.

1+3. ETC Group, 'Who owns nature? Corporate power and the final frontier in the commodification of life', ETC Group, Winnipeg, MB, 2008

2. R Patel, 'Stuffed and starved: Markets, power and the hidden battle for the world food system', Portobello Books, London, 2007

4. A Regmi & M Gehlhar, 'Processed food trade pressured by evolving global supply chains', US Department of Agriculture, Amber Waves Magazine, 2005

5. B Popkin, 'Part II: What is unique about the experience in lower- and middle-income less-industrialised countries compared with the very-high income countries? The shift in the stages of the nutrition transition differ from past experiences!', Public Health Nutrition Vol. 5, 2005, pp.205–214

6+8. 'The State of Food and Agriculture 2010–2011: Women in agriculture – Closing the gender gap for development', Food and Agriculture Organization of the United Nations, Rome, 2011, p.vi

7+9. R Nugent, 'The Impact Of Urban Agriculture On The Household And Local Economies', pp.79–80 [http://wentfishing.net/farmlit/Theme3.pdf], retrieved 16 July 2013

Movements opposing the global monopolies of Big Food are gaining strength. To name a few, the ideals of Via Campesina, the Slow Food movement and Occupy actively protest and promote alternative practices. Pertinent to the study of urban space, the Occupy movement saw the invasion of public, urban spaces globally by a movement opposed to the control and distribution of wealth and resources and the global social and economic systems in the world today. The actions of Occupy and similar movements, such as Tahrir Square in Cairo and the Puerta del Sol in Madrid, show how the city has emerged as a portal through which global trends can be analysed; not purely a reflection of the industry of a single place and its immediate surroundings. Further, these urban spaces are emerging as sites of transformation out of the monopoly of the food industry. As sociologist Saskia Sassen argues, 'the city is a space where the powerless can make history.'[10]

Transition Town Totnes

In the British town of Totnes a uniquely powerful movement is taking place. Relative to similar sites in the UK, the town has an independent character. It has a small population of just below 8,000 residents and has become renowned as a place where people can live a 'New Age' bohemian lifestyle.[11] Labelled by Time magazine as the capital of 'New Age chic', the residents of Totnes have actively campaigned against the presence of large corporations in their local food markets.

Totnes has joined the Transition Towns (TT) movement; a community-based response to the pressures of globalization and globally declining fuel stocks. A key area of the movement is creation of a sustainable food industry for their communities. The TT community believe in 'food feet, not food miles!'; that their food should be sourced from their immediate local environment. The town has even introduced a local currency! Accepted by over 70 businesses, the aims of the Totnes pound are to preserve the circulation of income within the community and its local industry.[12]

In Totnes, the greengrocers deliver boxes of produce to the cafés, the bakeries prepare cakes for the delis; everyone knows each other and is interested in each other's business plans. Darren Thorne and Lucy Hornsey, from Seeds2Bakery agreed, 'It's bringing people into town, but what's best is that all the retailers here are working together instead of trying to compete with each other'.[13]

Unsurprisingly, in 2012, faced with the prospect of a Costa Coffee opening in the town, Totnes declared war on the global food giant. The story of the anti-Costa sentiment in Totnes is a pertinent case study of how the notion of localism, a phrase used by the town's politicians, is tried and challenged.

The contested site is in a prime location and transport hub where most tourists first arrive in the town, and previously belonged to a local wholefood business. Frances Northrop, the manager of Transition Town Totnes, has voiced the concern: 'they'll come straight in, and they'll see a Costa Coffee. And if people are in a new place, a lot of people think: "I'm not going to try the unknown – I'm going to go somewhere that I recognise".'[14] The Chief Executive of Whitbread, the conglomerate that oversees the coffee outlet in the UK, has also spoken about the extensive reach of the coffee shop. 'People really don't want to walk very far for a coffee,' he has said. 'We can have them a couple of hundred yards apart on a

facing page from top left clockwise: Cairo, Ipoh, Mumbai and Seoul. Low investment food practice can offer women a stable source of income.

10. S Sassen, 'The Global Street', The Huffington Post Blog, 2011 [http://www.huffingtonpost.com/saskia-sassen/the-global-street_b_989880.html], retrieved 15 March 2011

11. J Hodgson & R Hopkins, 'Transition in Action: Totnes and District 2030, an Energy Descent Action Plan, Transition Town Totnes', 1st Edition, 2010

12. R Sharp, 'They don't just shop local in Totnes – they have their own currency', The Independent, 2008 [http://www.independent.co.uk/news/uk/this-britain/they-dont-just-shop-local-in-totnes--they-have-their-very-own-currency-818586.html], retrieved 18 August 2013

13. R Wearn, 'Totnes: The way forward for the UK's ailing High Streets?', BBC News, 2013 [http://www.bbc.co.uk/news/business-209471620], retrieved 18 August 2013

14. J Harris, 'Totnes: the town that declared war on global capitalism', The Guardian, 2012 [http://www.guardian.co.uk/business/2012/aug/15/totnes-war-global-capitalism], retrieved 18 August 2013

really busy high street, then another at a retail park and another at the station.'[15]

The town has responded to the perceived threat of an impending Costa Coffee by using the communal urban space to celebrate and communicate the independent character of Totnes. Residents held a two week Independent Coffee Festival, the culmination of which was a barista competition on World Fairtrade Day. Baristas from all of the unique coffee shops in Totnes were offered prizes for the quality and credentials of their fairtrade coffee, as well as in the calibre of their 'coffee art' – the ability to draw images in the froth.

The 'No To Costa' campaign was based on the legal obligation of councils to consider a planning application's effect on the 'vibrancy and vitality' of the area; however the planning committee would go on to approve Costa's plans by 17 votes to 6. Of the decision panel, only four of the councillors directly represent Totnes. There has been strong local opposition to the application at local planning meetings; at one, 100 people were ordered to leave a single planning hearing.[16]

The Totnes community are now mobilizing contingency plans for how to respond if, or when, the Costa actually opens in town. Residents are planning various acts of civil disobedience – such as regularly visiting Costa, ordering tap water and drinking it painfully slowly; another proposal is to constantly paste anti-Costa posters on the windows. The activities of the residents of Totnes are evidence of a movement by local communities opposed to a pervasive multinational capitalism encroaching on their food markets. Transition towns are emerging throughout the world, with 380 initiatives listed in the UK alone.[17]

The Golden Export
Other cities have embraced and capitalized on the global market. Butter exported from Ireland built the city of Cork into a powerful economy that dominated world dairy markets during the late eighteenth century. Cork was the great emporium of the butter trade, and its rural economy was largely orientated toward dairy product production. Land became exclusively devoted to maintaining dairy herds as market capacity grew during the Industrial Revolution and beef become a byproduct of milk production in the region.

The geographical location of Cork was vital to its expansion. Located at the head of one of the finest natural harbours in the world, the city became a crossroads of the food trade between northern Europe, the Americas and further afield. The role of the butter merchants was not only central to its commercial development, but also to the civic, social, religious, educational and artistic life of the city.

Trade in the city peaked in the eighteenth century. The butter trade was generating considerable wealth in the city and would shape its use to present day. The centre of the city had become a zone of industry accommodating the production of butter, slaughter houses and tanneries. To avoid the disease and stench of the centre, the wealthier residents moved to the waterside suburbs to live. These distinctions still persist, and nowadays people still prefer to live outside the commercial centre.[18]

To control demand at its peak, 'The Cork Butter Exchange' was established by a voluntary organization to oversee the public inspection, branding and making of butter for export from the city in 1769.[19] Daily price quotations were monitored as closely as the stock exchange is today in a large building located in the centre of the city. Specialist routes to facilitate the butter trade were built through Cork. Dairy farmers would deliver butter in simple wooden containers, colloquially known as 'firkins', on horse-drawn carts to be unloaded at the Butter Exchange, along main routes that became known as 'butter roads'.[20]

The rich grassland in the countryside around Cork city provided an appropriate landscape for grazing cattle. Dairy cows generally fed with high-quality forage, produce more milk with less supplemental concentration than cows generate on lower-quality forage. Natural grasslands provide grazing animals with a richer and more diverse diet than pastures used for more intensive farming.

37

Cork is now the second largest city in Ireland. The butter market has since declined. This is largely attributed to the Exchange's reluctance to modernize in the face of foreign competition. Amongst other reasons, the introduction of margarine, labelled a 'rogueish compound' by the Exchange, offered a tasty, cheaper butter supplement.[21] The landscape of Cork city continues to be influenced by its predominant trade. Fittingly, for a city which was built on the strength of its ability to capitalize on the global market, Cork now is a hub for pharmaceuticals and IT technology with an established global reach.

Kobe Beef

'Kobe beef' is considered by many to be the best type of beef available in the world. As with Cork's 'golden export', Kobe beef is a highly specialized product. The acclaimed meat refers to cuts of beef from the black Tajima-ushi breed of Wagyu cattle, raised according to strict tradition exclusively in Hyogo Prefecture, Japan.[22] Gourmet chefs worldwide prize Kobe beef for its full flavour, tenderness and the high amount of intramuscular fat, called 'marbling'.

As beef consumption increased in Japanese society, farmers began seeking ways to distinguish their product in the market. Kobe beef farmers hire workers to massage the backs of their cows, claiming that the soothing action relaxes the animals and tenderizes the meat.[23] Some cultures practice force-feeding of cattle which increases the weight of the animal, and they believe, the quality of the meat. Kobe beef farmers believe these practices stress the animals, encouraging them to drink beer to increase their appetites for the high quality feedstock offered instead.

Kobe beef is prohibitively expensive and importation from Japan is virtually impossible. The one essential rule concerning Kobe beef is that the Wagyu cattle must be slaughtered in the Kobe region of the country. However, due to a severe shortage of available land, Japanese beef growers have recently allowed a select group of international cattlemen to raise the Wagyu cattle in their native countries.[24] The terms of the license, nevertheless, require the cattle to be transported back to Kobe in Japan for final processing.[25]

The culture of the quintessential American burger is discussed in more detail in the chapter on food and culture in the city. However for a time, Burger King offered a special limited edition Kobe beef burger on its menu. The home of the Whopper charged £85 for the delicacy,[26] the proceeds of which went to charity. Only 100 of the burgers were offered, and food critics descended on the fast food chain to critique

15+16. J Harris, 'Totnes: the town that declared war on global capitalism', The Guardian, 2012 [http://www.guardian.co.uk/business/2012/aug/15/totnes-war-global-capitalism], retrieved 18 August 2013

17. 'Transition Initiatives Directory' [http://www.transitionnetwork.org/initiatives], retrieved 18 August 2013

18. 'Cork Travel Guide' [http://www.insightguides.com/destinations/europe/ireland/the-southwest/county-cork/cork-city/overview?leadimage.position=3], retrieved 18 August 2013

19. 'History of Butter', The National Dairy Council [http://www.ndc.ie/butter/history-butter.asp], retrieved 18 August 2013

20+21. C Ryne, 'At the Sign of the Cow: The Cork Butter Market: 1770–1924', The Collins Press, Cork, 1998, p.54

22, 24+25. L Augustin-Jean, H Ilbert & N Saavedra-Rivano, 'From Products of Origin to Geographical Indication in Japan: Perspectives on the Construction of Quality for the Emblematic Productions of Kobe and Matsusaka Beef', 'Geographical Indications and International Agricultural Trade: The Challenge for Asia', Palgrave Macmillan, Basingstoke, 2012, pp.139–163

23. JW Longworth, 'Raising Wagyu Cattle in Japan' [http://www.luciesfarm.com/artman/publish/article_39.php], retrieved 20 August 2013

26. 'Haute Cuisine Rapide', The Economist, 2008 [http://www.economist.com/blogs/freeexchange/2008/04/haute_cuisine_rapide], retrieved 20 August 2013

the reinvention of the everyday burger. The Kobe beef burger was embellished with an array of luxuries; garnished with blue cheese, foie grois, balsamic vinegar and sandwiched between buns made of white truffle flower dusted with Iranian saffron. Instead of the traditional fries, the Kobe beef Whopper was accompanied by a side of banana shallots fried in a tempura batter made using Cristal champagne.

Cornish Pasty

In February 2011, the 'Cornish pasty' won official preservation under the EU protected food names scheme.[27] The new prestige elevates the humble pasty's status to a culinary pedestal that sits alongside the likes of Camembert cheese, Parma ham, Champagne and Balsamic Vinegar. A far cry from the nineteenth century tin-miners who originally cooked up the 'pasty' as a handy form of packed lunch.

The Cornish Pasty Association, formed in 2002 by 50 pasty makers based in Cornwall, exists to protect the quality and the reputation of the popular snack. They advise that a genuine Cornish pasty should be 'D' shaped, and 'crimped at the side', with a filling of 'chunky' beef (making up at least 12.5% of the pasty), swede, potato, onion and a light seasoning with no artificial ingredients.[28] It is also suggested that the pasty is cooked raw in the oven. As for the pastry itself, they demand that the casing must be 'golden in colour, savory, glazed with milk or egg, and robust enough to retain its shape throughout the cooking and cooling process without splitting or cracking'.[29]

The Cornish pasty joins 47 other British products in receiving protected status.[30] The ruling from the European Commission means that only pasties made in Cornwall, following the traditional recipe, can use the name. However, authentic Cornish pasties can be baked elsewhere in the country so long as they are at least prepared in the West Country. Protected Geographical Status is a legal framework defined in EU law to protect the names of regional foods. The UK's other 47 protected products include Cornish clotted cream, Melton Mowbray pork pies, Arbroath smokies, Kentish ale, Whistable oysters, Gloucestershire cider, West Country farmhouse Cheddar cheese, Welsh beef, Jersey Royal potatoes and Yorkshire forced rhubarb.[31] These commodities all have a close connection to a specific part of the country and are closely bound into the lives and identities of the communities that produce them. As highlighted by David Roda of the Cornish Pasty Association, 'Thousands of people in Cornwall are involved in the pasty industry, from farmers to producers, and it's important that the product's quality is protected for future generations.'[32]

The food protection legislation came into force in 1992, with the purpose of protecting the reputation of the many regional foods and delicacies that exist throughout the country.[33] By promoting rural and agricultural activity, the law helps producers to obtain a premium price for their authentic food products. The enforced status eliminates any unfair competition and prevents consumers being mislead by non-genuine products that may be of inferior quality or of a different flavour. Intellectual property is now one of the most valuable assets in commercial transaction. Companies are forging alliances with each other in order to heighten the value of their intellectual property assets and to obtain mutually beneficial competitive advantages through cross licensing. As in the case of the Champagne region, protecting or controlling a food trade can be profitable. Successful strategies often specialize in a particular segment of the market or method of trading or in developing a holistic system of production, distribution and marketing to prevent external syphoning of profits.

left: At Shad Thames in London, a century of spice storage has infused the brickwork of the buildings with pungent odours.

27. 'Protected food names: guidance for producers' [http://www.defra.gov.uk/food-farm/food/protected-names/], retrieved 18 June 2010

28+29, 32. 'Cornish Pasty – Historical Information' [http://www.cornishpastyassociation.co.uk/pasties.html], retrieved 18 June 2010

30. K Salter, 'British Food: Protect and Serve', The Guardian, 2012 [http://www.guardian.co.uk/lifeandstyle/wordofmouth/2012/aug/08/british-food-protect-and-serve], retrieved 22 August 2013

31+33. Agriculture and Rural Development, European Commission [http://ec.europa.eu/agriculture/quality/door/list.html?locale=en&filter.country=GB&recordSelection=all], retrieved 18 June 2010

Seasoned Monopoly

The Oostindisch Huis, located upon a picturesque canal in the city of Amsterdam, was once the headquarters of the powerful 'Dutch East India Company'. Founded in 1602, it was the first multinational company to hand out shares, thanks to a lucrative food business.[34] For decades the company dominated global trade, transporting spices using large ships on many expeditions to the East to bring back spices, herbs and other riches that fuelled Amsterdam's 'Golden Age'. Ships sailed from the city to the Baltic Sea, North America and Africa, as well as present-day Indonesia, India, Sri Lanka and Brazil, and formed the basis of a worldwide trading network.

The demand for spices in Europe continued to increase throughout the sixteenth and early seventeenth centuries. At the start of the 1600s, the Portuguese were the only Europeans who imported spices from the Far East.[35] Before long, the Dutch expelled the Portuguese from the Spice Islands and became the exclusive supplier of spices to Europe. The spice business allowed the city of Amsterdam to prosper. The city became one of the most important ports in the world during the 'Dutch Golden Age', as a result of its innovative business developments in the food trade.

Similarly in London, the rapid expansion of the East India Company in the seventeenth century saw the city embracing ships bringing spices from Java and Sumatra, chests of tea, bales of silk and crates of porcelain from Canton, now modern day Guangzhou.[36] These great ships, known as the 'East Indiamen', were too large for the Pool of London, so they had their aromatic cargoes unloaded onto large flat bottom barges down the River Thames and brought to the Company's warehouses at East India Docks.

Shad Thames

At the beginning of the twentieth century, when London was still the world's most prolific port, the Docklands in the East End employed thousands of people, who sent and received goods from all over the world. Today the area has been redeveloped into high-rise apartment blocks, banks and offices and only remnants of the aesthetic of the buildings are reminiscent of the area's industrial past.[37]

The converted warehouses retain their original characteristic features of brickwork, winches and large lettered signage. Most of the signs name the commodities which were originally stored in them. 'Vanilla & Sesame Court', 'Cayenne Court', 'Wheat Wharf', 'Tea Trade Wharf' and further buildings named after cinnamon, cardamom, fennel, caraway, ginger, cumin, tamarind, clove, anise and coriander, adorn the weathered storage buildings, bringing an air of fantasy to the cold industrial environment. A century of spice storage has infused the brickwork of the buildings with pungent odours. Residents of the now converted flats report that they can still detect the scent of spices from the distant countries after which their buildings were named.

Deindustrialization

There are 374 shrinking cities in the world.[38] The countries with the most are the United States with 59, followed by China, Germany, Brazil and Italy. Detroit, the largest city in the US state of Michigan is one of these shrinking cities and currently has 40 square miles of vacant land, as much area as the entire city of San Francisco. Recent US Census results have published that the population of Detroit has decreased by 25% in the past decade, and a further 60% since 1950.[39] In 2010, the city had a population of 713,777 and was ranked as the eighteenth most populous city in the United States.[40] At its peak in 1950, the city was the fifth largest in the US, but it has since seen a major reduction in its population.[41]

Once referred to as the 'Paris of the West' for its architecture and elegant boulevards, many of the city's thriving neighbourhoods have become barren wastelands. The slow departure of people from a once prosperous city is the result of a declining auto industry.

After decades of decline, plans are taking root in Detroit to save the vitality of the city by reducing its size. Fields and farmland are slowly replacing entire neighbourhoods of gutted, burned-out houses that will return parts of the city to prairie land, more reminiscent of its nineteenth century appearance.

In 2011, the city's mayor, Dave Bing, pledged to knock down 10,000 structures in his first term as part of a radical plan to reconfigure the city of Detroit to reflect its shrinking population.[42] Bing recognized opportunities to save resources and instead focused development efforts in healthier areas of the city. However, even this ambitious goal has been criticized for only taking care of approximately one-ninth of the city's 90,000 abandoned properties.[43] In support of the new directive, the Bank of America has also pledged to demolish a further 100 abandoned Detroit homes currently in its possession.[44] The costs are estimated by the bank to be in the region of approximately $1 million,[45] with plans to donate the newly gained land plots to the city for green space, urban farming or redevelopment. Until recently, the city did not have adequate funds to tackle its growing list of houses slated for demolition. But $20 million in government funding has helped to kick-start the effort.[46]

Demolition, particularly of historic buildings, is a sensitive issue in Detroit, often leading to battles between developers, residents, city officials and preservationists. Abandoned expanses of land and structure in the city have become a playground for criminals, with many residents pleading with the city to tear down decaying structures that are attracting crime and repelling homebuyers.

No city has experienced the magnitude of abandonment that the city of Detroit has endured. Preservation is important but in many Detroit neighbourhoods, remaining buildings are too dilapidated or unsafe for rehabilitation. Detroit is at a crossroads to which no city of its size has ever come before. This presents both apprehension and a huge opportunity for the city to adopt a new agenda for rebirth. A re-sizing programme should remain committed to targeting growth opportunities.

Unused land throughout the city is being put to a new productive use. There is a growing urban agriculture movement that community groups are using to reclaim parts of the abandoned city. The practice is creating greater access to fresh produce for the population and is also mobilizing people to work on their own behalf.

With large amounts of new vacant land, Detroit has a realistic potential to become a self-sustaining green city. It is perhaps this green model which can sustain, refocus and revitalize the glory days of Detroit. Urban farms increase food security by growing food locally. They give under-served urban neighbourhoods access to fresh foods, whilst strengthening local economies by keeping dollars circulating within the community. Urban farming can create local jobs and grow community.

34. M Dunford, 'The Rough Guide to The Netherlands', Rough Guides, London, 2010, p.69

35. G Ames, 'The Globe Encompassed: The Age of European Discovery, 1500–1700', Pearson, London, 2007, pp.102–103

36. S Mazumdar, 'Sugar and Society in China: Peasants, Technology and the World Market', Harvard University Press, Cambridge, MA, 1998, pp.104–106

37. E Walford, 'Bermondsey: Tooley Street', 'Old and New London: Volume 6', 1878, pp.100–117 [http://www.british-history.ac.uk/report.aspx?compid=45269], retrieved 2 August 2013

38. 'Recovery Park' [http://recoverypark.org/faq], retrieved 25 August 2011

39, 42+43, 45. M Strachan, 'Bank of America Will Help Demolish Detroit's Abandoned Homes', The Huffington Post, 2011 [http://www.huffingtonpost.com/2011/03/23/bank-of-america-detroit-abandoned-homes_n_839817.html], retrieved 26 August 2011

40. 'State & Country QuickFacts: Detriot City, Michigan', United States Census Bureau, U.S. Department of Commerce [http://quickfacts.census.gov/qfd/states/26/2622000.html], retrieved 26 August 2011

41. J Wisely & T Spangler, 'Motor City Population Declines 25%' [http://usatoday30.usatoday.com/news/nation/census/2011-03-22-michigan-census_N.htm], retrieved 26 August 2011

44. C Morran, 'Bank of America Donating 10 Homes to Detroit to Attract Cops to LIve in the City', Consumerist, 2011 [http://consumerist.com/2011/03/bank-of-america-donating-10-homes-to-detroit-to-attract-cops-to-live-in-the-city.html], retrieved 26 August 2011

46. AP Kellogg, 'Detroit Shrinks Itself, Historic Homes and All', The Wall Street Journal, 2010 [http://online.wsj.com/article/SB10001424052748703950804575242433435338728.html], retrieved 26 August 2011

Yet to make their business work, urban farmers must contend with two challenges that rural farmers typically do not encounter: access to land for growing produce, and the ability to scale operations large enough to be profitable. Urban land suitable for farming is expensive and, even when land is available it comes in smaller sized patches rather than in large pieces of land. Urban land is at such a premium that farmers must be innovative to grow more densely and make their business viable.

Re-localizing even part of the food system is about much more than providing food. New strategies must recognize the value of creating more jobs, providing more fresh fruits and vegetables to underserved communities and reconnecting people more innovatively with their food. Cities may not need urban farms to survive, but given the social, environmental and economic returns that the urban food system can deliver, we should find ways of developing them.

The social and environmental benefits of urban agriculture are easy to understand. However, as compelling as they are, these benefits are not enough to motivate policy makers to help urban agriculture succeed on any kind of scale. The economic benefits that many proponents have long acknowledged in theory have yet to be demonstrated. The concept still needs to be proven. Communities need a farming model that can be learned and practiced across all economic classes and geographical boundaries. Cities need an engaged rather than an escapist agricultural system that allows farmers to return to the urban environment and rebuild local food systems that are human in scale.

Local Legislation

In Michigan, Governor Jennifer Granholm signed two cottage food licensing laws in 2011. The new legislation, aimed at local farmers, allows anyone who makes less than US$15,000 annually to prepare items in a home kitchen and sell them at roadside stands and farmers' markets without having to abide by excessive state regulations.[47]

The bill makes small-scale homemade food operations exempt from the licensing and inspection provisions of food safety laws. This means that a 'commercial kitchen' is no longer required for people who want to sell their own cookies, jams, and so on. However, labels must be applied to the packaging containing the same information as on most commercially available food products, such as ingredients, allergy information and weight. These labels must also carry a disclaimer, stating that the product was made in a home kitchen and has not been licensed by the Michigan Department of Agriculture.[48]

The New Dot Com

In general, sustainable agriculture has shunned technology and treated profitability as an afterthought, which gives it limited appeal to commercial investors. To infuse the sustainable agriculture industry with much-needed capital and authority it is crucial that it can be demonstrated to be profitable. Waves of innovators are developing profitable models for sustainable alternatives to industrial agriculture. These new entrepreneurs are developing breakthrough technologies, approaches and business ideas that are helping to create a post-industrial food system that is less resource intensive, more locally based, and easier to monitor and control.

facing page: De-industrialization has presented Detroit with the potential to become a self-sustaining food city.

43

47+48. T Perkins, 'Gov. Jennifer Granholm signs bill into law allowing residents to make food at home, sell it', AnnArbor.com, 2010 [http://www.annarbor.com/news/state-eases-cottage-food-industry-regulations-1/], retrieved 12 August 2011

'SPIN Farming' (SF) is a franchise-ready sustainable farming system that can be deployed quickly on a large scale. SF is a non-technical, easy-to-learn and inexpensive-to-implement vegetable farming system that makes it possible to earn significant income from land bases that are under an acre (4,000m2) in size.[49] The system is open to people who are new to farming, or want to farm in a new way. 'SPIN', which stands for 'Small Plot INtensive', is a relay system of agriculture that downsizes traditional organic farming methods. Invented by Canadian farmers Wally Satzewich and Gail Vandersteen in the 1990s, it is based on sequentially raising a variety of rapidly growing, highly marketable crops in multiple small growing patches.[50] The idea is to generate maximum edible output using minimal space, simple tools and a nearby municipal water supply. Planting, weeding, pest management and crop harvesting are all done by hand. The system allows small teams to raise large amounts of produce on limited amounts of land. The hand grown food is then sold directly to the community it serves.

Revenue targeting formulas, strategic crop-selection and organic-based techniques make it possible to realistically generate an income. A feasibility study funded by Pennsylvania's Department of Community and Economic Development estimated that with 200 growing patches in a half acre plot (2,000m2) with up to four rotations per plot, it would be theoretically possible to generate up to $120,000 per year.[51] Land does not need to be owned, as it is possible to comfortably afford a rent or barter a small piece of land adequate in size for SF production. Start up costs range from $10,000 to $25,000 and farmers typically work 30 to 60 hours a week.[52]

SF fits into many lifestyles. It is a modern concept that is being practised by a new generation of farmers, hobby farmers, as well as by established farmers who want to diversify or downsize. The ease of establishing a SF is possible because it removes the two barriers to entering the agriculture sector: land and capital.

SPIN's growing techniques are nothing new. The key aspect is the way a SPIN Farm business is operated. In regulating a food production system and creating a reproducible process, the approach of SF is unlike that of a hamburger restaurant chain. Restricted planning laws, competition for land from developers, insecure water supplies, pollution management and the many working parts of even a simple food system can be a daunting prospect for many. Urban agriculture is a sector that is usually viewed as marginal. It has never had its full potential released to the mainstream financial community. It can be demonstrated to investors that there are real economic and commercial prospects inherent in sustainable agricultural food production methods.

Modern consumers increasingly want a direct connection to the food they eat. The reasons have become personal, not selfish. Diet-related diseases, food-safety concerns, pollution created by transporting food great distances, water shortages and extreme weather events are encroaching directly on people's lives. Even when events do not have direct impacts, media coverage still brings the problems close to home, promoting a widespread awareness that the most pressing problems we face in our modern society are directly linked to the health of our food system. As a result, urban consumers expect greater transparency in the creation, storage and distribution of their food.

facing page: Constructed environments of a theatrical and awe-inspiring scale generated in the pursuit of transporting urbanites to foreign places. In Las Vegas (top), a restaurant absorbs unsuspecting punters into a chamber constructed to recreate the resplendent Piazza San Marco in Venice, complete with a perfect painted sky and idyllic cotton wool clouds. In Tokyo (bottom), an altogether utilitarian approach sees the manufacture of an urban fishery – the ideals of the rural transplanted into the city.

49+50. W Satzewich & R Christensen, 'Spin-Farming Basics: Thinking of Farming? Think Again. There Is a New Way to Farm', Spin Farming LLC, 2011

51+52. R Christensen, 'SPIN-Farming: Advancing urban agriculture from pipe dream to populist movement', Sustainbility: Science, Practice, & Policy, http://ejournal.nbii.org [http://www.spinfarming.com/common/pdfs/SPIN%20Article-SSPP%20essay.pdf], retrieved 12 August 2011

City planners and policy makers are acknowledging that the value of broadening quality of life issues will attract residents back to cities. Urban agriculture could be part of a response to the growing pressures on urban communities, who are concerned about the impacts of urbanization and the effects of this on the well being of residents. Sustainability has gone beyond a buzzword and is now spurring specific plans for significant change in how cities function. Producing food for residents within municipal borders could be a cornerstone of these plans. More cities are considering and actually implementing initiatives that require meeting a quota of their needs through local food producers. This has very positive implications for commercial urban farming. In July 2011 the unemployment rate in the US was approaching 10%.[53] With 13.9 million people out of work,[54] could urban farming be this generation's way to handle unemployment?

Jamaica Cottage Industry

Family food production systems in backyards provide a low-cost, sustainable strategy for increasing household food security by providing direct access to a reliable food supply. They may be the oldest production system known and their continued existence is proof of their intrinsic economic and nutritional merit. The strategy is not limited to rural areas and can also assist the poorest members of the urban population.

A project implemented on the Caribbean island of Jamaica by the Rural Agricultural Development Authority (RADA), as part of the Food and Agriculture Organization (FAO) 'Improve Household Food Security' policy, aimed to implement and promote the practice of home-based food production in urban Jamaica.[55]

Having successfully completed a series of rural programme implementations in backyard gardens throughout Jamaica, a new policy to expand the concept of the home garden to the urban areas of the island was proposed. Approximately 40% of the population lives below the poverty line in urban Jamaica, which also suffers from pockets of malnutrition.[56]

The main objective of the project was to improve food security through increased food production and income generation within the community. The project assisted 30 participants in each neighbourhood to produce their own food, and, by selling the excess, to purchase other goods or services. An advantage of this home-based income generation was that people were able to work within their communities and have more time to take care of their families.

The project sought to work with one urban community, and one peri-urban community. The inner city community, categorized as one of the most deprived areas in Jamaica, was based in Bowerbank in the east side of the capital, Kingston. The peri-urban area chosen was Watson Grove. The two city areas allowed for direct comparison and the identification of constraints and progress. In each community, the project sought to involve 20 women in vegetable production and 10 in poultry production. The participants deemed suitable for the latter were chosen according to the space that they had available for the chicken coops in their backyards, alongside their willingness and ability. Feeders, waterers, vitamin and mineral mix, lanterns, feed and chicks were provided free of charge under the project. Women in Watson Grove each received 55 chicks, while in Bowerbank they received 30 due to lack of space.

The total costs of the inputs provided for poultry production were US$140 and $125 per participant.[57] This enabled the first batch of chickens to be reared in approximately six weeks without any additional costs. It was expected that at least five batches of chickens could be raised per year. Any surpluses of eggs and meat from the participants' personal needs could be sold. The additional income provided by the scheme helped to financially support families and develop a sense of positive self-esteem.

The '5-to-9ers'

Dubbed the '5-to-9ers', many people are getting out their mixing bowls after a day at the office. They are part of the new baking mania that has generated an entire cottage industry, and provided retailers with the sales equivalent of an instant sugar high, in an industry that is now worth millions in the UK.[58] The mix of childhood nostalgia with solid business brains has become the key to modern cupcake marketing. Cupcakes are a decadent, affordable, small piece of luxury, offering instant gratification in times of austerity.

Due to tough economic climates and the onslaught of unemployment, many people are reverting to practising something that they love, such as baking. The production of cupcakes has become a cottage industry that is attracting many people who have typically either packed in their jobs to start their own cupcakeries, or are running cake Internet businesses and looking to scale them up to full-time. Vogue magazine proclaims that, 'Owning a cupcake bakery is the career fantasy of our times'.[59]

In an age when discretionary feel-good spending is at its lowest point, cupcakeries are trying to persuade people to upgrade from cheaper sugar-delivery vehicles such as doughnuts. Yet, the most exclusive cakes can cost £10 each for just a couple of sticky mouthfuls. The sugar rush that a typical cupcake contributes lasts only as long as it takes to walk back to the office. The small cottage industries are a stark contrast to the large-scale food conglomerates and the systems whereby food can be prepared, processed and packaged on a different continent to the end consumer. People respond to the homemade history behind the cupcake, making it a lucrative local industry.

Many from outside the farming world are starting to grow and make food to generate money, whilst others opt for a more leisurely approach. There is much global effort to reconnect with the source and the practice of cultivating, selling and cooking the food we eat, taking on political dimensions as urban areas become sites of convergence between 'Big' and 'Small' food practice. What unites them all is the ability to view and practise food production in a new, sustainable way.

No other economic development activity has had as much appeal to those concerned with sustainability as urban agriculture. Urban agriculture has many beneficial social and environmental impacts alongside its value as a community-building tool. It is the viability that the practice offers as a mode of economic development that is often put under question. However, the answers usually depend on how one defines economic development. Many projects are driven by non-profits and are far from being financially self-sufficient. They are dependent on grants, donations and government programmes. Although they experiment with entrepreneurial activities, their main mission is to be of social service, and because of this they are less likely to be economically successful as measured in revenues and profits. Yet, for some, economic self-sufficiency is not even a goal. The good citizens of cities who take up a business in urban farming have a sense of idealism and romanticism, embrace independence and have a pioneering spirit that is tempered by a pragmatic capacity for consistent effort.

47

53+54. M Fleury, 'US Unemployment Rate Down', BBC News, 2011 [http://www.bbc.co.uk/news/business-14420702], retrieved 12 August 2011

55–57. A Valstar, 'Home-based Food Production in Urban Jamaica', FAO Corporate Document Repository: Agriculture and Consumer Protection' [http://www.fao.org/docrep/X2650T/x2650t08.htm], retrieved 12 August 2011

58. M Thomas, 'Cupcake Business', EDP, 2010 [http://www.edp24.co.uk/what-s-on/food_and_drink_2_5148/creative_greenwich_cupcake_business_mixes_it_up_1_657100], retrieved 8 September 2011

59. S Richmnan, 'Being Modern: Cupcakes', The Independent, 2011 [http://www.independent.co.uk/life-style/food-and-drink/features/being-modern-cupcakes-2267863.html], retrieved 8 September 2011

Taste the Difference

'As he sat on his balcony eating the dog, Dr Robert Laing reflected on the unusual events that had taken place within this huge apartment building during the previous three months. With its forty floors and thousand apartments, its supermarket and swimming pools, bank and junior school – all in effect abandoned in the sky – the high-rise offered more than enough opportunities for violence and confrontation.'

– JG Ballard, 'High Rise: Critical Mass',1975

In order to understand the role of communities in combating hunger and malnutrition it is important to review the systems and institutions that hold power over food. Hunger is not simply defined by not eating enough calories and the concept of 'food security' acknowledges the role of social, economic and physical factors in determining the likelihood that people will go hungry. Global movements advocate 'food sovereignty' through which communities have the right to define their own food and agriculture policies and the ways in which they interact with corporate and foreign interests in their food systems.

facing page: Madison Avenue in New York, one of the world's busiest streets, closed to all motor traffic to facilitate a bustling community food market, and with it a new kind of energy abounds.

The global food crisis of 2007 and 2008 saw a sharp increase in the global price of food. The Food and Agriculture Organization (FAO) Food Price Index, an indicator of the global change in international prices of a basket of food commodities, showed the cost of food increased by almost 100%.[1] The impact was felt globally in both poor and wealthy economies, resulting in global sites of economic, political and social unrest. This crisis was not the result of an overnight phenomenon or a sudden unforeseen ecological disaster. Violent food riots, the result of communities outraged and unable to meet sudden price increases, coursed through cities to protest against the political and economic systemic failures that had facilitated such a disaster.

Since 2008 prices remain high, and a second 'global food crisis' in 2011 maintained prices at almost 200% of pre 2007 levels.[2] These crises have had significant impacts in small import-dependent countries, particularly in east and sub Saharan Africa. In the Horn of Africa, everyday staples have become unaffordable for communities; maize prices in Mogadishu, the capital of Somalia, were 100% higher in June 2011 than in June 2010.[3] Similarly, in sub Saharan Africa, the Millennium Development Goal (MDG) to halve the number of people who suffer from hunger by 2015 is unattainable under the current conditions. In 2010 food riots in Maputo, the capital city of Mozambique, were instigated by a 30% hike in the price of bread, which further added to a double-digit increase in water and energy prices. At this time, even before the increases, three-quarters of the average Mozambican household budget was already being spent on food.[4]

1+2. 'Food and Agriculture Organization of the United Nations: FAO Food Price Index', Food and Agriculture Organization of the United Nations [http://www.fao.org/worldfoodsituation/wfs-home/foodpricesindex/en/], retrieved 13 August 2012

3. D Carington, 'Food is the ultimate security need, new map shows', The Guardian, 2011 [http://www.guardian.co.uk/environment/damian-carrington-blog/2011/aug/31/food-security-prices-conflict#_], retrieved 15 August 2012

4. R Patel, 'Mozambique's food riots – the true face of global warming', The Guardian, 2010 [http://www.guardian.co.uk/commentisfree/2010/sep/05/mozambique-food-riots-patel], retrieved 15 August 2012

For communities in the most affected regions in the world, where it was once perceived as a role of the state to be in control of food production and food was locally attainable through subsistence farming and regional markets, neoliberal agendas have generated an altogether different scenario.[5] Global food crises have highlighted the rebranding of food as a commodity. Communities have become customers with degrees of purchasing power, rather than consumers with rights to livelihoods and survival.

Further, an amalgam of global crises of financial markets, energy supply, environmental disaster and food prices have led to increasing pressures to control the physical resources of land and water. Arable agricultural land in the global South, estimated to amount to between 445 million and 1.7 billion hectares, has emerged as a lifeline for a struggling global economy.[6] This land holds the potential to provide food and water for people and animals and for biofuel production. Labelled the 'global land grab', deals between transnational corporations (TNCs), foreign governments and national governments have seen huge areas of this land allocated to foreign investors.

Climatic conditions have been identified as catalysts for civil unrest and cyclical climatic changes have been seen to double the risk of civil wars. The climate phenomenon known as El Nino is associated with hot and dry weather around the tropics that drastically affects food production. Researchers at Columbia University have shown a correlation between the El Nino cycle and outbreaks of violence from Southern Sudan to Indonesia and Peru.[7]

Whilst the climatic condition is not a direct cause of conflict, phenomena like El Nino are cyclical. In understanding their impact on food cycles, and social behaviour as a result, communities can be empowered to take preemptive action against the causes of unrest. Some warn that the world is careering towards a 'perfect storm' of crisis by 2030. Chief Scientific Adviser to the UK government, Professor John Beddington, warned a conference in 2009 of the intimate connection between water, food and energy provision: 'You can't think about dealing with one without considering the others. We must deal with all of these together.'[8] This chapter reviews this emerging pressure on urban and rural land and the implications for communities in the global South.

Global 'Land Grabbing'

For millions in the global South, land is central to their livelihoods and culture, and carries huge significance in postcolonial politics and identity. For many economies in this region it is central to food security, subsistence farming providing the main source of food. It is also where land is cheapest, and where people's rights to land are weakest.[9]

In Africa, investors from the Middle East, East Asia, Europe, America and India are all leasing increasingly large tracts of land. These agricultural acquisitions are often combined with 'sweeteners' in the form of investment in the urban infrastructure such as the construction of roads and airports, welcomed by some politicians keen to be associated with visible built gains.

These acquisitions include government to government, as well as deals involving the private sector. For example, in 2008 a high profile deal over the potential acquisition of 1.3 million hectares between the South Korean company Daewoo Logistics and the government of Madagascar received global attention. Covering an area the size of Belgium and occupying nearly half of Madagascar's arable land, Daewoo Logistics proposed to grow maize and oil palm mainly for export.[10] Under the deal South Korea, the world's third biggest maize buyer, would not have paid fees for its 99-year

left: Effects of Climate Change. According to the United Nations and the Organisation for Economic Co-operation and Development (OECD), droughts, sea-level rise and floods will continue to render many areas uninhabitable and unsuitable for food production, thus causing agricultural losses and increased food insecurity in cities.

5. 'Reclaiming the resources for health', Regional Network for Equity in Health in East and Southern Africa, EQUINET in association with Weaver Press, Zimbabwe, Fountain Publishers, Uganda and Jacana, South Africa, 2001, p.53

6. SM Borras Jr. & JC Franco, 'A "Land Sovereignty" Alternative? Towards a Peoples' Counter-Enclosure', TNI Agrarian Justice Programme, 2012 [http://www.tni.org/sites/www.tni.org/files/a_land_sovereignty_alternative_.pdf], retrieved 15 August 2012

7. D Carrington, 'Climate cycles linked to civil war', The Guardian, 2011 [http://www.guardian.co.uk/environment/2011/aug/24/el-nino-cycle-deadly-conflict], retrieved 24 August 2012

8. I Sample, 'Beddington: World faces 'perfect storm' of problems by 2030', The Guardian, 2009 [http://www.guardian.co.uk/science/2009/mar/18/perfect-storm-john-beddington-energy-food-climate], retrieved 15 August 2012

9+10. J Vidal, 'How food and water are driving a 21st-century African land grab', The Guardian, 2010 [http://www.guardian.co.uk/environment/2010/mar/07/food-water-africa-land-grab], retrieved 20 August 2012

lease of the land, arguing instead that the generation of farming jobs would adequately benefit the Madagascan economy. Hong Jong-wan, a manager at Daewoo Logistics said 'We want to plant corn there to ensure our food security. Food can be a weapon in this world. We can either export the harvests to other countries or ship them back to Korea in case of a food crisis.'[11]

The deal has been said to have contributed to popular anger with the then president. Following his resignation, new President Andry Rajoelina cancelled the deal, saying that the people had not been adequately consulted.[12]

China Zambia Friendship Farm

Chinese corporations, such as the China Zambia Friendship Farm that occupies 667 hectares to grow barley, maize and soybean, are also established in Africa.[13] In the Congo, Chinese corporations have secured rights to plant palm oil over 2.8 million hectares in what will be the world's largest plantation of the crop. In the Zambian capital Lusaka, the central market is a bustling centre with a vibrant fresh food market and every day a jostling crowd haggles to get the best deal. Within this urban furore, Chinese migrants now occupy a niche market in eggs and livestock.

A BBC report from 2011 describes the scene: 'You will probably not see a single non-African there. Until, that is, you get to where the chickens are sold. Here you will see a row of trucks piled high with cages, each packed with plump white chickens all fussing and squawking. The African shoppers will be weighing the birds in their hands and looking their prospective purchases in the eye. In the background you might spot the owners of the trucks – Chinese men and women holding wads of money and making sure things go smoothly.'[14]

It is estimated that Chinese farms produce a quarter of the eggs now sold in the capital and local communities are struggling to compete with these new businesses, that are able to undercut them with economies of scale.[15] Mildred, a local poultry trader in Lusaka central market, is genuinely afraid of becoming destitute if she remains in this industry. Many are confused to see people from so far away in their market, 'What she cannot understand is why anyone would want to travel halfway around the world to set up a chicken farm.'[16]

Across the border in Malawi's capital Lilongwe, Yang Jie from China's Fujian province migrated to the region at 18. Yang had visions of Africa as 'all one big desert' and so pooled his resources and created an ice cream factory. Now 25, his company is now the country's biggest supplier.[17] However, as in Madagascar, these are not comfortable partnerships. In Zambia, the most recent election in 2011 saw the inauguration of President Michael Sata who ostensibly ran a campaign to review foreign control of local markets. President Sata also pledged to implement capital controls to keep foreign-exchange earnings in Zambia, a move that would curtail the export of profits out of the country.[18]

In Mozambique, construction has been completed on the US$6 million 52 hectare Chinese Agricultural Technology Research and Transfer Centre 'to facilitate scientific research, training and technology

facing page: Grain wholesale market, Beijing. In Mozambique, the Chinese Agricultural Technology Research and Transfer Centre aims to facilitate a five fold increase in Mozambican rice production with a view to exporting the surplus to feed Chinese markets.

53

11. J Vidal, 'How food and water are driving a 21st-century African land grab', The Guardian, 2010 [http://www.guardian.co.uk/environment/2010/mar/07/food-water-africa-land-grab], retrieved 20 August 2012

12. 'Madagascar leader axes land deal', BBC News, 2009 [http://news.bbc.co.uk/1/hi/world/africa/7952628.stm], retrieved 20 August 2012

13. R Aliyu, 'Agricultural development and 'land grabs:' The Chinese presence in the African agricultural sector.' Consultancy Africa Intelligence, 2012 [http://www.consultancyafrica.com/index.php?option=com_content&view=article&id=925:agricultural-development-and-land-grabs-the-chinese-presence-in-the-african-agricultural-sector&catid=58:asia-dimension-discussion-papers&Itemid=264], retrieved 20 August 2012

14–16. J Rowlatt, 'Chinese chicken farmers ruffle Zambian feathers', BBC News – Home, 2011 [http://news.bbc.co.uk/1/hi/programmes/from_our_own_correspondent/9386678.stm], retrieved 23 August 2012

17. HW French & L Polgreen, 'Chinese flocking in numbers to a new frontier: Africa', The New York Times, 2007 [http://www.nytimes.com/2007/08/17/world/africa/17iht-malawi.3.7159493.html?pagewanted=all], retrieved 20 August 2012

18. 'A setback for China in Africa', Foreign Policy, 2011 [http://blog.foreignpolicy.com/posts/2011/09/26/a_setback_for_the_dragon], retrieved 20 August 2012

development'.[19] The aims of the project state the Chinese intention to facilitate a five fold increase in Mozambican rice production to 500,000 tonnes a year with a view to importing surpluses to feed Chinese markets.[20] Access to land for food and fuels, and to markets for trade has been accompanied by visible investment in the built environment. Across Africa, the presence of Chinese construction firms is unavoidable. On the continent, billboards, road signs and some cash machines even display Chinese symbols.

This investment in the built environment can be seen in everyday life in Mozambique. In Maputo, the capital city, a Chinese funded bridge across Maputo Bay is proposed and Chinese investment has contributed over 65 million US dollars to modernizing the Maputo International Airport. Chinese investment has funded the construction of a new Parliament, Ministry of Foreign Affairs, High Court and a national Conference Centre. Dubbed 'the second scramble' for Africa, the appropriation of land on the continent has been seen by some as a new wave of colonialism. In this context it is perhaps ironic that Chinese companies have refurbished the famous Polana hotel – 'a gracious haven that recalls the elegance and splendor of colonial times'.[21]

Chinese construction companies have built urban water supplies, cement factories, cotton processing plants and vehicle assembly workshops. Construction is simultaneously underway on a US$439 million housing project outside Maputo catering to a 5,000-house middle class suburb and a US$2.3 billion hydroelectric damn in central Mozambique.[22]

A Ghost Town in Angola

Angola is China's biggest trade partner in Africa. A comparison between the two countries shows their startling differences. China has 22% of the world's population and less than 7% of the world's arable land.[23] In contrast, Angola has a population of 16 million and an area of over 1.24 million km2.[24] Angola is China's biggest supplier of oil and, in line with China's interests over the continent, supplies China with meat, coffee, spices and tropical fruits.

Within this context of mutual investment, Angolan society is highly unequal and offers one of the most extreme cases of investment linked to access to resources. Built by the Chinese state owned China International Trust and Investment Corporation, Kilamba is an entire ghost town built by Chinese investment that lies unoccupied on the outskirts of Angola's capital, Luanda. The eerie satellite 'city' is composed of 750 eight-storey apartment blocks, a dozen schools and 100 retail units. Occupying a 5,000 hectare gridded city-scape, the brightly coloured towers are surrounded by landscaped gardens and dust swept roads.[25] Although after a year on the market, only 220 of the first batch of 2,800 apartments were sold, the city of Kilamba features in a glossy government promotion video and hired actors play the parts of happy residents. The government project falls under President Jose Eduardo dos Santos' 2008 election pledge to build one million homes in four years.[26]

The reported reality is even more perverse. A BBC dispatch from the city describes 'driving around for nearly 15 minutes and seeing no-one apart from Chinese labourers, many of whom appear to live in containers next to the site' and later a hired Angolan street sweeper.[27] Of the commercial units, only a few have been occupied (by utility companies) and there is only one hypermarket at the site entrance to provide food for the 750 apartment blocks. The country director of the Angolan Office of the Open Society Initiative of Southern Africa (OSISA) argues that the government need to prioritize building low cost housing to cater for the 'great majority of the population [who] live in shacks with no water, electricity or sanitation'. Despite this, Angola's deputy construction minister was adamant that, 'It is with absolute certainty, an excellent project.'[28]

Communities and Conflict

A site of some of the most extreme global conflict, food security is a constant challenge for people in the Gaza Strip. Several years of almost total blockade have led to devastating economic collapse and the Israeli 'Operation Cast Lead' in 2008–9 led to massive destruction of assets and infrastructure. The FAO reported in 2011 that direct losses to the agricultural sector alone amount to at least US$180 million. Israeli exclusion zones preventing Palestinians from accessing 85% of fishing zones and 34% of remaining arable land have led to annual losses exceeding US$50 million.[29]

With a yearly growth rate of approximately 3.2%, the Gaza strip has the seventh highest population expansion rate in the world.[30] The expansion of cities and refugee camps has placed a huge demand on its land area and food supply, to cater for a large growing population. Global food price and climatic crises have further compounded these man made problems and in 2011, of Gaza's population 44% of people were classified as food insecure (52% in rural areas) and 80% of Gaza's inhabitants were dependent on external assistance in some way.[31]

Urban agriculture has emerged as a realistic and desirable land use option in the Gaza Strip. The potential of urban agriculture for enhanced food security, as well as new employment creation and small enterprise development, environment management and productive use of urban wastes, is becoming widely recognized in the region. With decreasing land and water scarcity, urban agriculture is providing a sustainable alternative for families and farmers in the Gaza Strip.

The Palestinian Agricultural Relief Committee (PARC) in Gaza was created in 1998.[32] The project aims to develop different urban agriculture practices in several Refugee Camps and urban domains in the Gaza Strip. The project's objective is not only to improve the health, food security, environmental and social situation for the population of Gaza, but it is also a step into the research for the implantation and proliferation in the practice of urban agriculture in the region.

One of the projects the organization manages is the 'Urban Garden' initiative in Gaza. Since the project has been implemented, PARC has set up many urban gardens in the region. More than 80% of residents are dependent on food aid in Gaza.[33] Urban gardens provide a buffer against Israel's policies of occupation and blockade. United Nations food aid is often restricted from entering Gaza.[34] By learning how to plant an edible garden in a small urban space, the project offers the potential to ensure self-sufficiency. In an insecure and unstable zone, a simple urban garden can help to ensure food security.

PARC also runs a 'Farm-to-Table' programme that sources local food from Gazan farmers for the people of the region who are in need of food aid. PARC supports local farmers by paying them for their produce and then provides fresh, healthy food to needy local families. The scheme assists in strengthening the local community, instead of building dependence. The urban gardens in Gaza are vital not just for food security and a way to revitalize agriculture, but also as a way to empower women. Household gardens are a part of Gazan culture, and women are more likely to become the primary caretakers of these gardens. The project aspires to improve female status in the region as the vital food source expands in

19+20, 22. DA Robinson, 'Chinese engagement with Africa: The case of Mozambique', The Portuguese Journal of International Affairs, Spring/Summer 2012

21. 'Polana Hotel, Maputo, Mozambique', Africa Travel [http://www.africastay.com/polana-hotel.html], retrieved 20 August 2012

23. 'The Millennium Project– 15 Global Challenges – Challenge 3', Global Futures Studies & Research, The Millennium Project [http://www.millennium-project.org/millennium/Global_Challenges/chall-03.html], retrieved 25 August 2012

24. 'Mozambique and Angola within China's food security network', 2009 [http://www.clubofmozambique.com/solutions1/sectionnews.php?secao=social_development&id=15311&tipo=one], retrieved 25 August 2012

25. S Medina, 'A Ghost City in Angola, Built by the Chinese', The Atlantic Cities, 2012 [http://www.theatlanticcities.com/design/2012/07/ghost-city-angola-built-chinese/2608], retrieved 25 August 2012

26–28. L Redvers, ' Angola's Chinese-built ghost town', BBC News, 2012 [http://www.bbc.co.uk/news/world-africa-18646243], retrieved 29 August 2012

29+31. 'Urban agriculture in the Gaza Strip through vertical gardens and Aquaponics', Food and Agriculture Organization of the United Nations [http://www.fao.org/fileadmin/templates/FCIT/PDF/Fact_sheet_on_aquaponics_Final.pdf], retrieved 25 August 2012

30. 'Gaza Strip', Central Intelligence Agency [https://www.cia.gov/library/publications/the-world-factbook/geos/gz.html], retrieved 20 August 2012

32. 'Gaza Urban Agriculture Committee', Urban Agriculture Notes, City Farmer [http://www.cityfarmer.org/GazaUrbA.html], retrieved 25 August 2012

the community.

PARC provides people with vegetable and fruit seeds, and gives them rigorous training in how to maintain a garden. Over 200 locations, including houses, schools, kindergartens, health centres, hospitals, cemeteries and streets, have received an assortment in local types of vegetable seedlings and fruit-bearing trees.[35] Growers learn about composting, fencing, irrigation, and how to make and use natural pesticides. Advice is also given on how to turn any scrap of land, including rooftops, into a blossoming garden.

People are also being educated on how to raise rabbits, an animal notoriously easy to breed. PARC incorporates animal husbandry into its training because other sources of animal protein such as beef are prohibitively more expensive. The combination of horticulture and the breeding of farm animals, allows a number of households to be almost completely self-sufficient.

The projects have helped many families who have received intensive technical training in different aspects of urban agriculture and organic farming. Through the distribution of technical brochures, information has been made available to people covering growing techniques, crop selection, organic fertilizer and eco-pesticide use. The principles of rainwater collection and the safe handling of grey water are also part of the education materials in an attempt to improve water-use efficiency in the region.

Supporting the small-scale income generating activities, PARC has provided greenhouses for home growing. A 40m2 greenhouse, which has capacity for at least 100 plants, and a 20m2 greenhouse that has a capacity for at least 50 plants have been made available to families by the scheme.[36]

Rooftop gardening is key to a viable future in the region. Whilst providing a source of nutrition and income, the roof gardens also act as a layer of thermal insulation, keeping the city cool during hot summers and warmer during cold winters. 'We grow on our roof because we are farmers but have no land now,' says Moatassan Hamad, 21, who grows cabbage and eggplants in the winter, and endochriyya (a plant used for making soup) and chilli, garlic and onions in the summer from his rooftop garden. The house is a typical cement blockhouse, in the crush of a Palestinian refugee camp.[37]

Whilst community responses in Gaza and in Africa to the appropriation of land are emergent, in Latin America communities have long established networks mobilized towards food security. Belo Horizonte is one of the most progressive examples of this.

Belo Horizonte

Join 80,000 people for lunch at one of the 'People's Restaurants' in downtown Belo Horizonte, Brazil, and you will be supporting a community led food revolution.[38] Locally grown food has become the new frontier in a movement towards ending hunger and malnutrition in the Brazilian city.

Belo Horizonte is the fourth largest city in Brazil with a metropolitan population of over 2.4 million.[39]

57

33+34. 'Guide: Gaza under blockade', BBC News, 2010 [http://news.bbc.co.uk/1/hi/world/middle_east/7545636.stm], retrieved 25 August 2012

35+36. 'Gaza Urban Agriculture Committee', City Farmer's Urban Agriculture Notes, Canada [http://www.cityfarmer.org/GazaUrbA.html], retrieved 25 August 2012

37. E Bartlett, 'Without land, Gaza famers grow crops on roofs', The Electronic Intifada [http://electronicintifada.net/content/without-land-gaza-farmers-grow-crops-roofs/4873], retrieved 25 August 2012

38. 'Public Policies for Food Supplies in Belo Horizonte City – Brazil', United Nations Educational, Scientific and Cultural Organization [www.unesco.org/most/southa10.htm], retrieved 27 August 2012

39. C Rocha, 'Urban Food Security Policy: The Case of Belo Horizonte Brazil', Journal for the Study of Food and Society, Vol. 5, No. 1, Summer 2001, pp.36–47

In the early 1990s it was estimated that 38% of families in the region lived below the poverty line, including 44% of all children who also suffered a degree of malnutrition.[40] The city's population were experiencing food insecurity because of high prices, extreme inequality, uneven distribution of food outlets throughout the 350km2 city, and various problems in urban infrastructure.[41]

In 1993 the freshly elected Partido dos Trabalhadores (Worker's Party) of Belo Horizonte inaugurated a programme developing new initiatives to reduce food insecurity across the city.[42] In a time of social mobilization against malnutrition and hunger, the local government committed itself to start a comprehensive policy to improve both food availability and accessibility in the city that would secure a healthy food supply for its future.

A new food security law, Municipal Law No. 6,352, 15/07/1993, was initiated to set out an integrated policy framework for food security.[43] This policy signalled the formation of the Secretariat of Food Supply (SMAB), a new government body responsible for the development of the city's food programmes. Established as a separate administrative structure to the rest of the city government, the 'SMAB' was allocated its own budget to effectively centralize the planning, coordination and execution of all municipal food security policies in Belo Horizonte. Mainstreaming food security into one exclusive municipal public policy was crucial to allow nutrition and food-related programmes to have the same status as traditional public policies in areas such as health and education.[44]

Offering a systematic approach to food that included producers, distributers and consumers, the intention of the policy was to apply to every stage of the food chain. This would allow for research and development of farming technology, credits for family producers, support for farmers markets, waste disposal and decentralized distribution. The policy also included eating and health education programmes and subsidized the operation of restaurants.[45]

A series of projects initiated by the SMAB were created, centring on a sustainable production system that offered food at affordable prices governed under local control. The notion of food security was interpreted as a principle: that all citizens have the right to adequate quantity and quality of food throughout their lives, and that it is the duty of governments to guarantee this right.[46] An approach of 'food with dignity' was employed as an important perspective for the basis of the programme's projects.[47] Since being implemented in 1993 the projects administered by the programme have become increasingly comprehensive. The scheme is divided into six broad policy areas for achieving food security in the city.

Under the first policy, the 'Restaurante Popular' project is a low-cost no-frills subsidized lunch that has become a basic right for citizens in Belo Horizonte. The service offers healthy and well-balanced menus for less than $1.00 at four different 'People's Restaurants' in the city every day.[48] The majority of visitors are poor but everybody is welcome to use the service in an attempt to avoid stigmatization. For each Real one diner pays, the government pays two (approximately US$0.70).[49] People who eat at the 'People's Restaurants' walk out well nourished, reducing the strain on the city's health and social services.

The public 'Food Basket' project provides low-income families with a parcel of subsidized non-perishable food items. Even though this service existed prior to the new food programme, the scheme suffered from inconsistency. Communities would usually receive a basic food basket during the period prior to an election, only for it to be cancelled a short time after the voting finished.[50] Food items in the revised policy can be purchased with a magnetic card at 26 sales locations in poor areas regularly served by special buses, trucks and vans, which make deliveries every 15 days.[51] The food basket scheme is restricted to registered families with an income of up to minimum wages.

Under the second policy, the 'SMAB' programme provides a meal per day to all students enrolled in the public school system. In poor neighborhoods of greater need, the all-year-long school meals programme is extended to serve children at municipal schools during vacation time. In 2009, an average of 156,000 school children in 218 public schools ate freshly prepared meals every day, paid for directly by the government.[52]

The 'Food Bank' project was started in 2004 to reduce amounts of unnecessary food waste in the city. More than 20% of crops were already being destroyed at the point of harvest, while a further 8% were wasted during transportation.[53] The project aims to reduce food waste.The scheme coordinates a citywide network of food banks that receive fresh fruit and vegetable donations from farmers markets and grocery stores. After cleaning and vacuum freezing the perishable food it is distributed to charitable organizations and social service agencies. In 2007, 108 institutions received 600 tonnes of food.[54]

For the third policy, the city introduced 'Straight from the Country' and the 'Harvest Campaign', aimed at facilitating a direct interaction between small rural producers and urban consumers. Harvested crops are offered all year round to the citizens from fixed sale locations throughout the city. The rural producers get better prices for their products and the consumers buy healthy food for a price below market value. The price and quality of the produce is closely regulated to maintain a quality service for all parties. In 2008, 34 rural producers from eight different jurisdictions around Belo Horizonte participated in these programmes.[55] They offered a variety of fresh leaf vegetables, roots and fruits at lower prices than in other outlets.

Under the 'ABasteCer' programme, private operators are chosen through a transparent, public selection process, to run 15 fixed outlets located in poor regions of the city.[56] Under the 'Worker's Convoy', the outlets are mobile. In exchange for being allowed to operate in more profitable, central locations, sellers are required to serve periphery neighborhoods at the weekends.

Farmers markets in Belo Horizonte are supported with the open availability of public space use. District markets have been revitalized throughout the city by granting their transformation into multiple vacant spaces, which has encouraged supplies to be consolidated and local culture to be strengthened. Four markets are located at the intersections of major transit routes in the city's centre. Not only is new space being allocated for the creation of food markets, but parts of some existing market spaces are being transformed for other uses altogether. The Lagoinha market is one of the most traditional in Belo Horizonte. Plans to revitalize parts of its space to conduct new experiments for the promotion of citizenship are part of a new SMAB food project. Part of the market's interior will be refurbished to shelter a new cinema with 115 seats, a restaurant and a bar.[57]

Under the fourth policy, the project 'Productive Garden' creates community gardens that provide fresh

40. 'SMAB Public Policies: Innovating on the Supplies of Food in Belo Horizonte', Belo Horizonte, PHB, 1995

41+44. C Rocha, 'Urban Food Security Policy: The Case of Belo Horizonte Brazil', Journal for the Study of Food and Society, Vol. 5, No. 1, Summer 2001, pp.36–47

42, 45–47, 54+56. 'Case study: Belo Horizonte, Brazil', Future Policy [http://www.futurepolicy.org/3385.html], retrieved 27 August 2012

43, 48, 51+57. 'Public Policies for Food Supplies in Belo Horizonte City – Brazil', United Nations Educational, Scientific and Cultural Organization [www.unesco.org/most/southa10.htm], retrieved 27 August 2012

49+50. A Aranha, 'Interviews - Silent Killer', 2005 [http://www.silentkillerfilm.org/interview_aranha.html], retrieved 25 August 2012

52. LL Smith, 'Groundbreaking food policy: Belo Horizonte!' [http://www.youtube.com/watch?v=fegBrwfHZ80], retrieved 27 August 2012

53. R Queiroga, 'Closing the divide between those who are starving and those who waste food', City Mayors Society [http://www.citymayors.com/society/belohorizonte_food.html], retrieved 27 August 2012

55. M Gopel, 'Celebrating the Belo Horizonte Future Policy Award 2009: Solutions for the Food Crisis, Food Security Programme', World Future Council [http://www.worldfuturecouncil.org/fileadmin/user_upload/PDF/Future_Policy_Award_brochure.pdf], retrieved 5 October 2012

produce and plants as well as satisfying labour, neighbourhood improvement, sense of community and connection to the environment. They are publicly functioning in terms of ownership, access and management. Vacant lots are converted into spaces for the public. The policy promotes the use of sustainable methods in growing fruits, vegetables and medicinal plants in the urban environment. The gardens encourage an urban community's food security, allowing citizens to grow their own food or for others to donate what they have grown. In 2008 the city had 44 Community and 60 School Gardens, distributed over 1,600 seedlings for fruit trees and offered 62 workshops for planting in alternative spaces.[58] This scheme helps satisfy a hungry population whilst generating complementary nutritional alternatives to other areas of the food security programme. The public has access to the supplies at specially organized events, and community support centres and nurseries.

The fifth policy is to improve food education in the city, to which end experimental cooking workshops and booklets with low-cost, highly nutritious recipes are made freely available to the community. Information is regularly published online providing instructions on the safe handling and storage of food, alongside cooking tips and diet advice, to address malnutrition. In 2007, the project reached 3,500 people in the city.[59] The 'Agro-ecological Centre' is a project carried out jointly with the City Department for the Environment. Four centres were developed to supply seedlings and seeds, and places to exchange opinions and knowledge. The title 'agro-ecological' was chosen because the project spreads agricultural techniques that preserve the environment and use the available resources rationally.

In the pursuit of increasing employment in the food sector, the sixth policy has established cooking and baking courses in schools, as well as professional and recreational culinary programmes in the city, giving people a skill set that they can use to find jobs. In 2007, 800 people participated in programmes offering training in food-related professions.[60]

The alternative food system created and maintained by the government in Belo Horizonte has been successful in bringing food security issues into public policy. What has emerged is a highly effective but low cost scheme using less than 1% of the city's annual budget.[61] A greater access to nutritious and fresh produce, a reduction in childhood and adult malnutrition, a decrease in child mortality, increased and stable income for rural producers in the boundary neighbourhoods, and an increase in local and organic food production and consumption, have been successfully created by the food programme. With social justice as its central motivator, the success and durability of the Belo Horizonte food programme make it a highly attractive model that outlines a plausible solution to city food insecurity, particularly for contexts in which sufficient food is technically available but not accessible for the poor and marginalized groups of the population.

Ice Rink Greenhouse

Whilst this chapter has dealt with aspects of global economic crisis and their tangible effects on communities in the global South, the case of the 'Inuvik Community Greenhouse' highlights an ingenuity borne out of global climatic crisis. Located approximately 120 miles north of the Arctic Circle, the Community Garden Society of Inuvik established a greenhouse in 1998. Catering for over 100 members, the intention of the project was to utilize a large abandoned space in the town to allow for the production of a variety of crops in an area where fresh, economical produce is often unavailable, due to high transportation costs and the great distances that the food has to travel to reach them.[62]

The community greenhouse is situated in a decommissioned ice rink that has been converted into a nursery. By removing the tin roof and replacing it with transparent polycarbonate glazing, the nature of the original building has created a vast 16,000ft2 of growing area. Seventy-four garden plots measuring 16ft long, 5ft wide and 2ft tall are available to all members of the community group for an annual fee of just US$50.[63] Lined with insulation to protect the growing environment from permafrost, raised beds are built upon a gravel floor.

The extreme northern location Inuvik experiences offers interesting growing patterns. The town typically receives an average of 56 days of continuous sunlight every summer and 30 days of polar night every winter. During the town's 24-hour daylight, which lasts from about mid-May until mid-August, sun cascades into the building through the roof's polycarbonate glazing. This creates an excellent growing condition, allowing vegetables to mature early.

Community gardening offers an important solution for urban people to grow their own food on a small scale who lack space on their own property or an agricultural education. For the residents of Inuvik, the existing climatic conditions offer land that experiences the harsh environmental condition of permafrost and a very short and unpredictable growing season. Due to this situation the town experiences a limited variety and quantity of edible produce. However, controlled indoor growing using techniques such as raised planter beds make it possible to produce high quality produce in extreme environments.

Inuvik's local grocery store, 'North Mart' sells romaine lettuce for US$3.79, red peppers for $6.21 a pound and broccoli for $2.59.[64] By contrast, the local community produces spinach, chard, lettuce, tomatoes, carrots, peas, herbs, strawberries, rhubarb, zucchini and squash in a unique growing environment next door and at little cost. The greenhouse provides a stark contrast to the arctic environment outdoors. The greenhouse's growing season is from approximately the second week of May until early October. The last snowfall and frost in Inuvik is typically from mid-June and starts again in late August.

This chapter began with an investigation of the role of communities in addressing global issues of hunger and malnutrition, and the Inuvik greenhouse is a fascinating example of the power of a community to meet its immediate food requirements against seemingly insurmountable challenges. The greenhouse provides an outlet for the most un-Arctic of pastimes. A once dilapidated building is providing opportunities for recreational gardening and food production whilst building a strong sense of community through member support and the sharing of knowledge. This unique Arctic oasis has provided learning opportunities through various workshops, work placements, composting projects and agriculture education in a new ecosystem that has provided an unlikely focal point for community development.

Whilst the strength of Big Food may seem indomitable, the actions described in this chapter, of communities protecting their own food sovereignty, from farmland in Madagascar to Totnes High Street in Britain, show examples of the global power of food as a mobilizing force for residents of cities. The next chapter will explore how the identity of these residents can also be read through an analysis of the food available, and the means by which people access it in the city.

58–60. M Gopel, 'Celebrating the Belo Horizonte Future Policy Award 2009: Solutions for the Food Crisis, Food Security Programme', World Future Council [http://www.worldfuturecouncil.org/fileadmin/user_upload/PDF/Future_Policy_Award_brochure.pdf], retrieved 5 Octover 2012

61. LL Smith, 'Groundbreaking food policy: Belo Horizonte!' [http://www.youtube.com/watch?v=fegBrwfHZ80], retrieved 27 August 2012

62–64. J Mahoney, 'Inuvik Community Greenhouse', Urban Agriculture Notes, City Farmer, 2004 [http://www.cityfarmer.org/inuvik.html], retrieved 7 October 2012

All in Good Taste

'Decadent cooks go one step further and make sculptures of the food itself. If life is to be spent in pursuit of the extravagant, the extreme, the grotesque, the bizarre, then one's diet should reflect the fact. Life, meals, everything must be as artificial as possible – in fact works of art. So why not begin by eating a few statues?'

– Medlar Lucan & Durian Gray, 'The Decadent Cookbook', 1995

Food is an intrinsic and defining aspect of a city's identity. Its smells, textures and tastes manifest a city's cultural heritage, define its social habits and bring vitality and joviality to its streets. Whilst many cities have retained a homogenous and independent food culture, often defiantly so, the vast majority of modern cities have become less singular in their tastes and instead have come to embrace a pluralistic food culture consisting of numerous competing culinary cultures from around the world. Patterns of consumption in cities have subsequently shifted, revealing a trend towards a culturally varied diet consisting of a high percentage of processed foods with a high salt and carbohydrate content and a low percentage of dietary fibre, vitamins and minerals. The composition of urban food cultures is of paramount importance not just to the future prosperity of the cities in themselves but to the condition of the global food system as a whole.

Economic growth and urbanization have had a profound impact on food cultures in cities. They have facilitated the international proliferation of local cuisines and encouraged the production of innumerable new culinary fashions such that a homogenous food culture no longer exists anywhere in the world. The unprecedented rise of food variety over the last 50 years has radically transformed urban food culture. Whereas the availability of foreign food cultures in cities used to be exclusive, exotic and novel, food variety is now pervasive to such an extent that it has come to define the food culture of many cities worldwide. The modern city is no longer identifiable by its native cuisine but for providing a vast array of competing food cultures. London today is equally renowned for its curry houses on Brick Lane or the Vietnamese restaurants on Kingsland Road as it is for offering culturally indigenous foods such as tea and scones at Fortnum and Mason's or a Full English Breakfast at a greasy spoon café. The informal ephemera of smells escaping from kitchens and aromas wafting invitingly out of restaurant doors have come to define these urban territories in more meaningful and evocative ways than the formal prescribed street signs and postcodes.

This phenomenon is not confined to London but can be seen in cities around the world. Culture in New York is equally defined by the smell of roast duck in Chinatown and the white paper takeout boxes

facing page: Florence has a symbiotic culinary relationship with the land and is known for celebrating seasonal local eating. According to the Italian Trade Commission, Tuscan cuisine was favoured by Catherine de' Medici for its 'noble simplicity' and has its roots in peasant cooking, relying on basic staples such as olive oil, tomatoes and fava beans. Incidentally, the combination of fava beans, human liver and a nice chianti was the perfect meal for the cannibalistic serial killer Dr. Hannibal Lecter in Thomas Harris's 1988 novel 'The Silence of the Lambs'.

popularized by televisions programmes like 'Sex and The City', as it is for native foods such as hot dogs at Yankee Stadium or Waldorf salads in the Waldorf-Astoria hotel.

Pluralistic food cultures have become so pervasive that they have in fact marginalized many local food cultures and made some redundant altogether. Many historic and culturally significant culinary traditions have been reduced to novelty experiences where they used to account for an active constituent of an urban food economy. For example, it has become customary for tourists to eat haggis whilst in Edinburgh or frog's legs whilst in Paris simply to experience a culturally specific culinary tradition rather than to satisfy a hungry appetite.

The pluralism of urban food culture has also had a physical impact on many cities. In order to assimilate a diverse and international food culture, many cities have segregated their food cultures into defined regions in order to help residents and visitors to locate their desired cuisine. These regions are often defined both socially and typologically by the food culture they project. Nowhere epitomizes the physical impact of the segregation of food cultures in cities more than Los Angeles, which is composed of a profusion of territories identified by the cuisine on offer including Chinatown, Little Tokyo, Koreatown and even Little Ethiopia. Food variety has become so associated with modern cities that it has come to symbolize more than just luxury and freedom of choice; it has become one of the primary indicators of an affluent and successful society and the embodiment of a modern and liberal democracy.

To satisfy this urban desire for exotic tastes, special ingredients are regularly imported vast distances into the city in order to produce authentic meals, closely reminiscent of their original recipe. The resulting meal speaks as much of its origin as the distance it has taken to reach the plate of the consumer, a concept known as a 'high-embodied food mileage'.

There is enough food produced worldwide to provide a healthy and balanced diet for the entire global population, yet, due to the political forces on the international food market, giant cultural discrepancies have emerged where wealthy cities over-consume and poorer cities under-consume. Nowhere is the culture of over-consumption more pronounced than in America. The American trend towards over-consumption is symptomatic of a broader cultural appetite for all things in excess. A cross section of the typical American city reveals a food culture with the ability to deliver in over-abundant quantities to a society that has become familiar with the convention of over-consuming and can afford it. From the enormous drinks at McDonalds, which have increased in size by 457% since 1955, to giant fridges with double doors in the typical kitchen, American food culture is designed to deliver quantity and variety irrespective of economy, efficiency or sustainability. The growth of over-consumption in America is both a cause and a symptom of the simultaneous growth of the fast food industry. In 1970, Americans spent $6 billion on fast food compared with £110 billion in 2001.[1]

The transformation of urban food cultures towards a pluralistic food culture has caused a global increase in the demand for processed foods, for milk and for meat. As well as having a detrimental effect on the nutritional value of the typical urban diet, this change in demand has also had significant environmental consequences. Rearing livestock is much more energy intensive than producing vegetables or grains and requires more than five times the amount of land. The production of 1kg of beef, for example, uses 7–10kg of grain,[2] while 1,600 litres of water are required to cultivate 1kg of wheat.[3]

left: Territories in the city identified by cuisine - Korean BBQ restaurant in Koreatown, Los Angeles.

1. E Schlosser, 'Fast Food Nation: What the all-American meal is doing to the world', Peguin Books, New York, 2001, p.3

2. 'High prices on commodity market', UNCCD, United Nations [http://www.unccd.int/en/programmes/Thematic-Priorities/Food-Sec/Pages/Wors-Fact.aspx], retrieved 6 August 2013

3. MM Mekonnen & AY Hoekstra, 'The green, blue and grey water footprint of farm animals and animal products, Value of Water Research Report Series No. 48', UNESCO-IHE, Delft, 2010

Whilst the population suffering from chronic over-consumption continues to grow at an alarming rate in many developed cities, there continues to coexist a large population who suffer from chronic under-consumption in many developing cities. An even more perverse cultural contradiction is that many of the countries that are suffering from chronic under-consumption are also net exporters of food and hence contributing to the cultural of over-consumption in other parts of the world. Tim Lang, professor of food policy at City University, London, notes this apparent disparity and the lack of independent choice available to the consumer today, 'In an ideological world, where the consumer is ostensibly sovereign, the notion of a "food culture" is a more robust way of understanding people's beliefs and behaviours regarding food: the concept is central to food and health and to which ideas about diet will dominate the consumer's mind.'[4]

facing page: Tea Mäkipää's 'Sisters' (2003) sensationally depicts the vulnerability of urban existence with two ladies having rats for dinner in a dilapidated London tenement.

67

Snack Street

Travellers return from Beijing, China with two distinct memories of local cuisine: the perennial favourite, roast duck, and the fast food culture. For authentic Beijing fast food, walk along the bustling Wangfujing Street, past the Beijing Department Store and the Foreign Languages Bookstore, and at the first set of traffic lights, make a left turn onto Wangfujing Snack Street. Even though a 10m high traditional Pailou-style archway with ornamental dragons and Chinese characters marks the entrance, it is the wafting aroma emitted from the bubbling cauldrons and frying woks of the open-air food stalls that unmistakably identifies this urban hub within the city. The low-rise architecture of the street is faux Ming and Qing dynasty lime bricks construction with carved beams, upturned eaves and rich coloured details, and is dwarfed by steel tower blocks in the neighbourhood.

Traditional and modern subcultures of Chinese society are clearly dissimilar to those of foreign travellers, yet on Snack Street they are bonded by gluttony and curiosity about the bizarre plethora of food on display. The bustling crowds and the rhythmic invitation to food tasting by the vendors provide Snack Street's culture and its magnetic quality. Under the glowing red lanterns and light bulbs, the pedestrian area of 2,000m2 is divided into zones of vendors selling a multitude of obscure and exotic delicacies from both northern and southern China. Seahorses on skewers, scorpion kebabs and iguana tails are considered to be delicacies, while folk-medicinal food includes grilled snake, silk beetles and lizards. Setting aside food taboo and morality, Beijing night crawlers can acquire an entire supper-on-the-move walking from one end of the street to the other. Foreign travellers can only describe Beijing fast food as true test of taste, fortitude and trust in the Chinese culture.

A Dog Eat Dog World

Monkey brains, dogs and rats have been common ingredients in Chinese recipes for centuries. However, Scandinavian artist Tea Mäkipää plays on cultural differences and conservative western attitudes to food to make political art. 'Sisters' (2003) sensationally depicts the vulnerability of urban existence with two ladies having rats for dinner in a dilapidated London tenement. Rats have long infiltrated the urban fabric and our homes, and have successfully affirmed their existence in cities throughout the world, feeding on urban food wastes. The staged photograph questions the accepted culture of inefficient food systems, and inequality of food access of different communities in cities that divides society. At the same

4. T Lang & M Heasman, 'Food Wars; The Global Battle for Mouths, Minds and Markets', Earthscan, London, 2004, p.185

time, the image highlights human greed and the possibility of a nutritional link between the ubiquitous city intruder and the urban inhabitants.[5]

In 2008, India's welfare minister Vijay Prakash advised a deprived population of 2.3 million to farm rats for snacks as a way to beat rising food prices.[6] Members of the Musahar caste in the state of Bihar, east India were told that plans to set up 'rat farms' for rearing meat could not only provide a good source of protein for the community, but also aid their social development. The government claims that almost 50% of the region's food grain stocks are eaten by rodents in fields or warehouses.[7] Plans to sell the produce to up-market hotels, street stalls and restaurants in cities are part of a system designed to reduce the inflation costs in food prices by reducing the amount of grain that the rodents feed on in the fields and producing a cheap form of meat.

Throwaway Culture

The shocking suggestion that urban vermin could be an ingredient in our next takeaway relates to how cities treat food waste. Cities provide an ideal environment for rats and other vermin, offering both shelter and food from careless urban inhabitants living in a throwaway culture. Effective vermin control is as much about controlling what attracts them as about controlling the pests themselves.[8] The amount of food waste from homes, businesses and institutions is growing at an alarming rate. Most of the waste we never see or think about, and is created in the process of making, packaging and transporting food. Domestic households alone in the UK throw away 8.3 million tonnes of food every year, and most of it could have been eaten.[9] This waste consists of elements such as bones and peelings, but the majority is entirely good food. Waste produced in the UK alone would fill the Albert Hall in one hour, Trafalgar Square to the top of Nelson's Column in one day, and Lake Windermere in nine months.[10] The throwaway culture that we have become so accustomed to is the reason pests are becoming so prolific in urban environments.

Flying Rats

Since World War II, the feral urban pigeon population has thrived on the wasteful practices of our society, living off a diet of leftovers and over filled bins.[11] Numbering in the hundreds of millions, the pigeon is a potential local guilt-free protein source, overrunning many cities' skylines. According to biologist Daniel Haag-Wackernagel at the University of Basel, the birds have an enormous reproduction capacity and they'll just come back. There is a linear relationship between the bird population and the amount of food available.'[12]

All cities, without exception, are intolerant towards the urban rat; however the pigeon has divided public opinion. Many value the pigeon as part of our natural wildlife in cities, yet others consider the bird to be a major nuisance, which poses a harmful environmental threat to cities. The common unsightly appearance of sun hardened pigeon droppings can cause irreparable damage to sandstone and brick facades. The acidic droppings also corrode through many tar-based roof surfaces, with build-ups causing perforations leaving exterior areas vulnerable to leaks.[13] Nests and nesting materials are notorious for clogging rain gutters, drains and roof corners, as well as damaging ventilation systems, skylights and solar panels to the point of inoperability. Pigeon waste poses a serious health and safety risk, causing pavements, walkways and fire escapes to become slippery and unsafe. There are many attempts to manage the pigeon population in cities. In 2003, former London Mayor Ken Livingstone claimed pigeon droppings caused up to £140,000 damage to Nelson's Column and Trafalgar Square in London. A law was passed in the same year that made the feeding of pigeons illegal in the 110m x 110m urban space. There is a fine of £50 to anyone caught giving food to the birds.[14] To control the population, a bird of prey was hired to scare the pigeons from the area at lunchtime every day. The hawk has since reduced numbers from 4,000 to 140.[15]

Instead of wasting resources on controlling, hunting the feral urban pigeon is a direct waste-to-food converter. Since ancient times, pigeon meat has been regarded as a gastronomic delicacy and culinary tradition in Asian and Middle Eastern cultures often referred to as the 'meat of kings'.[16] Although mainly for the discerning diners at present, the pigeon could potentially provide a very real source of sustainable food for a large urban population and not just reserved for the rich. The organic and sustainable additions to our menu would not only encourage us to eat local but add curiosity and novelty value to the twenty -first century everyday dining table.

Open Season

For most of the world's population, the act of hunting has transformed from a practice essential to survival to a pastime and a sport. Whilst some feel the practice has become an essential part of traditional culture, anti-hunting organizations seek to mobilize against the perceived cruel treatment of animals. Across the world, governments have enacted legislation banning hunting, from fox hunting in the UK to anti poaching laws in Africa, and whilst such legislation serves a vital purpose in protecting animals, it is undeniable that human beings are becoming increasingly detached from the reality of their consumption.

Culling legislation, which allows people to kill certain monitored pest populations, could hold a clue for how a sustainable future of hunting in the city could work. For example, hunting readily available assortments of wild animals and vermin may be a valid sustainable culture for procuring food in cities. Rats, pigeons, foxes, squirrels, sparrows, rabbits and seagulls thrive in cities; eels and trout can be found in many metropolitan rivers and canals. Parks and back gardens as well as the usual illegal waste dumping barren land, quiet alleyways and hidden nooks within cities make fertile urban environments for hunting and gathering. Berlin's wooded parks, cemeteries and the training ground of Berlin's major-league soccer team, Herta BSC make it Europe's capital city for wild boar – the troublesome pest would be the ideal substitute for farmed swine. Though it may sound heartless, 'Skippy' kangaroos make excellent steaks and are commonly found roaming on peri-urban golf courses in Melbourne, Australia. Urban 'pest' populations, from rats to kangaroos, cannot be relied upon to sustain the burgeoning populations of the city today, however it could be argued that they should start to be thought of as a valuable part of the local food chain, as they would have been during our 'hunter-gatherer' days. In the Highlands of Britain, for example, deer populations now have no natural predators and as such have increased to extremely high levels, threatening the survival of the local woodlands. Local councils are even said to be encouraging local schools to introduce 'Bambi-burgers' to provide a use for the 70,000 deer the council kills each year to manage the population.[17]

The Urban Squirrel

In the UK, rabbits and non-native grey squirrels have also benefitted from a decrease in human consumption to the point that they live with negligible threat to their populations. Grey squirrels have

5. T Mäkipää, 'Sisters', 2003 [http://www.tea-makipaa.eu/Sisters/], retrieved 9 July 2013

6. A Tewary, 'India's poor urged to 'eat rats'', BBC News, 2008 [http://news.bbc.co.uk/1/hi/7557107.stm], retrieved 10 October 2012

7. M Lee & P Tait, 'Food Crisis? Try rats, says Indian state government', Reuters India, 2008 [http://www.reuters.com/article/2008/08/18/us-india-rats-idUSSIN34470120080818], retrieved 10 October 2012

8. 'What attracts vermin?' [http://www.greenshield.com/what-attracts-vermin.html], retrieved 12 October 2012

9. 'About food waste' [http://www.lovefoodhatewaste.com/about_food_waste], retrieved 12 October 2012

10. 'Waste Facts', Reduce the use [http://www.reducetheuse.co.uk/Page/Waste/Wastefacts.html], retrieved 10 October 2012

11+12. A Madrigal, 'Pigeons: The next Step in Local Eating (No, Really)', Wired, 2008 [http://www.wired.com/wiredscience/2008/07/does-pigeon-mea/], retrieved 10 October 2012

13. A Kecskes, '7 Ways Pest Birds Cause Damage', 2010 [http://birdcontrolblog.com/?tag=bird-droppings-destroy], retrieved 5 August 2011

14. 'Feeding Trafalgar's pigeons illegal', BBC News, 2003 [http://news.bbc.co.uk/1/hi/england/london/3275233.stm], retrieved 5 August 2011

15. E Rowley, 'Soaring cost of hawks to scare pigeons from Trafalgar Square', 2009 [http://www.thisislondon.co.uk/standard/article-23746422-soaring-cost-of-hawks-to-scare-pigeons-from-trafalgar-square.do], retrieved 5 August 2011

16. 'Squab Information' [http://www.squab.com/product/squab.htm], retrieved 5 August 2011

17. T Stuart, 'Happy Hunting', The Guardian, 2006 [http://www.guardian.co.uk/news/2006/oct/20/food.foodanddrink1], retrieved 10 October 2011

overrun cities and directly caused a national decline in the native red populations. There are approximately 2 million grey squirrels in the UK, whilst there are only 160,000 red.[18] In June 2010, a £120,000 campaign was set up in Cornwall to cull at least 8,000 grey squirrels over three years.[19] The campaign will be repeated across the rest of the UK if it proves successful. According to these plans, the grey squirrel from North America that was originally a novelty to adorn Victorian gardens and parks in cities across the UK in the nineteenth century will soon become an everyday human food source at the dining table. In an unusual proposal to save the red squirrel, the conservative peer Lord Inglewood has called upon TV chef Jamie Oliver to encourage school children to eat grey squirrels.[20]

In parts of the UK, squirrel meat has been reported to be popular in recent times. Kingsley Village shopping centre in Fraddon, Cornwall, and Ridley's Fish and Game shop in Corbridge, Northumberland claimed their game counter has struggled to keep up with demand for grey squirrel meat and squirrel pasties.[21] Each rodent cost £3.50, tastes like wild boar or duck, and a large squirrel is nearly big enough to feed two people.[22] The green credentials of this cheap, abundant food source make it an attractive addition to the British menu. In a time when rising demand for meat across the globe endangers the food system, and local eating is becoming more popular, it is important to reconsider our assumptions about what protein sources are fit for eating.[23] The grey squirrel is low in fat, low in food miles, completely free-range and eating it would aid the survival of the indigenous red. From the street to the dinner table, the grey squirrel may be the ultimate ethical meal.

The Last Supper

As ethical and environmental debate becomes globalized, the concerns and sensitivities of multiple cultures are forced to assimilate. In Tokyo and other cities throughout Japan, whale meat is sold at supermarkets and restaurants, and served in school lunches. The controversial meat is sold as a by-product of scientific research, a loophole within the International Whaling Commission (IWC) sanction. Lucky Pierrot, a restaurant chain in Hakodate on the island of Hokkaido, a traditional whaling hub in the north of Japan, serves a deep fried minke whale meat burger with lettuce and mayonnaise for $3.50 at its ten restaurants.[24] A spokesperson for Lucky Pierrot claims that the restaurant is helping to preserve heritage, 'People in other countries may think eating whale is strange, but it is our culture.'[25]

Another endangered species is the Ortolan, a small, native songbird that is considered to be the highest gastronomy of all cuisine in France.[26] Trapped on their migration through France, poachers kill approximately 50,000 Ortolans every year, despite the ban in 1996. The tiny bird is captured alive, force fed, drowned in Armagnac, roasted whole and eaten whole, bones and all. The gourmet is draped in white linen to preserve the aromas steaming from the dish. Legend has it that former French President Francois Mitterrand, dying from prostate cancer, decided to end his life by dining like a king and devoured two of these birds after a plate of oysters, foie gras and capons.

On a chaise longue at home near Bordeaux, France, the dying president, in the presence of his 30 dinner guests, tucked into his Ortolan under a white cloth. Some believe the drapery is intended to hide the actions of the diner from God.[27] Ancient Romans traditionally ate Ortolan in this fashion; such was the magnitude of this sinful deed. The act of transforming the bird from a figure of innocence to an act of gluttony is seen as symbolic of a fall from grace. The French president reportedly spent ten minutes hidden under the white cloth, much to the embarrassment of his fellow diners. He apparently emerged 'capsized with ecstasy, his eyes sparkling with happiness, ready to face death' according to close sources. Mitterrand ate nothing for the next eight days and died soon after.[28]

The wheat of Morocco, the salty air of the Mediterranean, the lavender of Provence, the grapevine of the South of France, and the dip and plunge of a high wind in Africa, have been reportedly savoured by the few enlightened consumers.

Birds Nest Soup

In George Town, the capital city of Penang state, Malaysia, another type of bird is causing friction. Granted UNESCO World Heritage status since 2008 for its unique colonial architecture, the city has become a site of the industrial harvest of edible bird's nests. A multi-million dollar industry, George Town's traditional 'shop houses' are being converted into swiftlet breeding grounds.[29] The bird's nests, considered a delicacy served in a soup in Chinese cuisine, are made completely from the swiftlet's saliva secretion and are harvested three times annually.[30]

The birds traditionally breed in cave-like, damp, cold and wet habitats, and the residents' efforts to recreate the conditions within the shop houses are creating a stand off between UNESCO, local residents and local government. The traditional 'shop houses' of the city are transformed in the pursuit of the coveted and profitable nests. Local businessmen have set up loudspeakers broadcasting the bird song to attract the birds and lay pools of water in the shops to recreate the cave-like conditions within the shops. Drawn to the city, the shops fill with the swiftlets, causing even further damage to the structures, as bird guano and humidity deteriorate the historic buildings.[31]

Oysters

Yet another example of a delicacy moulding the city, oysters were once so prolific they covered much of New York and the East Coast of the USA. Over time, these industrial molluscs would terraform the land undersea, creating undulations and contours in reefs.[32] The impact of the seemingly small actions of individual oysters carving out reefs is so huge that it has been attributed to tempering the wave action in the area; so much so that Shell Oil Company has even invested US$1 million in an oyster shell recycling scheme to reinvigorate the oyster populations around the coast.[33]

For many, oysters are the preserve of the rich – and a supposed aphrodisiac; they are also an integral part of many ecosystems. In addition to carving the underwater coastline, oyster populations act as filters, creating habitable conditions for other species. In Maryland, USA, government policy is actively encouraging the recycling of oyster shells to encourage the growth of the oyster population. A state incentive offers oyster houses a tax credit of a US$1 for every bushel of recycled shells. For one oyster house, whilst the financial benefit is a welcome boon, the urban environmental benefit is the real reason for their engagement. According to Gunter of Acme Oyster House, Maryland, 'I may be able to eliminate two of our waste dumps as a result of recycling ... If I don't save a dime in-house it's still worth it.'[34]

Royale with Cheese

The delicacy of an unusual flavour or characteristics of cultural underpinnings make certain foods desirable and rare. Exclusivity makes some food sources an uncommon feature of the everyday dining table. The hamburger, on the other hand, is the quintessential trouble free, universal, easy fast food on

18+20. 'Jamie must back squirrel-eating', BBC News, 2006 [http://news.bbc.co.uk/1/hi/4835690.stm], retrieved 1 May 2012

19. L Hickman, 'If you want red squirrels, you have to kill greys', The Guardian, 2012 [http://www.theguardian.com/environment/2012/sep/05/red-grey-squirrels-cornwall], retrieved 15 October 2012

21+22. C Davis, 'The ultimate ethical meal: a grey squirrel', The Guardian, 2008 [http://www.guardian.co.uk/lifeandstyle/2008/may/11/recipes.foodanddrink], retrieved 1 May 2012

23. A Madrigal, 'Pigeons: The next Step in Local Eating (No, Really)', Wired, 2008 [http://www.wired.com/wiredscience/2008/07/does-pigeon-mea/], retrieved 12 October 2011

24+25. 'Mmm? Fast food chain offers whale burgers', The Associated Press, 2005 [http://www.msnbc.msn.com/id/8324667/ns/business-consumer_news/], retrieved 15 May 2012

26. M Paterniti, 'The Last Meal', Esquire, May 1998 [http://www.esquire.com/features/The-Last-Meal-0598/], retrieved 8 June 2012

27. R Seal, 'Burger King unveils £95 burger', The Guardian, 2008 [http://www.guardian.co.uk/lifeandstyle/wordofmouth/2008/jun/19/the95burger], retrieved 15 May 2012

28. M Caro, 'The Foie Gras Wars: How a 5,000-Year-Old Delicacy Inspired the World's Fiercest Food Fight', Simon & Schuster, New York, 2009, p.34

29+31. M Crook, 'George Town fears losing World Heritage status over birds' nest soup', The Guardian, 2010 [http://www.theguardian.com/world/2010/aug/10/bird-farming-swift-penang-malaysia], retrieved 14 August 2013

30. 'Getting to know bird's nests' [http://www.naturalnest.com/articles/id/46], retrieved 14 August 2013

32. S Curwood, 'After Sandy, looking at oysters as a way to protect vulnerable coastlines' [http://www.pri.org/stories/science/after-sandy-looking-at-oysters-as-a-way-to-protect-vulnerable-coastlines-12045.html], retrieved 14 August 2013

the run. Its common nature is typically representative of the lifestyle expressed in the American way. The hamburger is mass produced in mechanized food factories, fabricated in mass volume polystyrene boxes, cooked in huge numbers and sold at franchised food outlets all over the world.[35]

The space for eating a hamburger meal exemplifies the 'standard' even further. The mechanized start of the hamburger's life has been translated into the repetitive habitat in which its life ends. The commercial hamburger is consumed, more often than not, in a commercial environment. Big American burger chains that now exist throughout the world create the same dining experience in every outlet in every city. The calculated efficiency of table space, the fixed chairs, the sterile lighting, the 'push flap' bins and the swivelling doors, accompanied by the virtually identical menu makes the sense of space completely indistinguishable. Any capacity of place or local identity is lost to a national and global aesthetic decision that was made in an office more often than not a great distance away. Even the white serviettes, the folded napkins, the trays and the salt and pepper shakers are the all same and typify an institutional uniformity and anonymity that is equally characteristic of American dining.[36]

In New York, USA, the most delightful hamburger is not at MacDonald's on Union Square or at Burger King at Broadway, but in a gallery space at the Museum of Modern Art (MoMA). Made in 1962, the Claes Oldenburg sculpture displayed stands as a symbol of commonplace food.[37] The hamburgers are interpreted as signatures of American culture that reflect the favoured appetites and culinary practices of the population. The hamburger is popular, primarily as it can be enjoyed and purchased by anybody regardless of affluence, age or sex. A hamburger should taste the same and provide an identical gastronomic experience for everyone in any city.

The McDonalds hamburger has come to occupy a position of global political importance. The 'golden arches theory' is founded on the thesis that no two countries in which a McDonalds burger can be purchased have ever gone to war against each other. Confirmed by the New York Times in 1996, the theory highlights the effect of the business of the hamburger on the global political agenda. Such is the global demand for the burger that researchers at Maastricht University successfully 'grew' and ate a burger from cow cells in 2013. Responding to the environmental concerns of such a global food culture, the lead scientist on the project, Prof Mark Post, said, 'We are doing that because livestock production is not good for the environment, it is not going to meet demand for the world and it is not good for animals'.[38] Whilst an incredible innovation, Prof Tara Garnett, head of the Food Policy Research Network at Oxford University, highlights the issues raised in the beginning of the chapter; that the solution to the world's food problem is not the technological production of more food, but a more responsible understanding of the chain of supply, access and affordability of the food we currently produce.[39]

Claes Oldenburg, and other pop artists of this time started to work amongst an explosion of mass production art. Artists celebrated this new popular culture by using motifs and processes of the bulk fabrication of the everyday as the subjects for their art pieces. In many examples food took the lead role. Andy Warhol's Campbell's Soup Can paintings represented information that had become diluted through repetition.[40] He wanted his art, like the adverts he was seeing all around him, to become so

facing page top: A multi-million dollar industry, Penang's traditional buildings are being converted into swiftlet breeding grounds.

facing page bottom: Millions of dollars have been invested in oyster shell recycling schemes to reinvigorate the oyster populations around the coast of the USA.

73

33. S Madere, 'CRCL and Shell Oil Company Announce New Oyster Shell Recycling Program', Coastal Connections, 2013 [http://crcl.org/blog-menu-item/post/crcl-and-shell-oil-company-announce-new-oyster-shell-recycling-program.html], retrieved 14 August 2013

34. F Glazer, 'Recycling oyster shells benefits restaurants, environment', Restaurant News, 2013 [http://nrn.com/seafood-trends/recycling-oyster-shells-benefits-restaurants-environment], retrieved 14 August 2013

35+36. S Sitch, 'Made in U.S.A.: an Americanization in modern art, the '50s & '60s', University of California Press, Berkeley,1987, p.78

37. 'Two Cheeseburgers, with Everything (Dual Hamburgers)', MOMA [http://www.moma.org/collection/object.php?object_id=81183], retrieved 12 July 2012

38+39. P Ghosh, 'World's first lab-grown burger to be cooked and eaten', BBC News, 2013 [http://www.bbc.co.uk/news/science-environment-22885969], retrieved 8 August 2013

40. 'Andy Warhol/Art 1900 onwards Main Art 1928–1987' [http://www.londonfoodfilmfiesta.co.uk/Artmai~1/Warhol.htm], retrieved 12 July 2012

monotonous that it did not have an effect on people. The soup as a food source was mass-produced and economical for consumers of the new modernist age.

facing page: In New York, the best hamburger is not on the street outside the Museum of Modern Art (MoMA), but in the museum's gallery.

Oldenburg's 'Hamburger' emulates the icon of American culture by craftily displacing its identity through its construction. The sculpture is made from burlap soaked in plaster, and painted with enamel, an ironic reality a world away from the enduring strength of America.[41] Its malleable cast and soft construction also sarcastically mock preconceived assumptions that traditional sculpture is solid and hard.[42] A symbol of automated investment in the commercial appearance of the fast food meal that has shaped global cities, the sculpture draws the viewers to fittingly consume it. The reality however, could not be further from the truth in the white minimalist space of the New York gallery. The most common, readily available food source of the twenty-first century is right in front of you, yet unavailable for lunch.

75

We fantasize about food in galleries, museums and in movie theatres. We also indulge ourselves by flicking through mouth-watering recipes in bookshops and public libraries, or on the Internet in the comfort of our homes. Food habits and practices represent a central element of civilization and the culture of cities. Intellectual greed or sensual nourishment, the relationship between life and art, and media share much common ground in food. Bizarre, unethical or sustainable, food ultimately promotes dilution of cultural boundaries, and restores the primal link between urban inhabitants and their sustenance.

41+42. 'Two Cheeseburgers, with Everything (Dual Hamburgers)', MOMA [http://www.moma.org/collection/object.php?object_id=81183], retrieved 12 July 2012

'**When I walk into my kitchen today, I am not alone. Whether we know it or not, none of us is. We bring fathers and mothers and kitchen tables, and every meal we have ever eaten. Food is never just food. It's also a way of getting at something else: who we are, who we have been, and who we want to be.**'
– Molly Wizenberg, 'A Homemade Life: Stories & Recipes from My Kitchen Table', 2009

Eating habits have always been determined by a complex combination of social, technological and economic forces. Given that the global food market is economically subservient to choices made by the consumer, information has a pivotal role to play in influencing public opinion and thus shaping patterns of food consumption and production. Information in the public realm, however, is both overwhelming and contradictory and hence often powerless to remedy any of the inherent problems that are pervasive in the global food system. Generally, urban food habits are becoming increasingly unsustainable, unhealthy and exploitative and yet persist as they are socially accepted and encouraged to remain by the numerous drivers that shape popular culture. Although food issues relating to food security, agricultural sustainability, diet-related diseases and social exploitation are of vital importance to the future prosperity of our cities, they are under represented in the public realm.

facing page: Every year Sydney Harbour Bridge hosts the city's 'Big Breakfast', bringing people together in the middle of a highway to share knowledge about food.

As a society we are becoming less concerned about what we put in our mouths, partly due to a growing culture of psychological indifference but also because the nutritional value of food, as well as its environmental and social impact, are becoming less accessible and more difficult to understand. Furthermore, the burden of responsibility on the modern consumer in an international food economy is so small that food choices made today are almost entirely self-indulgent. Consumers in today's cities make food choices according to taste, cost-efficiency and time-efficiency irrespective of where it came from, how it was produced or even what it contains. Whereas information through advertisements disseminated on behalf of the food industry only maintains the status quo, the information communicated by governments and NGOs broadly attempts to encourage ethical consumption and reform the global food economy. In order to encourage ethical consumption, food education must be radically counter-cultural and focus on the fundamental problem of how to reconcile good eating habits with the way in which people living in a modern society want to lead their lives.

Information about food in the public realm in the form of advertising is ubiquitous to such an extent that it is virtually impossible to journey anywhere in a modern city without exposure to it. International food retailers lavish astronomical budgets on the publication of food information in the form of brand advertisements that have a profound effect on urban eating habits. Billboards have become urban

spatial devices, manipulating and choreographing a culinary journey through the city with sumptuous images of the meals on offer.

Food retailers value the foods they distribute in terms of unitary demand and cost and thus the only information that is of use to them is information that improves the unitary profit margin of a food. Hence, advertisements describe foods in terms of their appearance, their taste and their cost and are broadly taciturn about their nutritional value or the social and environmental impact of their production. The advertising industry has developed a method of communication that most appropriately achieves the singular economic aim of the food industry it represents by producing visually colourful and idealized projections of foods which are limited in their scope yet broad in their urban appeal. The growth of the advertising industry and its influence on urban society has systematically marginalized our awareness of methods of food production in cities. It has taken advantage of the geographical dislocation of production from consumption to present foods as one-dimensional economic commodities that appeal principally to our sense of thrift and our taste buds. Even organic foods and foods which promote Fairtrade have become commercialized by the food industry. Their apparent ethicality has become their selling point and also their justification for high prices. Food information in the public realm is heavily reliant on seductive imagery and keeps written information to a minimum. What little writing there is tends to be short sharp half-sentences such as 'taste the difference', 'new improved recipe' or 'now with 50% more', each of which promote a carefully calculated and succinct aim based on the evidence of market research. The continued success of food advertising has led to the production of modern urban societies that are saturated with imagery and information and yet remain ill informed about global food issues and reluctant to accept any responsibility.

In recent years, TV chefs and independent documentary filmmakers and writers have taken on the mantle of counter-cultural food education in the mass media by broadly encouraging ethical eating habits and denigrating the fast food culture. Whilst specialized films such as 'Super Size Me' and 'Fast Food Nation', which expose problems in the global food system, are well received by a large audience, their influence remains small and unnoticed by the parts of urban society which would benefit the most. Jamie Oliver's popular 'School Dinners' TV series provided a very effective combination of social drama and responsible food information which was broadly successful in its unveiling of the poor nutritional diets of school children and the associated social problems caused by bad eating habits. The popularity of the programme in the UK and in America raised awareness and caught national press attention. It even activated interest groups such as the Merton Parents group who were motivated to reform school eating habits in many primary and secondary schools in their local borough.

Appearing as early as the 1950s, the advent of the TV chef transformed the living room into a sort of food 'classroom'. In the UK, the first TV chef, Fanny Craddock, assumed the role of headmistress of this new food 'classroom', enjoying a 20-year reign as queen of the British kitchen. In the USA, Julia Child enjoyed similar celebrity status, capitalizing on the unique visual quality of TV cookery programmes to achieve both breadth of dissemination and intimacy of individual connection. Her impact on the American cuisine and palate was so great her kitchen has been preserved in perpetuity as an exhibit in the Smithsonian

facing page: Food advertising, Las Vegas. The growth of the advertising industry and its influence on urban society has systematically marginalized our awareness of methods of food production.

Museum of American History.[1] This legacy continues to date and, ironically, all too often families are huddled together in the living room eating a quickly, easily prepared, pre-bought 'TV dinner', nourished instead by the magnificent meals being prepared before them on the screen.

Concurrently, and often in conflict with the information communicated by global food retailers in the mass media, information about food and the food industry transmitted by the state aims to be broader in scope, disinterested in and not curtailed by economic interests. Food is becoming an increasingly significant issue on the national agenda of many countries as it is inextricably linked to, and detrimentally affected by, the recent downturn in the global economy and the impact of climate change. Despite the importance of food to the future prosperity of cities, it still receives relatively little attention from governments. Furthermore, the information provided by governments is often adversely affected by ineffective administrations that are impassive or immobile due to conflicting interests or insubstantial campaign budgets. Their impact on public perception is dwarfed by that of the food industry, due to the difference between their respective advertising budgets. Food advertising has gradually become an intrinsic and powerful part of urban food culture such that its many detrimental influences upon what people choose to eat are ingrained and difficult to remove. Government intervention in the food industry generally attempts to release this stranglehold, but is too reliant on rhetoric and not enough on reform.

Whilst governments struggle to convey a clear and focused message to the general public, NGOs and lobby groups offer a much more immediate and vehement form of food education. Groups such as Food Aid, The Red Cross and UNICEF have a significant presence in many of the world's largest cities and are responsible for the proliferation of important food information that is not otherwise available. As well as informing public opinion, these groups also play a vital role in prompting governments into action and encouraging charitable donations. However, despite the vital importance of the information they deliver, the reach of groups such as Food Aid is very limited.

As the many problems which are symptomatic of the chronic global food shortage come to bear in an era of unrelenting urbanism, rapprochement to prevent an impending catastrophe can only be achieved if food education ceases to be dominated by pervasive yet deficient brand advertisements and instead by direct and impartial information which encourages ethically responsible eating habits. Whilst it is argued that intervention and volitional education by the state is unconstitutional and impinges on the boundaries of personal responsibility, given that the burden of responsibility is small and the consequences of the continuation of existing urban eating habits great, ethical consumption can no longer be left to personal choice.

Education Through Experience

Sydney Harbour Bridge is the annual setting to bring people in the city together to converse, connect and most of all share knowledge about food. Every year Australia's most famous icon is turned into a giant picnic location where 6,000 people share breakfast together at daybreak. 'Breakfast On The Bridge' marks the pinnacle of the annual Crave Sydney International Food Festival. People are chosen by ballot to enjoy croissants, sausages, bacon, eggs and coffee together in the middle of a highway that is normally full of cars in rush-hour traffic.

With traffic diverted, the picnic space is made from over 8,000m2 of artificial turf laid out onto the tarmac surface of the bridge. Cows are transported from a nearby agricultural college, and are allowed to graze unflustered amongst the outdoor diners in their new surroundings.[2] Ironically, it is the thousands of commuters who stand in amazement, being more used to sitting in traffic on the bridge.

Novel and unusual learning environments generate a more active discourse and education than in classrooms. Stimulating learning habitats promote ideas and teaching focused around experience. Education is also critical for promoting sustainable development and improving the capacity of people to address environmental issues themselves. While experience invigorates the senses and embodies a spirit of discovery, knowledge enables people to improve their contributions to the local economy and society.

81

A Wheat Field in the City

Similar to the presence of livestock in the midst of urban Sydney, downtown New York seemed an unlikely space for food education until a living field of wheat sprouted at a road intersection in the centre of the city in 2010. The memorable environment provided a novel opportunity to reach an urban population who may not be familiar with the agriculture industry or where their food comes from, and promoted more informed food choices.

Over a quarter of an acre, the Wheat Foods Council's 'Urban Wheat Field Experience' included a full-size combine harvester, a working mini mill, and a mobile nutrition laboratory. There was even a bread-baking station to transform the streets of the city into a mini 'farm-to-fork' experience.[3] Approximately one and a half million wheat kernels were planted in three hundred, one metre by one metre interlocking pallets to make a field.[4] A pedestrian path running through the enclosure encouraged visitors to engage with the exhibition at a hands-on level.

The message of awareness of wheat as a food source was enhanced by the memorable experience that this inner-city event provided. Over the course of the exhibition, wheat field tours were given by agriculturalists who emphasized the importance of where wheat is grown, what methods are used to grow it, and when the best time is to sew and cultivate a crop. Information regarding annual consumption was highlighted to show how grain yields directly affect the economy of the United States. Milling experts were on hand to explain the process of transformation that turns a kernel into flour, whilst gourmet chefs delivered bread and cookie baking demonstrations.[5]

'This grain is grown on 63 million acres of American land and we each consume nearly 138 pounds of it annually, but very few of us understand how wheat gets from the farm to our table,' according to Marcia Scheideman, president of the Wheat Foods Council.[6] 'With the Urban Wheat Field we're offering a unique experience that has the ability to educate people everywhere about the importance of wheat to our diets, economy and the world.'[7]

The ability of wheat to feed people, animals and economies throughout the world makes America's most-consumed grain a food source of global significance. However, it seems that many people knew very little about the life of the valued seed. False understandings of nutrition about enriched white flours

haha, a book on food and "sow" is misspelled. sow

1. 'Julia Child's Kitchen at the Smithsonian' [http://amhistory.si.edu/juliachild/], retrieved 15 May 2012

2. N Bryant, 'Picnic on Sydney Harbour Bridge', BBC News, 2009 [http://news.bbc.co.uk/1/hi/8324591.stm], retrieved 5 July 2011

3. 'Wheat Foods Council' [http://www.wheatfoods.org/], retrieved 5 July 2011

4, 6+7. M Levenston, 'Urban Wheat Field Sprouts on Streets of New York', City Farmer, 2008 [http://www.cityfarmer.info/2008/10/12/urban-wheat-field-sprouts-on-streets-of-new-york/], retrieved 5 July 2011

5. 'A Kernel of Wheat', Wheat Foods [http://www.wheatfoods.org/sites/default/files/atachments/kernel-wheat-how-flour-milled.pdf], retrieved 5 July 2011

in particular have resulted in many people becoming attached to flavours rather than nutrition.[8] Educating the public about wheat makes them aware of their role in the food chain from kernel to shelf. People do not often realize that they are directly connected to a chain that they directly affect through their buying actions. Through promoting awareness it is possible to improve the participation of everyone in the sequence. Knowing what the availabilities and demands are strengthens the entire process. Farming in participation, where buyers and producers collaborate in projects together, will empower the entire system. Bottom-up approaches place accountability at all levels. Therefore, there is a lot of responsibility for individuals who have direct roles in the advancing of large-scale initiatives. This should be promoted in agriculture especially in urban food cultivation, as it would place greater emphasis on personal obligations and have a direct effect on the quality of produce. The artist Agnes Denes eloquently questioned 'our misplaced priorities and deteriorating human values'[9] in her installation 'Wheatfield: A Confrontation' in which she planted a golden field of wheat amongst the gleaming skyscrapers of downtown Manhattan. In the autumn of 1982, Denes harvested a crop that had a value of US$93 on land valued at US$4.5 billion.

London – a World Food Encyclopaedia

From local food education to global food knowledge, the city of London is an encyclopaedia of world food, attributed to its rich diversity of cultures. Cuisine from former colonies of the British Empire can be found sprinkled across the city. More than a quarter of London's population is from an alternative ethnic background, which makes up an essential super-sized part of its cosmopolitan feel. New communities have infused London's kitchens with the smells of exotic spices, delicious sauces and ethnic delicacies from around the globe, presenting the casual diner with a few lessons on cultural and culinary traditions.

A walk through the numerous districts allows you to sample the diverse social and cultural communities that are exhibited in over 60 different cuisines provided in over 12,000 restaurants, which make up more than half the nation's total.[10] The framework of culinary London clearly defines the constituencies of this multicultural city – for example Greek and Japanese foods are predominantly in the north of the city, while Caribbean and African cuisines dominate in the south.

With London boasting more ethnic restaurants than anywhere else in the world, almost any kind of cuisine can be on the tip of your tongue within yards and minutes. Brick Lane's 24-hour takeaway bagels have become something of an institution in Whitechapel, East London. The shop has become a social mecca for late night clubbers, students and local Jewish old-timers alike, who stand around and chat all night in a place filled with wholesome smells and smiling people.[11] The huge influx of Bangladeshi immigrants has also made Brick Lane the curry capital of the United Kingdom. The street has myriad quality curry houses and genuine Bangladeshi cafés offering a melting pot of culture that will entice the taste buds of any good food enthusiast. Most of the South Asian restaurants serving curry to the British palate along Brick Lane are owned and run by individuals originating from Bangladesh. These proprietors not only offer the popular Anglo-Indian dishes such as 'Chicken Tikka Masala' and 'Chicken Korma', but also add a more authentic touch to the menu in an attempt to revive the original Bangladeshi cuisine.[12]

Curry has now become an integral part of British cuisine to the extent that Chicken Tikka Masala is now designated as a 'true British national dish' which is served 'on Intercity Rail, as a flavour for crisps, and even as a pizza topping'.[13] With over 9,000 restaurants nationwide, the UK Indian food industry has a big effect on the British economy, with an annual turnover of £1.8 billion through the employment of over 60,000 staff.[14] Further north, Kingsland Road is lined with restaurants and eateries that boast authentic Vietnamese cuisine at affordable prices.

Derived from an Anglo-French hunting call, 'Soho' is the name given to an area in the West End of London that until 1536 was agricultural, food-producing farmland.[15] Today, though the green pastures have been traded for concrete, Soho is still a food lover's paradise that boasts an array of over 400 late night restaurants serving a multitude of delectable global dishes.[16] Frith Street presents a choice of Mediterranean offerings and an authentic selection of coffees alongside Italian football matches that are screened throughout the night. Soho has also become the main focal point of the Chinese community in London.[17] A highly developed social infrastructure including shops, churches, travel agencies and a library exists in Chinatown, but it is most famous throughout London and beyond for its eastern food. With a wealth of almost 80 restaurants, it is possible to sample cuisine from all over Asia including Cantonese, Szechuan, Mongolian and Malaysian dishes. West London also boosts a big selection of Polish and Eastern European restaurants.

The incredible variety of cuisines leads the curious appetite to ponder upon new dining experiences, but traditionalists need not despair, as British cuisine remains alive and well in the capital. English favourites are still around, and can be found in the working class cafés of the Old Kent Road, and in the abundance of public houses that serve inexpensive tasty offerings throughout the city. Classics such as toad in the hole, bangers and mash, roast beef and Yorkshire pudding, cottage pie, sticky toffee pudding and trifle, can all be found on the plates of hungry locals.

English cockney delicacies like fish and chips and jellied eels are street foods that can still be found in London today. Fish and chips are cheap and can be enjoyed in one of London's many gardens, parks and even bus stops. Fish and chips, like jellied eels, may have their origins in immigrant cooking techniques, having possibly been brought over from Europe. The French brought us chips from their culinary repertoire, and Jewish immigrants introduced the battered fried fish, but it was the British genius which lay in the East End that combined the two.[18]

Having been a readily available food resource for centuries in the capital, with many fisheries in the Thames and nets set upriver as far as Tower Bridge, the eel is enjoying something of a cultural renaissance in London. Synonymous with the city's East End, the cheap and nutritious dish has been served chopped into rounds and boiled in water with vinegar, nutmeg and lemon juice since the eighteenth century. Perfect as a snack due to its convenient assemblage, the jellied eel has recently been the surprising refreshment of choice by people attending the opera. With around 80 eel, pie and mash shops in East London, the eel lends itself to many other cuisines, whilst offering a refined concept of quintessential British cooking at an affordable price that lets the taste buds do the talking.[19]

Tate and Rowntree

There are two characters that stand out in the history of the food industry of the United Kingdom for their remarkable contributions to the urban landscape and the philanthropic public education of the cities that provided them with huge personal success. Henry Tate, sugar refiner and the first benefactor of the

8. 'Wheat Growers Corner, Flour 101', Wheat Foods [http://www.wheatfoods.org/sites/default/files/atachments/flour-101.pdf], retrieved 5 July 2011

9. B Oakes, 'Sculpting with the environment – a natural dialogue', Van Nostrand Reinhold, New York, 1995

10. 'Health and Sustainable Food for London', The Mayor's Food Strategy Summary 2006, London Development Agency [http://www.london.gov.uk/sites/default/files/FoodStrategySummary2006.pdf], retrieved 8 August 2011

11. 'Night at The Brick Lane Beigel Bakery' [http://spitalfieldslife.com/2010/12/31/night-at-the-brick-lane-beigel-bakery/], retrieved 11 September 2011

12. 'Brick Lane food revival', Timeout [http://www.timeout.com/london/restaurants/features/2986.html], retrieved 11 September 2011

13. 'History of Curry', Brick Lane Curry Festival [http://www.curryfestival.co/Home/History], retrieved 11 September 2011

14. 'Curry Facts and Trivia' [http://www.curryhouse.co.uk/faq/oddssods.html], retrieved 3 October 2012

15. 'Survey of London: volumes 33 and 34 – St Anne Soho' [http://www.british-history.ac.uk/source.aspx?pubid=295], retrieved 3 October 2012

16. 'List of Soho Restaurants' [http://www.urbanspoon.com/n/52/5182/London/Soho-restaurants], retrieved 3 October 2012

17. 'Chinese London', BBC News, 2008 [http://www.bbc.co.uk/london/content/articles/2005/05/27/chinese_london_feature.shtml], retrieved 3 October 2012

18. S Round, 'Some like it cold', The Jewish Chronicle, 2009 [http://www.thejc.com/lifestyle/food/some-it-cold], retrieved 4 July 2012

19. S Jeffery, 'Eels', The Guardian, 2002 [http://www.guardian.co.uk/news/2002/apr/08/netnotes.simonjeffery], retrieved 4 July 2012

Tate public art galleries, and Joseph Rowntree, chocolatier and philanthropist, transformed the urban environments of London and York respectively.

The Rowntree family was engaged in the food trade for generations, as grocers and later confectioners. Whilst the Rowntree family are no longer engaged in manufacturing, the legacy of their production can still be seen on shelves today as their sweets, the Kit Kat, Aero, Polo, Fruit Pastilles and Quality Street, remain some of the most popular in the global market. Less well known is Joseph Rowntree's contribution to the urban landscape and welfare of his employees. A passionate campaigner against poverty, and the causes of poverty, Rowntree invested his earnings into public libraries for his workers, and later established the city of York's first public library. The Joseph Rowntree Foundation continues to be involved in philanthropic work improving urban environments and targeting poverty around the world.[20]

Henry Tate was the founder of the gallery, donating his collection of British nineteenth-century art and providing the financial backing for its original location in Millbank, London. The gallery has since grown and the Tate collections now occupy several locations around the UK, one of the most iconic and controversial, the Tate Modern, now occupying a former power station on the southern banks of the River Thames. A hugely popular site in London, the Tate Modern provides the city with free access to works that have challenged and elevated public notions of modern art. The building's beacon-like tower proclaims the Tate's legacy, and draws people from both sides of the river together. The presence of the 'Tate' can be felt all across the city, and a successful policy of public engagement sees the gallery's exhibitions advertised with the same graphical importance on the underground amongst advertisements for the latest blockbusters out of Hollywood. The doors of the building open the lower ground facade completely during the summer months and an inclined slope gently swallows people into the building. For a moment, the building is a huge whale's mouth and the city's residents, released from the pressures of urban life, are sucked into a world of immense richness in the phenomenal collection held within.

It is clear that mass media promoting food as commodity can be felt in the city at an individual scale, such as the nearly unavoidable presence of the TV chef or the onslaught of gastro-advertisements in one's living room. Food education has also burst out of the living room 'food classroom' and can be observed at an urban scale in the form of billboards, bus stop adverts (and even customized 'Golden Arches' zebra crossings!) that usurp the tectonic elements of urban infrastructure as surfaces for food advertisements.

Residents of the city are visually bombarded from all sides, and the trajectory of food education into the city shows that the advertisers are not content to stop at just the one sense. A recent ad campaign for the liqueur 'di Saronno' proposed to flood the London underground with a two week 'scent-wafting' campaign, pumping the distinctive almond aroma of the drink into the ventilation system and directly appealing to consumer's taste buds.[21] The campaign was pulled after only a day due to the coincidental release of an article the same day on the signs of terrorist activity in the popular broadsheet the Daily Mail. The article warned commuters to be cautious of the smell of almonds, especially whilst underground – an indicator of the presence of the dangerous gas cyanide![22] Perhaps the real assault in this case was the further erosion of the boundaries between advertiser or 'educator' and the consumer. Our living rooms may not be neutral territory any more, but surely, as the examples of the potential of the city to embrace multiple food cultures discussed in this chapter show, our taste buds still deserve some degree of agency!

left: The Tate Modern in London is a product of the philanthropy of the food industry in the United Kingdom. Tate & Lyle and Rowntree are known for their contribution to the urban landscape and wider public education.

20. Joseph Rowntree Foundation [http://www.jrf.org.uk], retrieved 28 August 2013

21+22. H Dawley, 'The Great Amaretto Caper, Gone Awry' [http://www.medialifemagazine.com:8080/news2002/nov02/nov25/2_tues/news4tuesday.html], retrieved 4 July 2012

Every Little Helps

'In summer I often eat lunch sitting on a bench in Hanover Square. The benches are crowded with office workers, shoppers and, invariably, people in black from the Condé Nast offices that overlook the garden, and one has to hover, eagle-eyed, waiting for a spare seat. Other people's lunches are always more interesting than one's own, ... If we were in another country – Italy or Sweden, say – we would be much more open about it, might even strike up a conversation. But this is England, and therefore a furtive peep is all one allows oneself, or gets.'

– Nigel Slater, 'Eating for England: Lunch on a Bench', 2007

As has been explored in previous chapters, the disconnection between consumer and producer is more pronounced today than ever before, both physically and ideologically. The effects of urbanization and the convenience of modern food transportation have claimed much land that was previously used for agriculture and relocated many primary industries to far-flung corners of the developing world. Food processing and packaging have introduced innumerable new phases into the supply chain and are responsible for the introduction of a multitude of new and artificially contrived foods each year, which continues to drive modern food culture away from traditional and organic diets. The ever-expanding gulf between the consumer and the producer leaves a huge number of people employed by the food industry vulnerable to the economically motivated decisions made by a powerful cartel of food retailers who control the global food economy.

The global food market is over reliant on a dominant model of food supply, which is anachronistic and increasingly unfit for purpose. Whilst it is very adept at achieving high profit margins and caters to the demands of wealthy consumer societies, the modern food economy is ill-equipped to cope with the impact of climate change, to respond to huger crises, to react to geographical unemployment, or to deviate in any way from its predetermined, economically motivated course. Thus, despite the abundance of people world-wide who are employed in the food industry, from farmers to food processing factory workers to checkout cashiers in supermarkets, the power over their fortune is held by a few corporate middle men who act on behalf of large food retailers. Whilst the agricultural sector and the food processing and packaging industries have both suffered heavy losses as they cope with the prolonged effects of the global economic downturn and climate change, many of the world's leading food retailers have continued to record large profits. Whilst the fishing industry has shrunk by 20% over the last five years, Tesco recorded profits in excess of £3.5 billion for the first time in 2011 and Sainsbury's profits rose by 15%.[1]

facing page: Before the arrival of rail, fresh meat could only be transported on the hoof, which took time and was wasteful, as it was reckoned that each cow lost about 20 pounds in weight on a 100 mile walk to Smithfield Market in London.

1. A Renton, 'British farmers forced to pay the cost of supermarket price wars', The Guardian, 2 July 2011

In the modern city, the farmer and traditional farming practices are almost mythical in their significance; seen only in children's books and on television. Scattered across the countryside, the contemporary agricultural worker has become merely a figure in the landscape, unacknowledged by city dwellers. The social invisibility of the agricultural worker has grown in proportion to urbanization and as our cities have grown, less attention has been paid to the manual efforts of those who fuelled their expansion. The social exclusion and vulnerability of the agricultural worker is summed up in a variety of nicknames that the urbanite has attributed to the lowly status of a supposedly 'unskilled' man of the earth.

The on-going price-wars between supermarkets have been achieved by pressuring food suppliers to reduce their asking prices, which has had a consequential and profound effect on profit and employment in the agricultural sector. Most agricultural sectors worldwide have seen the prices for raw foods fall in the last few years whilst the profits of the retailers they supply have risen. Supermarkets and food retailers have transferred the risks of an increasingly volatile global food market back to the producers by charging high mark-ups and enforcing promotions to get rid of stock. The balance of power in the food economy is such that farmers are powerless to do anything but sell their stock at reduced prices or risk it going bad. To compound the issue, agribusinesses that are responsible for the supply of agricultural infrastructure and supplements essential to the success of modern farming methods, also hold a monopoly. Their pricing is irrespective of the economic relationships between the producer and the retailer and often takes advantage of the dependence farming has on the products they supply. Hence, the maintenance costs of agriculture have risen whilst the prices received from retailers have fallen, leaving many farmers worldwide in an untenable position. At least one dairy farmer has gone bust in Britain every day for the last decade.[2]

Modern food production is becoming increasingly mechanized, involving processes that render traditional agricultural practices redundant. The necessary intensification of agriculture to meet the demands of a rapidly growing global population has forced many industries to relocate and created a universal reliance on modern infrastructure and artificial supplementation. The numerous transformations the agricultural industry has undergone have had a radical and often detrimental impact on the lives of the millions of people that it employs, causing mass migration and poverty. Agriculture today, is still heavily reliant on an extravagant use of non-renewable resources, in particular oil and freshwater. As these resources run out over the next 50 years, further transformations of the agricultural industry will occur which are likely to cause further migration, poverty and social exploitation.

If urban culture is largely oblivious to agricultural affairs, it is entirely ignorant of the procedures involved in the food processing and packaging industries. The rise of food processing has been an essential factor facilitating the global proliferation of food cultures. The numerous technological and industrial tools now available to the food industry have allowed for a greater control of over the look, taste, colour and content of the foods they manufacture as well as allowing for the production of many new artificially blended foods to satisfy the urban consumer culture's perpetual demand for variety. Food processing and packaging have introduced various new loops in the food supply chain which have increased the distance between the consumer and the producer both ideologically and literally. Food production factories are typically large and nondescript, sited on the edge of cities and in industrial parks. The processing and packaging processes they contain are carried out systematically, requiring manual labour to carry out repetitive tasks in shifts of eight hours a day or more. Because of its lowly social status, employment in the food processing and packaging industries is characterized by a high proportion of migrant workers. As a result of the lack of regulation or social justice, the industry as a whole is rife with illegal employment, overworking and payment below the minimum wage.

The millions of workers employed in the vulnerable primary and secondary sectors of the food industry have taken the brunt of the pressures in the food system resulting in underpayment and a climate of social discrimination. The modern food system is extremely unseasonal, due to food processing and transportation, yet incredibly responsive to changes in consumer demand that are very changeable and difficult to predict. The ramifications of changes in demand have a consequent and spontaneous effect on supply. Whilst food trends are flexible, growing foods and establishing food processing and packaging lines are not, thus, the sudden impact of a change in demand often results in a financial loss or unemployment somewhere in the supply-side of the food economy. Food production and packaging are still growing as industries. Each year the industries are responsible for the introduction of 15–20,000 new foods onto supermarket shelves in the UK alone.[3] Modern society's perpetual demand for variety is responsible for the continued growth of food processing and packaging, yet as they continue to expand and food retailers and supermarkets continue to dictate prices, there is little evidence to suggest that employment conditions are likely to improve.

Fuelling this trajectory is the culture of food purchasing which currently pervades cities globally. In this age of accelerated urbanization it has been proposed that 'the highest temple of the modern food system is the supermarket'.[4]

Concrete Honey

The roof of the Eiffel Park Hotel and a handful of other Parisian rooftops have one thing in common: a faint buzzing sound. Urban beekeeping has become an unlikely source of responsibility for many people in their spare time throughout the hidden rooftops of inner city Paris. Thanks to the swarms of industrious bees that have been enthusiastically introduced throughout the city, the production of honey is rapidly becoming a new clandestine industry in the French capital.

With over 400 registered hives throughout the city, from the unseen rooftop of the Paris Opera, the hidden glass dome of the Grand Palais exhibition hall, and secluded at the top of the skyscraper La Defense in the business district of the city, the pockets of concealed green habitats in Paris have become the new homes to hundreds of thousands of bee colonies that are far more productive than their rural counterparts.[5] Cities are free from the pesticides and fertilizers that are killing the rural bee communities. The warmth of the urban environment promotes earlier breeding as the climate encourages an early spring and a lingering summer. Most pollination in rural environments is over by early August, but in Paris many streets that are lined with non-native Sophora trees have just started to blossom.[6] This gives the secretive bees the extended opportunity to keep producing honey much later into the year.

The reclusive phenomenon of urban beekeeping has become so successful in the city that local Parisian apiculturists are claiming record production of up to 100kg of honey per hive every year. This is a huge increase from the comparative 20–25kg from the typical hives on the cereal-producing plains of the Ile-de-France, the surrounding region of the capital.[7] This capacity to generate so much honey is hugely accredited to the abundant quantity of flowers amidst the lush parks, rooftop gardens, eloquent

2. A Renton, 'British farmers forced to pay the cost of supermarket price wars', The Guardian, 2 July 2011

3+4. R Patel, 'Stuffed and Starved: Markets, Power and the Hidden Battle for the World Food System', Portobello Books, London, 2007, p.216

5+6. H Schofield, 'Paris fast becoming queen bee of the urban apiary world', BBC News, 2010 [http://www.bbc.co.uk/news/world-europe-10942618], retrieved 11 November 2012

7. B Toma et al.,'Weakening, Collapse and Mortality of Bee Colonies', Agence Française De Securite Sanitaire Des Aliments, 2008 [http://www.uoguelph.ca/canpolin/Publications/AFSSA%20Report%20SANT-Ra-MortaliteAbeillesEN.pdf], retrieved 11 November 2012

boulevards and the attenuated edges of roads that line the streets of Paris. Acacia, lime, chestnut and maple trees offer pollen havens in urban spaces that are well suited to a bee's pollen addiction. The flavour of the desirable urban honey is reportedly deliciously sweet, subtle and most importantly free from any city pollutants and exhaust fumes. Champs Elysees honey sold under the Grand Palais label has joined other meil de Paris brands costing a steep €15 (£13) for a 125g pot at high-end food outlets.[8]

It seems that the bees are dying everywhere but in the city. Rural beekeeping is in crisis due to a collapse in bee populations as a result of new and intensive farming practices. Monoculture agriculture, organized irrigations, the heavy use of pesticides, chemical fertilizers and plant growth regulators, alongside climate change has increased the mortality rate of bee colonies at an alarming speed. 35% of world production of fruits, vegetables and oilseeds depends on the activities of these flying pollinators.[9] The disappearance of bees endangers the beekeeping profession and threatens global agriculture that relies on pollination by bees to produce our human food supply.

A National Trust and BBC experiment in 2010, 'Bee Part of it', supported evidence that bees today often fare better in urban environments than in contemporary farmland. Bees are living better in the town than the country because of biodiversity.[10]

Not only is the practice of urban beekeeping creating an environment that offers a rich diversity of pollen, but it is also providing a novel hobby and source of relaxed employment for different age groups in many countries. In Germany, beekeeping has become part of an environmentally aware 'pension plan' for a small percentage of the country's ageing population. This unlikely source of casual employment for older people, occurring predominantly in the cities, provides a stage for new responsibility that cultivates a sense of independence. A self-sustaining support network of older people who act as social and team-building mentors for younger generations contributes an important aspect into community cohesion.

However, the pursuit of enthusiastic new beekeeping has not prevented nationwide bee populations in Germany to decline. Today there are only 82,000 beekeepers in Germany who manage approximately 700,000 bee colonies.[11] Expert apiculturists claim at least a million colonies are needed in order to maintain apple, cherry, berry and agricultural crop production in Germany.[12] This overhanging threat highlights the importance of hobby beekeeping.

Bee stings can be dangerous and even life threatening to a minority of people who are allergic to them. Introducing bees into dense living environments causes anxiety amongst inhabitants. This anxiety has resulted in beekeeping becoming a hidden practice away from the paranoia of public scrutiny. The sense of fear is the usual consensus of the many cities that have until recently banned urban beekeeping. Council policies apply strict guidelines for keeping bees within urban environments, such as in Paris, where beekeeping is only legal when the hives are at least 25m from hospitals or schools and have a 2m high security screen if they are not located upon a high building.[13]

In New York, beekeepers traditionally operated under the official radar, as Section 161.01 of the city

facing page top: The Tower Bridge Moorings community floating garden in London is a habitat for bees and other nectar-seeking insects.

facing page bottom: The abundant quantity of flowers amidst the Highline Park in New York offer bees the opportunity to keep producing honey much later into the year.

91

8. B Toma et al.,'Weakening, Collapse and Mortality of Bee Colonies', Agence Française De Securite Sanitaire Des Aliments, 2008 [http://www.uoguelph.ca/canpolin/Publications/AFSSA%20Report%20SANT-Ra-MortaliteAbeillesEN.pdf], retrieved 11 November 2012

9. M Tanguy, 'Can cities save our bees?', The Guardian, 2010 [http://www.guardian.co.uk/commentisfree/2010/jun/23/can-cities-save-bees], retrieved 11 November 2012

10. 'City bees show a richer diet than bees from farmland', BBC News, 2010 [http://www.bbc.co.uk/news/science-environment-10998318], retrieved 11 November 2012

11+12. 'Bee Mortality and Bee Surveillance in Europe', The Efsa Journal, European Food Safety Authority, 11 August 2008, pp.1–28

13. C Bremer, 'Paris rooftops swarm with bees as urban honey industry takes off', The Times [http://www.thetimes.co.uk/tto/news/world/europe/article2600836.ece], retrieved 15 November 2012

health code deemed their practice illegal until recently. The code banned keeping animals that exhibited 'wild, ferocious, fierce, and dangerous qualities', with offenders facing a fine of up to $2,000.[14] In 2010 the Department of Health and Mental Hygiene unanimously amended the law after it received a petition calling for beekeeping to be legalized in the city. Organized by the New York City Beekeepers Association, the amendment was considered after research was published showing the small risk honeybees actually pose to the public. 'Most people think they are dangerous, because they can't distinguish between bees, yellow-jackets (wasps) and hornets ... a honey bee is very unlikely to attack' claims New York beekeeper, David Graves.[15]

In the face of fear of bees, councils are acknowledging the sustainable and ecological necessity of their urban presence. Cities are beginning to encourage different ways of introducing beekeeping. In an attempt to reverse the rapid decline in the number of apprenticeships people are undertaking throughout Germany, apiculturists are introducing beekeeping on a trial basis. Over the period of one year, experienced apiarists lease individual colonies to young beekeepers and provide them with crucial advice and support. At the end of the trial term, the new beekeepers have the option to continue or return the bees and hives.

Self-appointed voluntary collectives and charities are raising awareness of the critical situation that bees face by helping to introduce new colonies into cities. Thanks to campaigning by the British Bee Keeping Association, bees can be found all over inner city London. The rooftops of the city are increasingly abuzz as a new safe haven for the honeybees away from the public gaze. With gardens declining, space always at a premium and the threat of wary neighbours, aspiring beekeepers have been pushed onto the rooftops of cities as favoured sites for urban apiaries. Green and brown urban roofs provide the perfect apiary conditions, secluded in the centre of a built-up environment. The Bank of England and the quintessentially English Fortnum and Mason food hall both have concealed rooftop beehives.

Luke Dixon, a theatre maker from London took over a year to find the perfect place for his first beehive in the city. After local allotment owners hypocritically raised concerns of scary swarms and honeybee stings even though dependant on them for the success of their crops, Dixon ventured into the inner city and installed his hives in the secretive haven of the Wildlife Garden at the Natural History Museum in South Kensington.

Since registering his interest in such a prestigious location, his presence has been noticed by an array of institutions around the city eager for his advice on the establishment of further small apiaries on their roofs. His success has subsequently been such that he has been employed to place hives on rooftops across London, including schools, churches, offices and theatres. The roofs of the Lancaster London Hotel, Pimlico Academy and National Magazine House have all been turned into wild-planted gardens providing the perfect bee microenvironments. His passion for beekeeping has found him new and rewarding responsibilities.

Beehives are a welcome addition to a city's skyscraper, out of sight from the public realm. The people

facing page: Hives on the rooftops of a hotel in Paris. Hidden urban beekeeping could be seen as a secret, private celebration of food within the places we live.

93

14+15. G Collins, 'For Hives and Honey In New York City; Rooftop Beekeepers Defy Law to Get That Sweet Central Park Bouquet', City Farmer, 1999 [http://www.cityfarmer.org/beekeepNY.html], retrieved 2 December 2012

that manage these flying honey suppliers carry out their work in some rather surprising locations, where the stunning surroundings inspire a passion to enjoy food. Hidden urban beekeeping could be seen as a secret, private celebration of food amongst the places we live. The urban experiment is carried out in locations that are not revealed.

Home Restaurants

Aiming to inspire a new trend in dining, 'Secret Supper Clubs' are the latest culinary trend to hit the underground restaurant scene in London. The movement spurred by a recession-beating drive involves venturing into to a stranger's house, being taken to their living room, loft or garden shed and having dinner cooked for you, often in the company of other strangers. The experience of sampling other people's old-fashioned home cooking in their secluded home environment provides the ultimate 'Come Dine With Me' experience.

Referred to in the USA as 'supper clubs', and in Cuba as 'paladares', these unseen home eateries are a cross between a restaurant and a dinner party. Like a restaurant, you are waited upon and have to pay for your meal, but like a dinner party, you are in someone's house with a regular person cooking. Home restaurants are much cheaper than a take-away, and exude a phenomenal sense of occasion.

Marketing executive Nicola Swift and social services worker Andrew Newman have run the discreet supper club, 'The Shed Likes Food', since 2009. Having served over 500 dinners from their modest shed at the end of their garden in Scunthorpe, northeast England, they typically charge a very reasonable £15 per head to cover costs.[16] Secret supper clubs are not licensed, and guests are asked to give a 'voluntary contribution'. The apparent formula for calculating cost per head is to take the cost of the ingredients, multiply it three times, and divide it by the numbers of diners.[17]

Home restaurateurs could be labelled as self-employed chefs who work from home, with the freedom to create their own menus in a unique environment. People do not do it for money and instead offer a genuine personal service that they enjoy as much as their guests. Reservations are strictly by word of mouth, or via guerrilla advertising, often on Facebook and associated blogs, with many requiring actual references to make bookings.[18]

A novel alternative to restaurants, secret supper clubs provide the opportunity for people to show off their culinary talents and sit down to chat with like-minded strangers. 'I love cooking and I love to cook for people ... I've met great friends at my supper clubs', 'You tend to have a lot in common with the people who come, you're interested in food, and it's nice to be in a slightly strange atmosphere in someone else's house where you're not exactly sure what you're supposed to be doing', certifies Alexis Coleman, a Lawyer who runs 'Lex Eat' in London during her spare time.[19]

Indoor Paddy Fields

Office workers in Japan are adding rural relaxation to their usual workday routines. Hidden in Tokyo's bustling business hub of Otemachi, a 1,000 square foot indoor rice paddy field is providing stressed out business people with a way to get back to their horticultural roots. The new urban farmers are part time office workers who cultivate the rice from a field during lunch breaks away from their desks. The idea is to get people interested in farming and to teach them the skills that have been taken over by machines, even in Japan's legitimate countryside. The project has provided full time employment to eight workers who have managed the paddy field since it was planted in the office lobby.

left top: Urban Home Restaurants? The ambiguous 'home restaurant' movement spurred by a recession-beating drive involves venturing into to a stranger's house, being taken to their living room, loft or garden shed and having dinner cooked for you, often in the company of other strangers.

left bottom: In Hong Kong on Sundays and public holidays, thousands of Filipino domestic helpers congregate around Victoria Park, HK Cultural Centre and in the foyer of the HSBC in Central District to socialize and picnic.

16+19. 'Dining on the sly at London's secret supper clubs', Moneycontrol [http://www.moneycontrol.com/news/features/diningthe-sly-at-londons-secret-supper-clubs_528220.html], retrieved 3 April 2011

17. Z Williams, 'The Secret Feast', The Guardian, 2009 [http://www.guardian.co.uk/lifeandstyle/2009/feb/10/underground-restaurants-london], retrieved 3 April 2011

18. Z Williams, 'Going underground', The Guardian, 2009 [http://www.theguardian.com/lifeandstyle/wordofmouth/2009/may/29/underground-restaurants-msmarmitelover-hardeep], retrieved 3 April 2011

Using lights inside office buildings to cultivate crops, the experiment could have big implications for Japan, which currently grows less than half the food it needs.[20] The rice harvested is served in the office canteen, redeeming the workers' effort with a rewarding meal. The employees of personnel recruitment firm 'Pasona Group' typically manage a considerable 50kg of rice per harvest. This is an impressive amount for an experiment but worryingly not enough to fill a rice bowl for the average Japanese person for even a year.[21]

Electric fans aid the numerous 1,000-watt lamps, constructed from a mix of high-pressure sodium and metal-halides. These simulated light sources are used to provide energy for the plants to photosynthesize in the confines of the indoor habitat. The paddy field is also open to the public, encouraging passers-by to try their hand at cultivating.

'People working in cities think a paddy field is something far from them and rare to experience, we want to give them a chance to experience it at the place where they are', declares Sayaka Itami, one of the farmers at the office field project.[22]

The implications for future food production are quite considerable. By incorporating the artificial system throughout Tokyo's offices, rice could be produced all year round. The vision is to transform agriculture and create a seasonless farm that will permit yields of up to three crops a year in the city. By restructuring salaried office worker timetables in order to formalize a window of agricultural productivity, indoor farming could not only provide refreshment from the daily grind in the crowded urban environment, but implement a workforce of food producing potential.

While the importance of local food growing is fast gaining ground, the ability to conceive of urban food production actually happening within the bewildering array of structures and surfaces of the city is a difficult concept. Can urban agriculture be the antidote for the many spaces that exist between utility and productivity in our cities?

Throughout the UK, seasonal workers, particularly from the EU, play an integral role in the food economy; from harvesting ripening berries to cockle and mussel picking. Coinciding with the promotion of locally sourced food, there has also been an increase in people visiting 'pick-your-own' fields in farms close to the urban fringe. Capitalizing on the romance of seasonal produce, some farms are even offering day trips and party packages: 'Not for us the bowling alley or pub – we are going a-hunting for anything berry-shaped!'[23]

SOLEfood

The hidden Astoria Hotel parking lot at the corner of East Hastings Street and Hawks Avenue in downtown Vancouver was once a meeting place for loiterers, binge drinkers and drug dealers. But since 2009 the urban planter collective SOLEfood has transformed the space into a successful farm. Cherokee purple tomatoes, French breakfast radishes, rainbow swiss chards, Tyee spinach and Red Knight peppers, amongst others have replaced litter, beer bottles and crack pipes on a newly revived site.

Established by the non-profit collective 'United we can', SOLEfood exists to provide affordable local food in Vancouver's Downtown East Side. The farm provides training and work opportunities to local residents, who build, plant, maintain and harvest the inner city farm all year round. Employing 12 local residents, who are paid wages of up to $12 per hour for their time, the collective produces over 4.5 tonnes of fruit and vegetables annually.[24] The locally grown food is sold to restaurants, at Farmers Markets and when possible, supplied to community organizations with similar aims of improving neighbourhood food security.

Led by the farmers themselves, educational opportunities during the growing season are available to the public who are interested in learning about urban agriculture. Employees see the farm as a place for self-growth and healthy community development, while beautifying their neighbourhoods. It is hoped that the future of SOLEfood will grow to include a network of farms that will help revitalize many new neighbourhoods, providing meaningful employment, to build relationships around healthy food.

97

Growing food for the city is a good idea but achieving it affordably is not often an easy task. Urban agriculture constantly struggles to exist in cities, as land values are extremely high. Farms like SOLEfood are looking to expand but often financially stretched city councils have no plans to provide more land at sustainable prices. To cover overheads and be self-sustaining the food grown by these collectives often, unfortunately, has to be sold to buyers who want high-end produce to sell at up market restaurants.

Implementing urban farms legally in inner city locations requires agreements with landowners to rent and use their land. Negotiations are aided by the incentive of land tax reductions brought on by the change of land usage.[25] The onset for something such as a garden can dramatically change classifications from 'business or commercial' to 'recreation or non-profit'. The attractive lower tax rates lead people to take advantage of the legal system in a process labelled 'land banking'.

City councils claim that they lose a lot of tax money and that more attention needs to be given to how they make up the lost revenue. However, the green collectives believe that the importance of providing tax abatements for private landowners is crucial in managing the high city land prices that urban farms depend on for their existence. 'What we are trying to do here is create a social enterprise that supports itself ... It wouldn't be possible to support itself at market value in the city', claims Sean Dory, project manager of SOLEfood.[26]

Urban farm collectives such as SOLEfood are a positive addition to inner cities and need to be supported by the city councils to exist. The fact that deprived urban neighbourhoods benefit economically and socially from the farms supports the need for a rethink in the way land property values are assessed. The city should support urban farming but needs an honest discussion about tax reductions with collectives like SOLEfood to stop private landowners taking advantage of these social enterprises.

FoodWorks
Food systems in cities have the opportunity to create thousands of jobs. By taking steps to create these jobs, cities can also improve public health and reduce energy consumption, alongside fighting child obesity and asthma. With no real long-term city food system plan however, many urban centres face potential opportunities being ignored. Many urban dwellers throughout the world are missing out on greener, healthier, more economically vibrant environments and lifestyles.

Food issues often get pushed to the fringes of public policies. People believe the only goal of food

20+21. R Buerk, 'Tokyo office workers turn into rice farmers', BBC News, 2010 [http://www.bbc.co.uk/news/science-environment-11617230], retrieved 5 April 2011

22. 'Tokyo office workers turn into rice farmers', City Farmer, 2010 [http://www.cityfarmer.info/2010/10/25/reuters-and-bbc-report-tokyo-office-workers-turn-into-rice-farmers/], retrieved 5 April 2011

23. 'PYO for the true taste of Summer', Localfoods.org.uk, 2013 [http://www.localfoods.org.uk/news/77-pyo-for-the-true-taste-of-summer], retrieved 10 July 2013

24–26. J Williams, 'Downtown Vancouver gardens replace trash with jobs', Thethunderbird [http://thethunderbird.ca/2010/11/25/downtown-eastside-urban-farm-costs-taxpayers-130000-a-year/], retrieved 15 December 2012 initiatives is to feed the hungry. Consideration over the origins of food is believed to be the reserve of the wealthy, who have the luxury of being the only ones able to really afford organically grown food. People do not appreciate that each step in the food cycle from the farm to the fork has a major impact on the lives and the economic wellbeing of every single city inhabitant. Each step also has the potential to create jobs that will improve public health and also preserve our share of the environment.

Aside from the Military, the combined branches of the New York City Council are the largest industrial buyer of food supplies in the United States.[27] The Department of Education alone serves over 860,000 meals a day, but spends the majority of the money used to provide this service outside the state of New York.[28] Recently, the Department of Education has started offering salad bars at many public schools, across the state. To stock these salad bars the city council spends approximately $300,000 a year to buy the 225 tonnes of romaine lettuce needed.[29] The lettuces do not come from the state of New York but instead are transported from fields in California, on the opposite side of the country.[30]

New York City Council has plans in motion to radically re-evaluate the city's food ecosystem. 'FoodWorks' is a long-term, comprehensive plan for the New York food system. The plan aims to redefine every step of New York City's food cycle by assessing the production, processing, transport, retail, consumption and post consumption needs of its inhabitants. The programme has also become a critical part of the efforts to create good jobs and promote nutrition in the city around food. Setting ambitious but achievable goals, the vision intends to better coordinate efforts across all levels of state government to improve the city's food system, by using both zoning and tax incentives to bring more grocery stores to underserved communities. The plan hopes to provide initiatives that can be achieved at little to no cost to taxpayers, and that will in many cases actually save money.

Food sales and services constitute a $30 billion market in the state of New York.[31] Only 2% of the food value consumed currently is actually produced in the city itself.[32] By changing state legislation to allow the city to prioritize local producers, the plan intends to change the market imbalance and keep more 'local food dollars' in the local economy. Supporting the localism ethic, farmers markets will be increased and more encouragement for wholesale retailers and restaurants to use regional products will be implemented.

In a city where 56% of adults are overweight and are classified as obese, one of the critical goals of the city's food plan initiative is to reduce diet related diseases and to combat the high level of diabetes that over 500,000 people suffer with in New York.[33] The new effort by the city council will aim to get more edible produce transported into New York by rail instead of truck to minimize the environmental damage brought on by the production, delivery and consumption of food. Approximately 97% of the food that enters the market in the city at present is transported by truck, whilst only 3% comes in by rail.[34] Studies show that by simply doubling the amount of food coming in to New York by rail, 58 million truck miles per year would be eliminated.[35] Through the 'FoodWorks' plan, the council aims to find ways of making the city's food system more transparent and sustainable. Expanding urban agriculture through community gardens, green roofs and urban farm projects will dramatically alleviate the dependency on the food transportation network.

Early Risers

Rodger Barton starts his working day under the cover of darkness at an early 1.15am. A fish merchant by trade, Rodger works at Billingsgate Fish Market in the East End of London. Billingsgate is Britain's largest inland fish market, selling approximately 25,000 tonnes of fish and fish products through its merchants each year.[36] His employment is in an environment of working with people around the commodity of food, hidden from public gaze.

Supplied by almost every port in the United Kingdom, the majority of fish entering the market is transported by road directly from the coast, arriving at the market in the early hours of the morning. Wares are set out in great competition amidst an atmosphere where the traders are loud and brash, eagerly trying to win over customers with cut price bargains.

Amazingly 40% of the market's products comprise fish imported from abroad.[37] Imported chilled fish is often air freighted from countries thousands of miles away, or transported by sea via roll-on, roll-off ferries. The choice of produce attracts customers of all nationalities to Billingsgate Market in the unseen hours of the morning, fighting to get the freshest fish in the whole country. 'They come from Jamaica, Poland, Russia, and they all want their own kind of fish, you name it, we gotta get it – that's our job' announces Barton.[38]

An abundance of fresh mackerel, cuttlefish, octopus, turbot, parrot fish, and halibut from Scotland can all be found in large refrigerated containers throughout the 13-acre large trading hall.[39] 'You couldn't get a better bit of fish, I swear to you if you went from here to the great China wall', proclaims Barton.[40]

Billingsgate is a thriving market and a remarkable place. The environment is crowded with people every day and it stands as a testament to the importance our culture and society places in the value of daily meal preparation for family, friends or even strangers. Food always plays a central role in society.

The merchants of Billingsgate share flavours of friendship and community in the hours they work together, hidden in the dark of the early morning. They have immense job satisfaction and enjoy being with the public, enjoying the tastes and textures of the fish in shared experiences based around food. 'The banter between the customers, the porters, the salesmen; you wouldn't get anywhere else in the world', declares Barton.[41] The market's few trading hours operate in the early hours of the day, in darkness, yet still provide an annual turnover estimated to be in the region of £200 million.[42]

Our Daily Bread

In recent years, a critical global shortage of bakers has emerged.[43] Older, experienced bakers are retiring and their younger replacements often do not have the right training due to the distance educational institutions currently have from the needs of modern business. Contributing to the shortage is social stigma that is also often attached to such lines of work. The nature of the work, and poor image of the profession makes it tough to recruit young people.

Although bakers rely on state-of-the art machinery and modern techniques, the profession has remained unchanged for thousands of years. Working through the night, bakers roll out cheese rolls, knot brioche, mix scones and whole grain loafs, shape sourdough loaves and baguettes, cut English muffins and model focaccia, making sure it is all hot and ready on the shelves by the morning. Bakeries are hot and

27–30, 34. 'Speaker Quinn Announces FoodWorks New York', New York City Council [http://www.youtube.com/watch?v=TGLYBiatNb0], retrieved 21 August 2011

31. M Barron, B Goldblatt, C Ho et al., 'Understanding New York City's food Supply', Columbia University, 2010 [http://mpaenvironment.ei.columbia.edu/news/documents/UnderstandingNYCsFoodSupply_May2010.pdf], retrieved 25 August 2011

32+33, 35. 'FoodWorks New York', The New York City Council [http://council.nyc.gov/d3/documents/foodworksny_12_7_09.pdf], retrieved 25 August 2011

36+39. 'Billingsgate Market', City of London [http://www.cityoflondon.gov.uk/Corporation/LGNL_Services/Business/Markets/Billingsgate+Market/about_billingsgate.htm], retrieved 27 November 2012

37+38, 40. 'City of London Billingsgate Market', Aboutbritain.com [http://www.aboutbritain.com/BillingsgateFishMarket.htm], retrieved 29 November 2012

41+42. 'Billingsgate Market', City of London [http://www.cityoflondon.gov.uk/business/wholesale-food-markets/billingsgate/Pages/default.aspx], retrieved 29 November 2012

43. 'Company Information', Bread Solutions [http://www.breadsolutions.com.au/about.html], retrieved 30 November 2012

noisy places of employment that operate while most people are fast asleep. However, for some bakers, the work is truly an art. Matt Jones, a 'craft baker' in Greenwich, London, describes it thus: 'For me, the best aspects of the job are the textures, the smells, the endless stream of creativity, and the joy of feeding happy customers ... baking is a touchy-feely kind of thing – if I hadn't started baking, I'd have been a sculptor' claims Jones.[44]

There is an increased public demand for 'real food'. Organic practices are increasingly accepted as in tune with marketplace demands but it is a market that is increasingly dependent on imports. Local baking could have the potential to alleviate this reliance and provide a healthy, fresh, nearby supply of unique foods to a supermarket-dependant society. Artisan bakers, such as Matt Jones, are capitalizing on the globalized appetites of urbanites. City dwellers have developed a taste for 'Breads of the World' and 'ethnic bread', from Indian naan and pitta to Scandinavian rye bread.

The baker's experience of the city is also changing. Where they used to work through the early hours of the morning to provide the rising city with fresh bread, the working day is no longer determined by daylight hours, as cities operate on 24-hour cycles to compete globally. As a result 'in store' and 'plant bakeries' have emerged to satisfy the demand for 24-hour access to fresh food.

The selling of food is by far the most familiar sector of employment in the global food system. From the waiters serving food in restaurants to the checkout cashiers in supermarkets, those employed in the selling of food are ubiquitous and unavoidable. The typical employees in the tertiary industry are monotonously uniformed and customer friendly, sometimes wearing badges indicating shortened versions of their first name to encourage a colloquial and informal atmosphere ripe for commercial enterprise. Cleanliness is paramount to success; hair is tied up and kept in hairnets, sleeves are rolled up and aprons and plastic gloves are worn. Work environments are similarly sanitized: the modern supermarket is filled with aisle upon aisle of processed foods in heavily branded, brightly coloured packaging which belie the notion they contain anything that is naturally sourced. Even the fruit and veg aisles contain waxy and unblemished foods in vacuum packed containers showing no trace that they were ever grown.

In the city, whilst there is a small portion of workers who run their own, independent food businesses, the vast majority of people employed in the tertiary industry work for international conglomerates, predominantly chain restaurants and supermarkets. Unlike the primary and secondary industries, employment in the selling of food generally comes from people who live in cities. Employees on the whole are paid low wages and work shifts which minimize the social obligations borne by the food industry in terms of health care, holiday pay and sick days. Whilst the supermarkets have evolved and capitalized on the dramatic increase in urban populations, there is dispute over the social and ecological sustainability of this mode of both food purchasing and employment. As discussed in greater detail in the chapter on food and health, city dwellers are beginning to demand alternative food practices; that the artisan butcher, baker and urban agriculturalist may actually propose greater socially, ecologically and economically sustainable future alternatives.

facing page top + bottom: In the early hours of the morning, fishing boats unload their catch at Sassoon Docks in Mumbai. Fishermen in small boats make day trips out to sea, while the larger boats would have been at sea for more than a week. Their wives and daughters sort the catch, carry it along the docks in baskets balanced on their heads and haggle hard with wholesale buyers.

44. 'Baker', MyJobSearch [http://www. myjobsearch.com/careers/baker. html], retrieved 30 November 2012

Five A Day

'It's amazing how pervasive food is. Every second commercial is for food. Every second TV episode takes place around a meal. In the city, you can't go ten feet without seeing or smelling a restaurant. There are 20-foot high hamburgers up on billboards. I am acutely aware of food, and its omnipresence is astounding.'

– Adam Scott, 'The Monkey Chow Diaries', 2006

In 1991, The United Kingdom Department of Health published the Dietary Reference Values for Food Energy and Nutrients which introduced a framework which valued food not according to the commonly established social indices of taste and cost, but according to its fundamental value towards the subsistence of a healthy human life. The subsequent Food Labelling Regulation, introduced in 1996, required that all food sold in the UK had to be labelled to reveal its nutritional information, its place of origin, a 'best before' date and the Recommended Daily Allowance (RDA). The RDA encourages responsible eating habits by expressing the food we eat in terms of the vitamins and minerals it contains in order to provide a healthy and balanced diet. The RDA also represents food in terms of its inherent energy potential through cellular respiration, in the form of food calories. The universal comprehension of food in terms of its inherent energy potential is vital to encouraging responsible eating habits and preventing the pervasive trend of over-consumption and diet-related diseases.

Energy efficiency in the global food system is reliant upon a complex interplay of agricultural, technological, social and economic forces. Whilst the free market is very good at achieving economic efficiency, it is not naturally inclined to value environmental efficiency or to support sustainable practices. In 2012, food was responsible to 30% of all global greenhouse emissions[1] and 70% of the world's freshwater supplies.[2] It is predicted that the global population will rise to an excess of 9 billion people by 2050, in addition to which, many of the resources upon which our current food system is dependent, in particular oil, gas and freshwater, are likely to be partially or entirely expended. In order to nutritionally provide for an increase in the global population of 2 billion people, with diminishing resources, the global food system will need to become radically more energy efficient in a number of ways. Whilst growing and eating local produce, reducing food miles and buying organic foods are all valuable in creating an efficient food system, the root of the problem is to achieve the sustainable intensification of the agricultural industry and simultaneously the transformation of the existing food distribution networks in such a way that more food is grown, more sustainably and delivered universally to all those who need it.

Farming has always been damaging to the environment. The organized cultivation of land in human

facing page: According to The City of Melbourne, the roofs of the Queen Victoria Market are equipped with 1,328 photovoltaic panels, covering 2,000m2, generating 252,000 kilowatt-hours of electricity and saving over 350 tonnes of greenhouse gas emissions in a year.

1. D Carrington & J Vidal, 'Global food system must be transformed on industrial revolution scale', The Guardian, 24 January 2011

2. T Smedley, 'Water and food security: where to next?', The Guardian, 13 September 2012

history has caused deforestation, destroyed ecosystems and used up an enormous amount of the world's freshwater supplies. The exponential rise in the global population over the last century has placed an enormous strain on agricultural production in terms of space and resources. The new farming methods of the 'green revolution' of the 1960s responded to these pressures by introducing chemical fertilizers and mechanized methods of sowing and harvesting crops that tripled grain yields without increasing the areas of agricultural cultivation. The research and development of new technological advances in the agricultural industry has continued since the 1960s in order to increase output whilst minimizing space, energy and labour. Farming practices in developed countries today are heavily reliant on chemical supplements, artificial fertilizers, diesel burning vehicles and automated mechanisms to maximize the agricultural output from the land available.

Organic farming is commonly regarded to be more environmentally friendly than conventional intensive farming because it is free from any chemical interference. However, it is also far less energy efficient, space-efficient and cost-effective than industrial practices as well as being reliant on crop rotation and compost in place of fertilizer. Research sponsored by the Department for Environment, Food and Rural Affairs has shown that a litre of organic milk requires 80% more land than conventional milk.[3] Whilst fostering an interest in organics is vital to raising public awareness, challenging the more intolerable methods of modern industrial farming, and supporting biodiversity, it should not be the primary strategy for addressing the problem of feeding a growing population with diminishing resources. To produce the world's existing agricultural output organically would benefit the ecology and the environment but would require several times as much land as is currently used for cultivation and several times the volume of agricultural labour.

The convenience of modern transportation networks and technological developments in food packaging and preservation have allowed the modern food economy to dislocate food production from food consumption and in doing so to profit from the economic deferential between developing and developed countries. Today, the global food system is reliant on a huge volume of food imports and exports; one of the reasons why food is responsible for 30% of all greenhouse emissions.[4] Localizing supply chains has, for a long time, been a counter-cultural government prerogative and green movement agenda in order to protect local and regional food economies and to reduce the environmental impact of food miles inflicted by the long haul transportation. However, local food economies are not always environmentally efficient. Taking into account the energy expended in modern methods of food production, especially in the EU and North America, it is often the case that locally produced food is in fact less energy efficient and more environmentally damaging than importing foods from far away. Producing lamb in New Zealand and shipping it to North America expends less energy than producing North American lamb, even in spite of the impact of its preservation, packaging and transportation, because farming in New Zealand is much less energy-intensive.

Rejecting imports on the basis of the environmental impact of the food miles they incur, without taking into account the efficiency of the supply chain as a whole, is not only misguided but also hypocritical. It punishes remote, and often fragile primary economies, which are typically very energy-efficient in

facing page top: Dough allowed to rise under the sun on streets in Cairo.

facing page bottom: Claypot cooking. In developing countries, in rural areas and cities, billions rely on biomass, such as fuelwood, charcoal, agricultural waste and animal dung, to meet their energy needs for cooking.

105

3. E Glaser, 'Is the food revolution just a great big fat lie?', The Guardian, 2 March 2012

4. D Carrington & J Vidal, 'Global food system must be transformed on industrial revolution scale', The Guardian, 24 January 2011

terms of production, for the carbon emissions caused by transportation and packaging, when they represent only a fraction of the emissions caused by consumer economies. Rather than concentrating on the efficiency of imports, the global food system would be better served by instead addressing the impact and sustainability of modern methods of production, by investing in better modes of transport and infrastructure and by encouraging a culture of buying locally and reducing the food miles.

All the cities in the world are reliant on a daily influx of a large quantity of food, much of which is internationally sourced. Whilst localizing the global food system may not always equate to environmental efficiency, it is paramount to reducing the current dependence of cities on imports and thus improving their food security.

Pigeon Power

For most city dwellers, pigeons are categorized along with rats, cockroaches and mice as vermin. In ancient Persia however, they were regarded as an important supply of energy. Hundreds of curious 'pigeon towers', dating largely to the Safavid period, peppered the vast fields of orchards and gardens in the vicinity of Isfahan, central Iran. The now derelict large-scale towers adorn the landscape in an abnormal context that is somewhat redolent of naval forts stranded hundreds of miles inland.[5]

The useful but unromantic purpose of the towers was to collect pigeon manure, a substance that had been found to be beneficial to the fields in the surrounding plains during the sixteenth century. Pigeon manure was mixed with ash and soil in varying proportions, and used as a fertilizer for different agricultural purposes including melon cultivation. A well-managed pigeon tower could provide fertilizer for more than 18,000 fruit trees over approximately 10 hectares of cropland.[6] Agriculture in the fertile but nitrogen-lacking Isfahan plains was largely supported in this manner, fuelling the energy of large melon crop production in the region.

The famous sixteenth century French jeweller and traveller Sir John Chardin, regarded as one of the finest western scholars on Persia and the 'Near East', noted his inquisitive observations of melon consumption at Isfahan in his ten-volume book 'The Travels of Sir John Chardin'.[7] 'Peasants live upon nothing else but melons and cucumbers ... there are some that will eat five and thirty pounds of melon at a meal without making themselves sick. During these four months, they come in such vast quantities to Isfahan, that I can't help believing they eat more here in a day, than they do in France in a month' observed Chardin.[8]

The pigeon towers are hand made cylindrical constructions built with unfired mud bricks, lime plaster and gypsum. Built on elaborate ground plans, the large towers range from 10 to 22m in diameter and stand approximately 18m high.[9] The towers actually consist of two separate cylindrical drums that are buttressed together internally to prevent collapse. The inner drum is taller than the outer and divided vertically by galleries, which cut the supporting buttresses and are connected by a circular stairwell. Inside the inner dome, internal barrel vaults and saucer domes support open space galleries. No timber was used in the construction and the structure is designed to work in compression.

facing page: The pigeon castles of Isfahan provide a glimpse into a sophisticated system for human–pigeon symbiotic living, the lessons of which can be gleaned and applied to other animal–human relationships in the city.

5. E Beazley, 'The Pigeon Towers of Isfahan', Iran, British institute of Persian Studies, pp.105–109, 1996 [http://www.jstor.org/stable/4299579], retrieved 4 July 2013

6. E Hansen, 'Castles of the fields', Saudi Aramco World, 2011 [http://www.saudiaramcoworld.com/issue/201102/castles.of.the.fields.htm], retrieved 4 July 2013

7. Sir J Chardin, 'Sir John Chardin's Travels in Persia', Cosimo, New York, 2010

8. 'Isfahan province' [http://wiki.worldflicks.org/esfahan_province.html], retrieved 4 May 2012

9. 'Burj-i Kabutar', Digital library, Arch Net [http://archnet.org/library/sites/one-site.jsp?site_id=8372], retrieved 4 May 2012

Pigeons enter the towers through perforations in the honeycomb brickwork of the domed cupolas at roof level. From here, the birds can enter the galleries through openings in the external buttresses or access the main inner drum vault at ground level through a set of archways. The enchanted character of the tower interiors comes from the mesmeric repetition of pigeon perches that adorn the entire surface of the vaults. Each perch is assembled from an asymmetrical mud pyramid of four unequal sides, and in their vast number give the space a certain sculptural quality. The inward slant of the interior wall of the pigeon perches ensured that the manure fell to the bottom of the tower for collection.

The pigeon manure was collected annually from the towers via a small entrance commonly positioned at roof level. This was to reduce the risk of snakes entering the building and alarming the birds.[10] Vibrations set up by the wings of thousands of startled birds posed a significant threat to the tower's construction. A mud brick building fabricated without timber to take tensile stress was dangerous. Today, structural cracks can be seen on the exterior of many towers, caused by the movement of terrified birds.

The external finishing of the pigeon towers served the dual function of letting the birds in and keeping the snakes out.[11] Bands of plaster typically coloured with red ochre or lime were finished extremely smoothly to minimize the probability of a snake getting a grip on the surface.[12] String courses of moulded mud and brick friezes, positioned at vertical intervals up the towers, created projections that snakes would find difficult to negotiate, whilst providing an added decorative feature.

The towers were never used for sourcing pigeon meat. The famous thirteenth century traveller Marco Polo observed: 'Turtle-doves flock here in multitudes ... the Saracens never eat them, because they hold them in abhorrence.'[13] Another possible explanation of why the Persians avoided the consumption of pigeon meat is due to their association with the Prophet Muhammad. Islamic tradition proposes that a fantail pigeon perched and fed on the Prophet's shoulder as he preached. Similarly, people of medieval Europe believed in the sacredness of doves and refrained from eating them because of their association with Christian tradition.

The pigeon towers of Isfahan represent one of the most remarkable examples of eccentricity in Persian architecture and an unusual arrangement of mutual interest between humans and nature. Today, even in their dilapidated state, the pigeon towers at Isfahan still remain impressive constructions. Small flocks of wild pigeons occasionally roost in the towers, despite collapsed ceilings and huge cracks in the walls that expose the roosts to the weather. The view upward from the bottom of a tower still reveals a sculptural quality and haunting beauty that transcends its utilitarian purpose as a place to collect the dung of wild birds.

The pigeon towers are an important part of Iran's architectural heritage. Beyond the preindustrial mud-brick engineering that so efficiently solved complex structural problems with a perfect marriage of form and function, they remain as an enduring tribute to the ingenuity of unknown master builders who have left their unique creations for all to see, still standing on the fields of Isfahan. These castles in the Iranian landscape provide a glimpse into a sophisticated system for human–pigeon symbiotic living; the lessons of which can be gleaned and applied to other animal–human relationships in the city. Whilst providing a resource for the builders, guano as fertilizer, the towers afforded the birds a nocturnal refuge from predators. Contrary to the perception that such sophisticated systems require a large budget, or highly engineered construction, here the skill was passed down, not as drawings, but as word of mouth between family and villages.

Water Power

Until recently, crop yields in agricultural systems depended on internal resources, the recycling of organic matter, built-in biological control mechanisms and rainfall patterns. Agricultural yields were modest, but stable. Production was safeguarded by growing more than one crop in a field as insurance against pest outbreaks and severe weather. Inputs of nitrogen were gained naturally through crop rotation cycles, which in turn suppressed insects, weeds and diseases by effectively breaking the life cycles of these pests. A family with occasional hired help did most of the labour, and no specialized equipment or services were purchased from off-farm sources.

But as agricultural modernization has progressed, the link between ecology and farming has often been broken as ecological principles are ignored or overridden to feed our growing appetites. Today there is concern about the long-term sustainability of food production systems. Modern day farms have become nothing more than chemical factories producing food. They are dependent on pouring massive amounts of fertilizers onto their fields in order to meet profit and quotas. These practices are destroying our environment, wasting gallons of water, and are even adversely affecting the health of local residents.[14]

In order to solve these problems agricultural production methods must change. 'Aquaponics' is a sustainable food production system that combines a traditional aquaculture system with a hydroponics procedure in a symbiotic environment.[15] Aquaponics is a relatively new form of farming that could solve our agricultural dilemmas, combining the two techniques of aquaculture (farming fish and aquatic plants in controlled conditions) and hydroponics (growing plants in mineral and nutrient rich solutions in water). The philosophy of aquaponics is centred on recycling wastes into resources in a closed loop system. The process works by initially creating an aquaculture environment with a collection of fish in a tank or a body of water. In the fish tank, effluents accumulate in the water and increase toxicity levels for the fish over time. This water is led to a hydroponic system where beneficial bacteria break down the toxic ammonia in the fish waste to Nitrite, and then to Nitrogen, a key nutrient for plant development. After the by-products from the fish waste are filtered out, the now cleansed water is re-circulated back to the fish in the tank and the process starts all over again.

The efficiency of food production systems can be judged on their inputs and outputs and their ability to generate more from less. Aquaponics is a closed loop system. By eliminating the need for soil and using fish waste to feed the plants, aquaponic farming also eliminates the need for chemical fertilizers, agrochemicals and pesticides. As the system takes nutrients from the fish instead of oil-based fertilizer, it relies on a mere fraction of the inputs and outputs compared to conventional field agriculture.

There are many different plant species that are well adapted to living in an aquaponic habitat. Lettuce, herbs, spinach, chives, basil and watercress, all have low to medium nutritional requirements and are well adapted to survive in aquaponic systems. Fruit producing plants, such as tomatoes, peppers and cucumbers, can all be grown but they have a higher nutritional demand and therefore perform better in heavily stocked, well-established aquaponic systems.

10. A Amirkhani, H Okhovat & E Zamani, 'Ancient Pigeon Houses: Remarkable Example of the Asian Culture Crystallized in the Architecture of Iran and Central Anatolia', Canadian Centre of Science and Education, Vol. 2, No. 2, July 2010

11–13. E Beazley, 'The Pigeon Towers of Isfahan', Iran, British institute of Persian Studies, pp.105–109, 1996 [http://www.jstor.org/stable/4299579], retrieved 4 July 2013

14. 'Factory farming's hidden impacts', Friends of the Earth, 2010 [http://www.foe.co.uk/resource/briefings/factory_farming.pdf], retrieved 6 July 2012

15. S Bernstein, 'Aquaponic Gardening: A Step-By-Step Guide to Raising Vegetables and Fish Together', New Society Publishers, Gabriola Island, BC, 2011

Several warm-water and cold-water fish species are adapted to recirculating aquaculture systems, including trout, perch, arctic char and bass. However, most commercial aquaponic systems are based on tilapia; a warm-water species which naturally grows well in the recirculating tank.

By transforming hydroponic operations into aquaponic operations, increasing the amount of urban farming and thus minimizing the distance food needs to travel, and decreasing the use of water compared to conventional farming, aquaponics will create a food production for the future which is both economical and ecologically sound. The attention to the 'true cost' of our food is changing our attitudes to what we demand for our diets. Open field, long distance transported produce is increasingly giving way to locally grown sustainably produced food. To achieve this, cites and urban environments need to become the locations for the new farms.

Based in San Francisco, 'Cityscape Farms' is an urban collective aiming to produce sustainable aquaponic food within the confines of the city. Their vision is to introduce urban greenhouses that will serve as aquaponic food centres in vacant spaces, unutilized strips of land and rooftop terraces, throughout the built environment of San Francisco.

Commercial aquaponics is a young sector of agriculture but one with great potential. Aquaponic farming is not limited to seasons as it is a process that can be controlled indoors. In a controlled greenhouse environment, a grower has the ability to enforce a bio-security programme that will keep the grown food free of contamination. In addition, the ability to be close to the marketplace eliminates the long-distance travel that most fresh food endures. Cityscape predicts that by eliminating transportation costs and fertilizer, a 10,000 square foot greenhouse could produce $500,000 in profit and 20 to 30 tonnes of food a year for local supermarkets and cafeterias.[16] Local and organic produce like strawberries and tomatoes being produced all year round is an attractive investment for local restaurants.

The rapid growth cycle aquaponic cultivation allows, encourages crops to be produced at a higher frequency than in traditional agricultural methods. This is due to the unique relationship aquaponics creates between a plant's environment and its energy resources. In aquaponic systems, plants are able to grow with shallower root systems, allowing more energy for leafier, more vertical vegetable growth. Aquaponic cultivation systems can be accommodated in lightweight frame structures, which are quickly and easily constructed – a further benefit to the potential success of aquaponic farming.[17]

New urban farming and aquaponics is about creating ecosystems in areas where they would not otherwise exist. Aquaponic systems could exist in homes to enhance self-sufficiency, and encourage people to take more control of what they eat. The processes behind aquaponic farming could be taught in schools to empower a growing generation, and give them the techniques that will allow them to grow food in their back gardens forever. By engaging all sectors of the community, aquaponics could be part of an array of new and sustainable farming solutions that will create food security resilience.

To close the loop in our current food production system, and meet our global challenges, we need to produce 50% more food by 2030.[18] We need to produce more food with fewer resources. Ultimately, in order to feed our growing population we need to produce food in more environments than the traditional crop field. To achieve this we need to reconnect people with the food they consume. This is a particularly pertinent issue in urban communities where children and adults do not get access to seeing many of the foods they eat, simply being grown. It is important to excite, inspire and engage the next generation to give them the skills to meet our global challenges.

Floor Power

Global population growth and rapid urbanization increase have placed a huge demand on our resources. Soon, our traditional soil based farming model that has developed over the last 10,000 years will not be a sustainable option.[19] The implications of rapid urban growth will make the sustainability of our cities a major priority. The ideal future urban settlement will reduce environmental impact with the recycling of wastes for production of energy and foods as products of consumption. 'You can't be an ecosystem without producing your own food. That is gardens and big buildings with food inside and three story versions and empty lots that are used in the summer – all of this has validity towards making a city more independent of its food supply from the outside', declared Dr Dickson Despommier,[20] professor of public health at Columbia University.

The 'Vertical Farm' is a concept that seeks to address the major concerns of environmental degradation and the failings of the current food production system in our modern cities. The vertical farm will make use of what is now considered waste to create energy and food. The concept proposes that we can reduce the ecological footprint of the city and create a more sustainable habitat than our current system offers.

Most densely populated cities consume the resources of their surrounding land areas at an alarming rate. Vertical farming, in which agricultural products are produced within the city limits, stems from a need to address this concern. Urban agriculture can not only decrease the amount of land used but also eliminates the need for transportation of food into the city. This effectively decreases fuel consumption as well as the emission of greenhouse gases associated with the food industry.

Efficient land utilization and self-sustainability are the key aspirations of urban agriculture. The current situation is one in which the city imports produce and exports waste. Urban agriculture strives to reverse this process by recycling waste and other resources within the city for crop production, closing the loop and creating a more self-sustained city. By making use of these resources, urban agriculture should also be effective in lowering the cost of food. This is especially important for the poorer areas of the city where food cost is a concern.

The resources sought after for the vertical farm are the common outputs from the city's normal processes. Resources being considered as inputs for the farm include wastewater, post-consumer organic wastes from supermarkets and restaurants, alongside unutilized space, and abandoned building spaces.

Approximately 6% of New York City's land is classified as vacant, with Staten Island alone having more than 4,200 acres going spare.[21] Most of these vacant plots have the advantage of needing little demolition to use, and have already been deemed unsuitable for other development use. This land is particularly useful for urban farming, which can utilize odd shaped plots of land for production, such as those along railway tracks or streets.

111

16. 'Urban farming 2: No soil, no sun', Cable News Network, 2010 [http://money.cnn.com/2010/12/23/technology/urban_farming_high_tech/index.htm], retrieved 6 July 2012

17. A Starr, 'Why aquaponics may be the future of urban farming, and one solution to our local food problem', City Farmer, 2010 [http://www.cityfarmer.info/2010/01/24/making-urban-farming-scalable-with-fish/], retrieved 6 July 2012

18. 'Water and food security', United Nations Department of Economic and Social Affairs [http://www.un.org/waterforlifedecade/food_security.shtml], retrieved 6 August 2013

19. DD Despommier, 'Windy City', Ted Talks, 2010 [http://www.youtube.com/watch?v=XldP00u2KRA], retrieved 6 July 2012

20. 'Interview with the Father of Vertical Farming' [http://urbantimes.co/magazine/2012/03/interview-with-the-father-of-vertical-farming---dr-dickson-despommier/], retrieved 5 August 2013

21. 'New York City Land Use', New York City Department of City Planning [http://www.nyc.gov/html/dcp/html/landusefacts/landusefactshome.shtml], retrieved 5 August 2013

Vertical farms will bring urban habitats one step closer to self-sustainability and an enclosed energy feedback system of recycled outputs. The concept could change the traditional conception of 'waste', demonstrating its value as a source of energy for food production. The ecological footprint left by the vertical farm will be minimal in comparison with traditional farming methods. Future consideration must include social considerations of community, land use, and a smooth integration into neighbourhoods with available vacant landscape, as well as employment opportunities made available by the vertical farm concept.

The concept of the vertical farm is not building specific. Whilst there would be key structures exclusively for the intense production of food they are not the only settings that could house urban farms and spaces for food production. Farms of various dimensions and crop yields could be built into a variety of urban locations such as schools, restaurants, hospitals, public buildings and rooftops of apartment complexes. The definitively urban broadsheet, the New York Times, is a proponent of the vertical farming movement, inviting the world to 'Imagine a farm right in the middle of a major city'. The article goes on to assert that for every indoor acre converted to urban farming, a greater 10–20 outdoor acres could be returned to their 'original ecological' states.[22]

Vertical farms would bring a great concentration of plants, crops and vegetables into cities. These plants would absorb carbon dioxide produced by vehicle emissions and give off oxygen in return. This process would improve urban air quality and create a better environment for city inhabitants. A continuous quantity of fresh vegetables and fruits for city dwellers would also aid overcoming health problems such as obesity in the city centre.

The technologies needed to create a vertical farm are currently being used in controlled-environment agriculture facilities such as greenhouses, but have not been integrated into a seamless source of food production in urban high-rise buildings.

Yet indoor farming using hydroponics, aeroponics and aquaponics has existed in the agriculture industry for many years. Crops such as strawberries, tomatoes, peppers, cucumbers, herbs and spices have grown in this system and have been sold to the world's markets in large quantities. Most commercial indoor farming operations are small when compared to 'factory farms', but unlike their outdoor counterparts, they produce crops year-round. The vision of vertical farming using indoor cultivation is to produce a wide variety of foodstuffs that can be harvested in enough quantity to sustain even the largest of cities without significantly relying on resources beyond the urban footprint.

The restaurant industry produces a lot of organic waste within our cities. Methane generation from this single resource could contribute significantly to energy generation, and may be able to supply enough to run vertical farms without the use of electricity from the grid. For example, in New York City there are more than 23,000 food service establishments, all of which produce significant quantities of organic waste, and they have to pay to have the city for refuse disposal.[23] Refuse waiting to be collected also encourages vermin, and presents a threat to public health.

facing page: Farms of various dimensions and crop yields could be built into a variety of urban locations such as schools, restaurants, hospitals, public buildings and rooftops of apartment complexes.

113

22. DD Despommier, 'A Farm on Every Floor', The New York Times, 2009 [http://www.nytimes.com/2009/08/24/opinion/24Despommier.html], retrieved 5 August 2013

23. 'NYC Statistics' [http://www.nycgo.com/articles/nyc-statistics-page], retrieved 5 August 2013

Slum Power

City populations have dramatically increased with the influx of new migrants displaced by natural disasters and conflicts. The increase has caused slum populations to rise in cities and urban environments. 62% of the urban populations in sub-Saharan cities are slum dwellers.[24] Slums are characterized by urban decay, high rates of poverty, illiteracy and unemployment, with inhabitants having restricted access to adequate and safe water, sanitation and food.

Urban agriculture holds promising solutions to the issues of urban poverty and human rights in sub-Saharan Africa. The importance of having affordable, nutritious food in the urban setting is heightened in a period when you have high food prices and potential for unrest and political instability. Those involved in the practice of urban farming are more likely to maintain an adequate food supply for their families than those who are not.

'There is increasing recognition of the urbanization of the world and the role that urban and peri-urban agriculture plays to provide food supplies for the population that is most vulnerable in cities', says Daniel Gustafson, Director of the Food and Agriculture Organization (FAO).

Overcrowded slums in Nairobi have been part of a campaign looking to educate malnourished urban dwellers on the potential of urban agriculture. The Italian organization 'Cooperazione Internazionale' has led the 'farm-in-a-sack' project, which provides impoverished families with more than 40 seedlings that can be grown into food in just a few weeks.[25] Even though the slum is not a gardener's paradise – the streets are narrow and refuse is strewn everywhere – small farms are starting to appear on the areas of vacant land. The capability provided by urban agriculture promotes independence for slum dwellers by giving them full control of their own growing production.

Nairobi's urban centres are increasingly cramped, forcing farmers to innovatively use minimum amounts of space to get the maximum amount of output. Vertical gardens that make use of recycled sacks and biodegradable cement bags, alongside rooftop gardens that harvest and treat household wastewater, are all being used to grow food in the city. To protect their crops from pests within the urban habitat, farmers are planting vegetables such as capsicum and spring onions that naturally deter pests, instead of using chemicals that could harm the soil.[26]

As slums of sub-Saharan African cities continue to grow, efforts need to be directed towards the development of supportive government policies to establish urban agriculture into more permanent city plans. Formal education on the practice and consumption of urban agriculture products along with food safety information is also an important aspect of formalizing urban policies on food production. Polices encouraging urban agriculture enterprises can create jobs and build life skills. Not only can they enhance the urban environment but also provide food security and promote community cohesion.

Innovative urban farming practices in slum areas of cities in sub-Saharan Africa are crucial in order for people to start having better access to food. The progress of urban agriculture to improve the quality of life in the slums must be paired with political measures and supportive structures to ensure a stable food supply that can become a staple convenience.

Mulch Power

An urban agriculture renaissance is happening in San Francisco. On 20 April 2011 Mayor Ed Lee signed a new planning bill to approve an urban agriculture-zoning proposal that will revise city-planning codes to welcome vegetable gardens in all areas of the city and provide the ability to sell produce from them. Gardens less than an acre in size are now permitted in all zoning districts of the city, with permission to sell food products between the hours of 6am and 8pm.[27]

The new approach to planning in the city of San Francisco encourages a modern urban lifestyle that combines traditional city living with more agrarian sustainable food practices. Many abandoned freeways, dilapidated back yards, institutional dumping grounds, back gardens and pockets of underutilized land can now be more freely transformed into areas for urban cultivation.

The soil that is found in urban environments frequently offers distinctive challenges to urban farmers. They are often compacted, contaminated, poorly drained, low in organic matter and competing with residential lawns for nutrients. These soils require practical methods, which can ensure a successful outcome for city planting. However, organic green waste provides an excellent raw material as a base for an urban farm to grow on. Forests take hundreds of years to make an inch of topsoil, but layering green waste artificially can create this fertile layer, making it possible to grow plants that can thrive on surfaces where cars once drove.[28] Green waste is biodegradable waste composed of garden or park waste, such as grass or flower cuttings and hedge trimmings.[29]

Since 1998 'Bayview Greenwaste' have been recycling wood products from tree professionals, gardeners and landscapers, and turning their scrap wood into greenwaste, mulch (soil fertilizer), wood chips, compost and biofuel. By charging a collection fee for removing plant waste it is then subsequently offered for no charge to anyone wishing to use the organic fertilizer.[30] Charities, municipalities, private citizens and schools have all benefited from the innovative scheme.

The San Francisco Central Freeway was damaged and subsequently closed after the Loma Prieta earthquake in 1989. Following the road's closure, in 2010 abandoned slipways were activated by the city council as sites for temporary green space use. This change of land use attracted a group of farmers and permaculturists who converted the urban space into usable farmland. With a border of mature trees and areas of direct sunlight, the location was well suited for gardening and food production but suffered from polluted soils that lacked any nutrients.

Employing Permaculture methods, 'Hayes Valley Farm' explores strategies for farming in the urban setting, using minimal inputs, recycling local waste, replenishing the landscape and maximizing community involvement and resources.[31] The farm aims to become an agricultural hub to encourage local residents to connect with one another, and learn about sustainable ecological food systems.

Lawn Power

Increasingly people are worried about the distances food endures to reach our dining tables and satisfy our huge appetites. Keen to eat wholesome organic produce, an increased number of people are opting to grow their own food, in their back yards. This phenomenon is occurring so rapidly that sales of vegetable

24. BC Arimah, 'Slums as Expressions of Social Exclusion: Explaining the prevalence of slums in African countries', UN-HABITAT [http://www.oecd.org/dev/pgd/46837274.pdf] retrieved 6 August 2013

25+26. D McKenzie, 'Nairobi's slum farms', Resource Centres on Urban Agriculture & Food Security, 2010 [http://www.ruaf.org/node/2193], retrieved 12 July 2012

27. 'Overview of San Francisco's Urban Agriculture Zoning Ordinance', San Francisco Urban Agriculture Alliance [http://www.sfuaa.org/uploads/4/8/9/3/4893022/overview_of_sf_urban_ag_zoning_changes_final.pdf], retrieved 12 July 2012

28, 30+31. M Baume, 'Bayview Greenwaste provides fertile ground for San Francisco's urban agriculture revolution', Grist [http://www.grist.org/urban-agriculture/2011-02-22-bayview-greenwaste-provides-fertile-ground-for-san-franciscos-ur], retrieved 12 July 2012

29. 'Garden Waste', Recyclenew [http://www.recyclenow.com/how_is_it_recycled/garden_waste.html], retrieved 12 July 2012

seeds have now overtaken those of flowers![32] Parents in Camden, London, have started signing their children up to become allotment holders. Bizarrely, their intention is that they hope to secure them a place by the time they reach middle age. Waiting lists for allotment plots have hit record lengths, with residents of the borough facing a 40-year wait for their own vegetable plot.[33] Similarly, in Islington it can take 25 years to secure a plot, while most lists in Haringey are so long they are closed.[34]

Likewise in the USA the design collective 'Visual Logic' has proposed to re-purpose the lawn service industry in order to set up a distributed backyard farm network across the country.[35] There are over 5,000 professional lawn care companies in the USA employing a phenomenal 921,900 document workers, far outweighing those employed in the farming, fishing and forestry occupations combined (438,490 workers).[36] Such companies maintain the front lawns of over 34 million American households every day.[37]

Crews of three take no more than 30 minutes to complete a service that costs homeowners a small fraction of their disposable incomes. The use of lawn-service providers has, over the last three decades, become less of a luxury and more an indispensable part of everyday life for many families in modern day America. In contrast to vast, monolithic crop factory-farming, lawn-service providers constitute an under-appreciated mode of 'farming' in America, one in which the farmer goes directly to the consumer. The demand for lawn care continues to rise with the continued construction of single-family homes in innumerable suburban developments across the USA. With readily available cheap labour and a relatively modest investment cost in equipment as the only requirements for entry into the field, the lawn-service industry now comprises a diverse multitude of overlapping networks of providers and customers spanning the entire country in many differing climatic zones and geographic regions.

The lawn-service industry's highly mobile infrastructure of trucks and portable equipment to farm grass and maintain yards for millions of Americans is the perfect vehicle to sustain a new urban agriculture network. The actual key to the productivity of America's residential landscapes lies not with the homeowner, but in tapping the remarkable potential of the existing lawn-service industry.

There is an increasing demand amongst consumers for fresh and locally grown produce, for healthier foods, and for more sustainable lifestyles. American lawns are a reservoir of arable land. The lawn-service industry serves as a model for how the farming of produce can become integral to the lifestyle of American families, without the requirement of the homeowner to invest in tools, time and agricultural education. Networks of local urban farmers, acting as lawn-service professionals, could provide farming as a service to homeowners, at a low cost.

The proposal suggests that the homeowners would obtain the majority of the crop harvest delivered from their personal gardens onto their front doorsteps. The remainder of food produce would be sold to local restaurants and markets. Suggestions render a single garden of 800ft2 capable of providing over 180kg of fresh vegetables for each household.[38]

facing page top: The lawn-service industry serves as a model for how farming of produce can become integral to the lifestyle of American families.

facing page bottom: Many city planners are supporting urban agriculture in abandoned municipal spaces.

117

32. 'Gardening Guides', BBC News [http://www.bbc.co.uk/gardening/grow_your_own/expertgrowers_nsalg.shtml], retrieved 05 August 2013

33+34. R Jones, 'Allotment demand leads to 40-year waiting lists', The Guardian, 2009 [http://www.theguardian.com/money/2009/jun/02/allotments-shortage-waiting-lists], retrieved 18 July 2012

35. N Twilley, 'Best of the Blogs: Mammoth's Backyard Farm Service' [http://www.good.is/post/best-of-the-blogs-mammoth-s-backyard-farm-service/], retrieved 18 July 2012

36+37. BE Cantrell, 'Backyard Farm Service', Reactscape [http://reactscape.visual-logic.com/2010/08/backyard-farm-service/], retrieved 18 July 2012

Every homeowner is offered the means to become a local food producer without requiring them to abandon their jobs and take up farming on their own. The strategies can be implemented anywhere homeowners and yards exist, while relying on local knowledge and farmer-to-household relationships. 'Backyard Farm Service' suggests how we can diversify and localize food production in order to enhance each neighbourhood's ecological diversity and food security. By physically reintegrating agricultural production into the fabric of our cities and suburbs, the vision could bridge the gap between farming and everyday consumption that has formed over the last century with the advent of modern agriculture.[39]

One of the most significant inefficiencies in the global food energy cycle is food waste. Whether it's uneaten food left on the plate or the millions of tonnes of fruit and vegetables unsold by supermarkets, 30% of the food produced worldwide is never consumed.[40] Irresponsible eating habits and food waste are a symptom of the transformation of urban food cultures around the world. The frugal post-war eating attitudes which encouraged eating all the food on one's plate and cooking with leftovers have been replaced by a food culture characterized by casual over-consumption and the nonchalant disposal of unwanted food.

Anaerobic digestion, the generation of biogas from the decomposition of organic waste, offers a constructive means of ameliorating the inefficiency of urban food waste. However, only a tiny fraction of food waste is successfully transferred into energy due to both our failure to recycle food waste, the vast majority of which ends up as landfill, and the lack of available recycling infrastructure to convert what little food waste is recycled into energy. As of 2012, only 13% of homes in England have separate food waste collections.[41]

The profligacy of urban food culture is sustained by a lavish and unregulated food industry, as has been discussed in the previous chapters. The lucrative, yet unpredictable nature of urban food culture is such that food retailers are better off by hedging their bets and flooding the market with numerous options, in spite of the fact that many of them will remain unsold and contribute to food waste. Furthermore, food waste in cities is particularly inefficient as the foods that are wasted typically have a high environmental impact due to the relatively large number of food miles they incur and the high amounts of the food processing and packaging they require. Food waste is not only environmentally and energy inefficient, but financially detrimental to the consumer. A recent report from DEFRA concluded that in rich cities, such as London, preventing food being unnecessarily thrown away could save a family as much as £500–700 a year.[42]

The issue of waste also raises the health, hygiene and sanitation issues that pertain to food in the city. Whilst the urban case studies explored in this chapter offer insights into the innovative solutions city dwellers have designed to maximize food energy efficiency, the sombre note on food waste in the conclusion highlights how much potential energy is simply discarded by the inefficient cycles in the city.

facing page top: Dandora slum located only a couple of kilometres from the centre of Nairobi, holds the biggest rubbish dump in sub-Saharan Africa with 1,500 tonnes of food waste and re-useable rubbish dumped daily.

facing page bottom: In the large garbage dump on the outskirts of the West Bank city of Hebron, Palestinians living in poverty search for food and other items they might be able to use or sell.

38+39. BE Cantrell, 'Backyard Farm Service', Reactscape [http://reactscape.visual-logic.com/2010/08/backyard-farm-service/], retrieved 18 July 2012

40+42. J Gustavsson, C Cederberg & U Sonesson, 'Global food loss and food waste', Food and Agriculture Organization of The United Nations, Rome, 2011

41. D Carrington & J Vidal, 'Global food system must be transformed on industrial revolution scale', The Guardian, 24 January 2011

Feed A Fever

'Although I have been prevented by outward circumstances from observing a strictly vegetarian diet, I have long been an adherent to the cause in principle. Besides agreeing with the aims of vegetarianism for aesthetic and moral reasons, it is my view that a vegetarian manner of living by its purely physical effect on the human temperament would most beneficially influence the lot of mankind.'

– Albert Einstein, 'Translation of letter to Hermann Huth', 1930

The fragile state of food security that affects people in both the northern and southern hemispheres is evident. The pressure to secure food supplies for communities facing imminent ecological and fuel crises has corresponded with a pressure on other communities with weak land ownership rights facing food crises of their own. These pressures have erupted in cities globally, and progressive movements exist fighting for fair practices to ensure food sovereignty for all. This chapter will examine the ways in which people in cities are feeding themselves through these global struggles. It will investigate the changing way people have fed themselves through the development of cities and explore the various ways in which people access food in urban areas and how this affects their health.

The notion of public health emerged in the mid nineteenth century in England, continental Europe and the USA fuelled by social reform movements and a deeper understanding of biological and medical knowledge. People began to understand causation, that certain practices had negative effects on peoples' health, and how to manage and control the spread of infectious diseases. Crucial to the understanding of public health was the cholera that from humble beginnings would become one of the most widespread and deadly diseases of the nineteenth century. It would kill an estimated tens of millions of people until John Snow, a British physician, studied the case of the Broad Street outbreak in Soho, London. He was the first to identify the importance of contaminated water as its cause in 1854.[1]

In the mid nineteenth century, the Soho district of London had experienced a huge influx of people and was unable to manage the resultant increase in filth. The London sewer system had not yet reached Soho and the basements of buildings filled up with excrement. The local government at the time decided to clear the cesspools by dumping the waste in the River Thames, which then contaminated the water supply, leading to a cholera outbreak. On 31 August 1854, there were reports of outbreaks of cholera across the city and a major outbreak erupted in Soho. Over the next three days, 126 people died on or near Broad Street and by the next week nearly three-quarters of the residents had fled the area. By 10 September, 500 people had died and the mortality rate was 12.8% in some parts of the city.[2]

facing page: Commuters can enjoy their 'most important meal' of the day, breakfast on the Star Ferry within the 10 minute journey across Victoria Harbour in Hong Kong.

1. 'John Snow and the Broad Street Pump' [http://www.makingthemodernworld.org.uk/learning_modules/geography/05.TU.01/?section=2], retrieved 3 August 2012

2. 'Origins of Cholera', City of Westminster Archives [http://www.choleraandthethames.co.uk/cholera-in-london/origins-of-cholera/], retrieved 6 August 2013

The overriding medical theory of the time concerned 'miasma'; that diseases such as cholera or the Black Death were caused by a form of 'bad air'. The germ theory was not widely accepted at this time, but Snow was a sceptic about the miasma theory. He began an elaborate investigation into the effect on the water supply in the Soho outbreak of 1854 and together with the Reverend Henry Whitehead interviewed local residents. By drawing up a spot map indicating incidences of the disease and illustrating how outbreaks of the disease were concentrated, he identified the source of the outbreak as the public water pump on Broad Street (now Broadwick Street). Although his chemical and microscopic evidence was not conclusive enough to prove the contamination, his studies of the patterns of the disease were able to convince the local council to disable the pump by removing its handle. Snow also showed that the Southwark and Vauxhall Waterworks Company was taking water from sections of the river Thames polluted with sewage. The homes which had received water from the company had shown higher incidence rates of cholera.[3]

Contrary to Snow's pattern in Soho, the monks in the adjacent monastery were all unaffected by the disease. Further investigation showed that this was not an anomaly but mounting evidence. The monks had preserved themselves by only drinking beer that they had brewed themselves.[4]

This association of health with everyday activities, such as eating and cleaning in the case of the Broad Street tap, was infiltrating thinking in society. Reports and investigations into urban outbreaks and consideration of society as populations rather than individuals led to a greater understanding of how disease spreads in communities. The work of leading physicians at the time, among them Koch, Farr and Pasteur, led to a shift in thinking towards an emphasis on prevention rather than a cure. Narrators of the time, Hogarth and later Dickens, would illustrate the filthy inequalities in the city and start to engender ideals of social justice and equity.

Epidemiologists often refer to the Winslow definition of public health: the 'science and art of preventing disease, prolonging life and promoting physical health and efficacy through organized community efforts for the sanitation of the environment'. The definition has implications for the built environment and further states that public health includes the 'control of communicable infections' and that it is society's responsibility to ensure that every individual has access to a 'a standard of living adequate for the maintenance of health'.[5]

Although this definition is more than 90 years old, and the incident of the Broad Street tap over 150 years old, simple and avoidable problems in the provision of services urban environment are still affecting people today.

Street Food

With the massive increase in urbanization an increase in urban poverty has been observed. Between a quarter and one-third of all urban households in the world live in absolute poverty.[6] A source of income and a cheap means of feeding the urban masses, street food vending is a widespread phenomenon across the world. A source of employment, particularly for women, the street food industry turns over

facing page: Street dining next to a construction site adds grittiness and colour to what is an increasingly homogenous city. Decades of urban transformation have made Hong Kong's street food an endangered species, supplanting it with big eateries, and indoor food courts.

123

3. J Summers, 'Soho, A History of London's Most Colourful Neighborhood – Broad Street Pump Outbreak', Bloomsbury, London, 1989, pp.113–117

4. S Johnson, 'The Ghost Map: The Story of London's Most Terrifying Epidemic – and How it Changed Science, Cities and the Modern World', Riverhead Books, London, p.206

5. 'History of Yale School of Public Health' (http://publichealth.yale.edu/about/history/index.aspx), retrieved 4 August 2012

6. 'Food Safety in Emergencies', Fact sheet No. 3, Division of Prevention and Control of Non-Communicable Diseases Food Safety and Nutrition, WHO Africa

considerable sums of money. In Cotonou in the early 1990s it was estimated that the street food industry had an annual turnover of US$20 million and in 2000, a survey in Accra of 334 vendors indicated that the sector employed over 60,000 people with an annual turn over of approximately US$100 million.[7]

Whilst the informal food sector provides an important source of food and income for the urban poor, outbreaks of foodborne diseases have been traced to contamination of street foods. A microbial study of the quality of street food in Accra, Ghana found traces of 'Shigella sonnei', enteroaggregative 'Escherichia coli' and 'Salmonella arizonae' in some of the food samples.[8] The stations from which food is traded often lack safe, sanitary storage or the necessary refrigeration and cooking facilities to prevent disease. Access to clean water cannot always be guaranteed and this too contributes to the risk of contamination.

Incidence of illness from street food in Bangladesh shows the impact of these conditions. On average, more than 500 people a day are hospitalized due to contaminated food and water on the streets of Dhaka.[9] Due to mass illiteracy and lack of appropriate protective laws, the state of awareness on consumers' rights and responsibilities among the people in Bangladesh is generally poor. Thanks to a new local initiative however, the street vendors are cleaning up their act. Food vendors have received training in basic food hygiene to reduce incidences of food contamination and related food-borne illnesses. Portable carts have been provided free of charge from the Consumers Association of Bangladesh (CAB). Part funded by the United Nations and the USA and European aid agencies, the campaign is expected to boost the number of organized street food vendors in the city. Rapid urbanization in Dhaka has turned street-food vending into an important business.

A food cart run by Jarina Begum serves breakfast and lunch on a bustling Dhaka road in the city centre. Her new wooden, healthy portable stall provided by the scheme can now provide clean food and water to her diners, 'I was trained by the CAB and now, following their advice, I keep food clean and always sell fresh food ... people from all walks of life, from rickshaw pullers to office workers come to my shop because they love my food and my sales have also increased.'[10]

Many consumers, covering a range of economic circumstance from the urban poor and local office workers to tourists, appreciate the convenience of purchasing food from informal street vendors. One local customer, Prashanta Kumar, spoke of the food carts, 'I work here in an office, so every day I come here to eat my lunch ... the food over here is very fresh and good. She is trained to make fresh food.'[11]

City inhabitants are frequently faced with problems of access to and availability of food products and services. Rapid urban expansion, population growth and rising urban poverty, have placed huge pressures on the food security of many cities. The 'informal' food sector (IFS) offers an important division of support to improve and strengthen the food supply and distribution systems of urban environments throughout the world. The IFS is a division of the food system that includes small producers, manufacturing enterprises, traders and service providers, involved in legal as well as unrecognized activities related to food. The practice can be characterized by the absence of food specialization. The informal trade develops by diversifying products sold with very low capital investment.

The sector can contribute to food security by providing small quantities of affordable food products at convenient locations for consumers rich and poor alike, by providing employment and income to under privileged households, and

left: The informal food sector provides an important source of food and income by diversifying products sold with very low capital investment. Street vending can enhance the quality of urban public space when properly managed.

7. 'Food Safety in Emergencies', Fact sheet No. 3, Division of Prevention and Control of Non-Communicable Diseases Food Safety and Nutrition, WHO Africa

8. P Mensah et al., 'Street Foods in Accra, Ghana: How Safe Are They?', Bulletin of the World Health Organization, Geneva, 2002

9. 'Bangla street food on health drive', Reuters [http://www.blinkx.com/watch-video/bangla-street-food-on-health-drive/QNl1GYuhbiP57Ab4CP-sew], retrieved 7 August 2012

10+11. 'Bangladesh Healthy Food Carts' [http://www.youtube.com/watch?v=ZZh4sUUvWMl], retrieved 7 August 2012

by bringing food to marginal urban districts furthest from the city centre and the organized secondary markets. The IFS exists in all countries of the world. It often provides nutritious low-cost food to a variety of urban inhabitants. It has continued to grow, even when illegal or state-oppressed. The informal food sector offers independence and a source of income to a wide variety of people who suffer economic difficulties. Numerous consumers, including the urban poor, office workers and tourists, appreciate the convenience of purchasing food from informal suppliers. The practice is therefore unlikely to vanish.

Street food is one of the most prevalent and visible examples of the informal food sector in action. The people that run portable food stalls play a part in strengthening the vitality and effectiveness of a city's food supply and distribution system by providing healthy and reasonably priced food throughout the year. Street vending can also enhance the quality of urban public space when it is properly managed. Portable stalls can alleviate the conflicts between pedestrian and vehicular traffic. The locations of street vending, often near to schools and offices, bus stops and stations, facilitate easy consumer access to a resource of nutritious food in the city. This saves time and transport costs that would otherwise be absorbed by other means. Street vendors sell small units of food, which are affordable to the poor and the more under privileged members of the community.

The informal sale of raw and prepared food activities has the potential to adjust to socio-economic circumstances. In times of economic crisis, the decline in purchasing power and drop in employment opportunities in the formal sector often spurs the development of the informal food sector as it has the ability to create employment and income to households that are suffering hardship. In situations of economic uncertainty, the ability of poorer households to produce their own food products and services can be crucial for their own food security and personal health.

Informal Sector Unions

The city of Makati is the economic centre of the Philippines, yet suffers from a very high level of unemployment. The 'Makati Vendors Program' (MVP) was established in 1992.[12] The Scheme involves 760 street vendors, who are mostly women and between the ages of 30 and 45.[13] Vendors are registered and allocated sites on the condition that they maintain certain standards of health and cleanliness. Credit is offered through the support of local associations. Municipal authorities distribute aprons and head-covers to vendors and arrange for clean water delivery to their stalls.

Suffering from a high level of unemployment, the principal objectives of the programme in the city are to provide the urban poor of Makati with an alternative source of income, to guarantee the safety of street food, and to protect the urban environment at the points of sale. To achieve this, the MVP supports the creation and management of micro-enterprises and street food vending. The programme participants are tolerated even when they do not pay any land occupancy tax. The street vendors are also made aware of sanitary regulations and penalized for failing to comply when they are not wearing the proper clothing. The MVP provides its participants with uniform market stalls and allotted them a vending space. The vendors have been able to improve their standard of living thanks to the programme and no longer fear being detained through their actions of selling food.

facing page top + bottom: Istanbul and Saigon. The locations of street vending, often near to schools and offices, bus stops and stations, facilitate easy consumer access to a source of nutritious food in the city.

127

12+13. 'Makati Vendors Program' [http://kwentongmayor.com/ gpsolutions01/articles/1999/ MakatiVendorsProgram.html], retrieved 7 August 2012

Street vending from portable food stalls has the ability to respond to urban development and the expansion of cities. The informal food trade offers a large number of 'sales points' in the urban districts furthest from the city centre and the organized secondary markets. This characteristic offers the ability to bridge the inadequacies of the formal distribution structure.

The IFS can offer new services and be easily shaped by changing social patterns and dietary habits. Street food and the sale of fresh produce have served to alleviate the increasing distance between work and home. Some informal food traders have demonstrated a keen sense of creativity in the food products and services they offer. Concerns about cleanliness and freshness often discourage people from eating street food. Portable stalls frequently suffer from a lack of refrigeration and consumers can interpret this as a lack of cleanliness or hygiene. To alleviate this however, street food often uses exceptionally fresh ingredients.

Despite the health hazards, street foods are popular. A large part of the urban population, particularly from the lower income groups, meets a substantial part of its dietary and nutritional needs through meals and beverages offered by outdoor vendors. Occupational health and safety issues related to food vending would be more adequately addressed if vendors were organized in a more economically and spatially secure position. A critical assessment of the street food situation was followed by actions to promote awareness and application of hygienic practices among informal operators in the Philippines.

The 'Cebu City United Vendors Association' was founded in 1984 by vendors in Cebu City in the Philippines.[14] The association represents 63 organizations involving over 7,000 members who sell predominantly food items.[15] Through years of working in close dialogue with the city council, the CCUVA has become a powerful and legitimate urban voice in the local community.

Food vendors who are located outside public market places are the most in need of organization. With no formal access to a fixed selling location, street vendors commonly obstruct pedestrian and vehicular traffic. This activity results in conflicts with municipal officials. Vendor selling spaces in these environments are classified as illegal. Street sellers are often asked to relocate their stalls or risk facing closure and possible demolition. The IFS manifested here in the form of unorganized portable food stalls, is seen as trespassing on public space.

Clarity in local policy practice is the role of organizations like the CCUVA. In Cebu, property has become very valuable, and access to space is the predominant issue facing sidewalk sellers. The CCUVA attempts to secure access to space by employing a strategy of forming vendor associations. Securing access to urban space is a political issue that is best addressed when small food entrepreneurs are well organized. Persistent demonstrations with other community-based groups in Cebu city are organized by the CCUVA. The association continues to expand its membership and perfect its strategies to engage with, rather than to simply challenge, the local council's policies and legal systems in order to have its members recognized. The CCUVA is a model for food vendors in cities who are in need of organization at grassroots level.

In many cities street vending exists outside official regulations pertaining to the safe sale and consumption of food. Various attempts to organize and regulate the practice can be found throughout the world. There are a number of organizations that communities have mobilized to protect street food vending, to promote local and small-scale production, and facilitate the access to 'home made' products at the local market through portable stalls. Attitudes and policies that are favourable to informal food operators need to be promoted in order to understand their role better.

Local government policy makers need training to identify informal activities, operators and consumer practices in the purchase of food. The formation of groups and associations of informal food operators needs to be encouraged whilst reinforcing those that already exist. Meaningful dialogue with the representatives of the informal operators must be sustained and they should be actively invited to participate in the formulation of the programmes of action that affect them.

The needs and constraints of informal food operators should be integrated at the level of city planning. Areas for the sale of food from portable stores, and ensuring the supply of clean water to IFS locations and the removal of refuse from markets and locations at points of sale need formal land occupancy planning strategies in urban environments. Land is also required for urban and peri-urban food production, and communication routes should be improved between markets and outlying districts. These key issues will improve access to healthy food and local food production.

The absence of monetary accounts and the non-payment of all or some council taxation is a typical characteristic of trading within the IFS. In many cases, the IFS can complement the 'formal' food sector by satisfying a differing demand and consumer base. The IFS overwhelmingly addresses the needs of households and micro-enterprises with varying and limited purchasing power. It is important for local councils to consider informal street vendors as companions in local development initiatives. New policies and programmes aimed at creating adequate conditions for informal sector activities to be efficiently undertaken while minimizing risks to society consistently need to be implemented. To make the IFS more viable, proactive dialogue with municipal authorities is needed. Other improvements to the IFS, such as hygiene, can also take place with investments in the social capital of food vendors resulting from more effective dissemination of information.

Regulating the Urban Kitchens

The 'National Association of Street Vendors of India' (NASVI), was registered in 2003 to bring together street vendor organizations in India.[16] It campaigns for changes to support the livelihood of approximately 10 million street vendors who face closure due to outdated laws and attitudes of the Indian government.[17] It is formed from a coalition of trade unions, community based organizations, non-government organizations and professionals.

The initiatives of the NASVI are focused on securing the livelihood of street vendors through policy interventions and amendments through dialogue with administrators and planners. The association organizes national conferences and demonstrations to highlight the campaign and draw attention to its concerns. Financial services, legal aid and advice are made available to those people who are unable to afford the costs. The NASVI also collects and disseminates information through leaflets and websites

14+15. G Yasmeen, 'Workers in the in the urban "informal" food sector: innovative organizing strategies', FAO [http://www.fao.org/docrep/004/y1931m/y1931m05.htm], retrieved 12 August 2012

16+17. 'National Association of Street Vendors of India', Women in Informal Employment: Globalizing and Organizing [http://wiego.org/wiego/national-association-street-vendors-india-nasvi], retrieved 12 July 2013

about the issues concerning street vendors, sensitizing society about the issues of the informal food sector.

IFS activities are often carried out despite being strictly illegal. They can empower marginalized members of society and contribute to fairer distribution of resources. Women are often overwhelmingly responsible for retailing fresh produce, small catering operations and street food. This allows them to feed their families at lower costs and therefore contribute to their own food security. Women are disproportionately represented in the informal sector, thus much of women's work is invisible to policy makers.

Governments and labour unions that protect the interests of formal sector workers often neglect the needs of IFS operators. IFS activities are not recorded in national financial records and are rarely considered in development plans. In times of economic crisis, city dwellers tend to resort to the informal sector for both employment and the purchase of goods and services. The practice can serve as a safety net economy when more formal structures break down. In order to manage the sector effectively, particularly with respect to traffic and hygiene issues, a proactive dialogue needs to be established among those earning their livelihood in the IFS and the local councils.

The creation of membership-based organizations comprised of food vendors and others who gain their livelihoods from the preparation and sale of food in cities, gives people increased access to food. Having access to healthy food in urban environments is associated with a health-promoting diet. Despite the analysis and exploration that may be needed on the various ways in which these developing organizations function, associations such as the CAB, the NASVI, the CCUVA and the MVP, are needed in developing countries to act as collective voices for people in the informal food sector. Associations have the potential to access government funding and campaign for social protection for workers. They can also help to secure an affordable city space in which to carry out food selling. Street vending is an important sector of the food system and needs to be encouraged through training and support by local government policies and actions.

Street Food Vs Big Food

Whilst street vending is easily vilified as a source of contamination and disease, its largest competitor is the 'Big Food' industry. As discussed in a previous chapter, 'Big Food' is the name given to the large companies that dominate the food and beverage environment. Benefitting from economies of scale, the Big Food industry is able to supply fast food cheaply to a vast market. Aggressive marketing, often targeted at children, and nutritionally poor food has seen health problems related to nutrition across the globe.

In South Africa there has been an increase in sales of packaged foods; sales of snack bars, ready meals and noodles rose more than 40% between 2005 and 2010.[18] In 2010, up to half of young people were reported to consume fast food, cakes and biscuits, cold drinks and sweets at least four days a week and carbonated drinks are now the third commonly most consumed food/drink item amongst South African children aged between one and two years (less than maize meal and brewed tea, but more than milk!).[19]

This issue of the health impact of the Big Food industry is widespread across the globe. Nutrition-related health problems are reaching epidemic levels in the USA.[20] One in eight Americans uses food stamps; 4.8 million Americans relied on food banks in 2009.[21] High unemployment rates are impacting the way that people eat. The number of adults and children who are obese or at risk of obesity has increased dramatically during the past 20 years.[22] Low-income and minority

left: Participants of the 'Supplement Nutrition Assistance Program', popularly known as 'Food Stamps', lack access to healthy food options because low-income areas are often served only by mini-marts with limited and generally unhealthy selections.

18. E Igumbor, '"Big Food", the consumer Food Environment, Health and the Response in South Africa', PLOS Medicene [http://www.plosmedicine.org/article/info%3Adoi%2F10.1371%2Fjournal.pmed.1001253], retrieved 21 July 2012

19. M Theron, A Amissah, IC Kleynhans, E Albertse & UE MacIntyre, 'Inadequate dietary intake is not the cause of stunting amongst young children living in an informal settlement in Gauteng and rural Limpopo Province in South Africa: the NutriGro study', Public Health Nutrition, Vol. 10, No. 4, 2007, pp.379–389

20. 'Chronic Disease Prevention and Health Promotion – Obesity', Centres for Disease Control and Prevention [http://www.cdc.gov/chronicdisease/resources/publications/aag/obesity.htm], retrieved 21 July 2012

21. 'Hunger and Food Access', Repair the World [http://werepair.org/knowledgebase/issues/hunger-food-access], retrieved 21 July 2012

22. 'Overweight and Obesity – Adult Obesity Facts', Centres for Disease Control and Prevention [http://www.cdc.gov/obesity/data/trends.html], retrieved 4 November 2012

communities are the hardest hit as obesity and diet-related disease rates increase throughout America.

Health variations among US population groups are usually related to inequalities in socioeconomic status. This can be affected by unequal access to healthy food. Attainable access to abundant fruits and vegetable supplies differs among residents in the city of Philadelphia. Research concludes that approximately 71,000 residents find that it is difficult to locate fruits and vegetables in their communities.[23] Eight out of ten of these residents, who reportedly do not consume the recommended five servings of fruits and vegetables a day, risk an increase in malnutrition from an unbalanced diet.[24] Living in a food desert can mean an unreliable and limited diet, high food prices, soaring diabetes rates and an increase in childhood obesity.

Philadelphia has the second lowest number of supermarkets per capita in the United States.[25] Incapacitated communities endure the negative health impacts of food retail disinvestment from their urban neighbourhoods. In Philadelphia, nearly 228,000 residents believe that the quality of the groceries available in their neighbourhood is fair or poor.[26]

After high levels of obesity were recorded in a deprived area of Los Angeles, USA, the city council passed a law prohibiting the construction of new fast-food restaurants in a 32 square mile area inhabited by 500,000 low-income people.[27] Defining fast-food restaurants as 'any establishment which dispenses food for consumption on or off the premises, and which has the following characteristics: a limited menu, items prepared in advance or prepared or heated quickly, no table orders and food served in disposable wrapping or containers.'[28] The campaign strives to support new potential developers with healthier eating on their menus.

People should be able to decide what sort of restaurants can operate in their neighbourhood. Fast food is generally high in calories and fat, whilst offering low levels of nutrition. Such characteristics are associated with obesity, diabetes, heart disease and other health problems, which present unwelcomed additions to modern communities. French fries and hamburgers should perhaps be treated like cigarettes or alcohol in the eyes of city planners.

Slow Food

The Slow Food movement is as much a political movement as a gastronomic one. Armed with a statement of intent, the aims of the movement supersede a mantra of simply eating well and incorporate the rights of workers and global land use. The manifesto is a backlash against the age of Industrialization, and a century which first invented the machine and then modelled its lifestyle after it. Speed became our shackles. We fell prey to the same virus: the fast life that fractures our customs and assails us even in our own homes, forcing us to ingest fast-food. The manifesto is against the infestation of speed into everyday life arguing that it is certain to lead to human extinction; the fast life has changed our lifestyle and now threatens our environment and our land (and city) scapes. The Slow Food movement proposes that the considered, paced enjoyment of eating, cooking and cultivation can provide an antidote to the frenzied pace of life: 'Slow Food is the alternative, the avant-garde's riposte. Real culture is here to be found.'[29]

One-time food journalist, Carlo Petrini, who wrote restaurant reviews for communist dailies in the 1970s, started the Slow Food movement in the mid 1980s. The movement was initially a reaction against the opening of a McDonalds in Rome's Piazza di Spagna. Unsuccessful in this attempt, the movement has since become, in Petrini's words, a 'revolution'. One of its main achievements, the movement now hosts a conference every two years drawing 180,000 people over five days to Turin for the Salone del Gusto, which literally translates as the 'Big Room of Taste'. The festival hosts food stalls from around the world in 'two cavernous hangars' especially celebrating Italian food with 'stalls from every region in the country, clamorous with Tuscans, Pugliese, Piedmontese, Lombards, Emilians and Sicilians, all vying to convince passers-by of the merits of their cheese, their chocolate, their prosciutto, their limoncello.'[30]

In line with the movement's ideals, it is not simply a food festival and has joined forces since 2004 with Terra Madre, a global network of small-scale farmers opposed to the threat of homogeneity, globalization and unsustainable environmental practices.[31] During the festival, there are lectures, calls to action and treaties. One Telegraph journalist wrote of the conference, 'It's amazing they find time to eat anything with their mouths so busy.'[32]

Grow Your Own
There is an emphasis on local production amidst the ideals of the Slow Food movement. Urban agriculture is not a new phenomenon and has been in practice since 3,500 BC when Mesopotamians farmed plots within their emerging cities.[33] The use of urban agriculture as a tool for alleviating poverty is also not a new concept. In reaction to the sprawling slums of a rapidly urbanizing London, urban agriculture was viewed as a way for people to become self-sufficient. Ebenezer Howard, influenced by thinkers from Peter Kropotkin, exiled from Tsarist Russia for pushing social reforms, and Henry George and Edward Bellamy, would create the utopian Garden City concept. The successes of the British Garden City would influence communities around the world. The Vegetarische Obstbau-Kolonie Eden is a vegetarian community established in 1893 near Oranienburg, Germany, concentrating on the cultivation of fruit trees. It is still functioning and profitable today.

Philadelphia has a growing number of new urban farms. The well-established 'Philadelphia Green' programme, which has been promoting green infrastructure in the city for more than 30 years, has been investing more resources in urban agriculture.[34] A total of 2,812 families are involved in the vegetable gardens.[35] Philadelphia Green has created an association amongst local residents, community groups, government and businesses to develop and preserve community green space. The organization has become the nation's largest urban greening programme.[36]

Despite the growing interest in urban agriculture, urban planners and landscape designers are often inadequately equipped to integrate food-systems thinking into future plans for cities. The challenge and opportunity is to design urban agriculture spaces to be multifunctional, whilst matching the specific needs and preferences of local residents, and also protecting the environment. Food is one of the basic essentials of life, yet is often avoided as an organizing strategy for improving cities and communities. A 10x10m plot and 130-day temperate growing season will sustain a family annually with fruit and vegetables and a nutritional intake of vitamins A, C, B complex and iron.[37]

Historically, physical solutions to urban agriculture have taken many different forms depending on climate, available technologies and cultural preference. During the Middle Ages, kitchen gardens became

23+24. 'Food Geography: How food access affects diet and health', Community Health Data Base, 2006 [http://www.chdbdata.org/datafindings-details.asp?id=38], retrieved 12 August 2013

25+26. 'Needs Assement Methodology and Findings', Pennsylvania Nutrition Education, 2012 [http://www.patracks.org/public/documents/StatewideNeedsAssessmentFY2012.pdf], retrieved 12 August 2013

27+28. M Hennessy-Fiske & D Zahniser, 'Council bans new fast-food outlets', The Los Angeles Times, 2008 [http://articles.latimes.com/2008/jul/30/local/me-fastfood30], retrieved 13 January 2013

29. 'Slow Food Manifesto' [http://www.slowfood.com/_2010_pagine/com/popup_pagina.lasso?-id_pg=121], retrieved 23 August 2012

30+32. R Colvile, 'Foodies of all lands unite!', The Telegraph, 2010 [http://www.telegraph.co.uk/foodanddrink/8159491/Foodies-of-all-lands-unite.html#], retrieved 23 August 2012

31. L Hickman, 'Slow Food: Have we lost our appetite?', The Guardian, 2009 [http://www.guardian.co.uk/environment/2009/feb/04/slow-food-carlo-petrini], retrieved 2 August 2012

33. J Green, 'Urban Agriculture Isn't New', ASLA, 2012 [http://dirt.asla.org/2012/05/09/urban-agriculture-isnt-new/], retrieved 23 August 2012

34+36. 'The Pennsylvania Horticultural Society' [http://www.pennsylvaniahorticulturalsociety.org/phlgreen/about.html], retrieved 23 August 2012

35. 'Urban Agriculture in Philadelphia', Urban Agriculture Notes, City Farmer [http://www.cityfarmer.org/Phillyurbag9.html], retrieved 23 August 2012

37. P Sommers & J Smit, 'Promoting Urban Agriculture: Strategy Framework for Planners in North America, Europe and Asia', The Urban Agricultural Network, 1994 [http://community-wealth.org/sites/clone.community-wealth.org/files/downloads/report-sommers-smit.pdf], retrieved 1 August 2013

popular throughout Europe for growing vegetables, fruits, medicinal herbs and cut flowers primarily for the residents of the household. On a larger scale, Machu Picchu is an example of a sixteenth century city constructed physically to support food production, that included critical infrastructure such as terraces and irrigation, as well as management systems for waste, microclimate control and food storage.

Many modern opportunities exist to retrofit existing buildings with the appropriate infrastructure to support food production. The large number of flat rooftops in many cities such as New York could serve as a platform for urban agriculture. Agricultural production systems can take advantage of the close proximity of resources and consumers, despite appropriating environments that are driven by high land values and competing land use needs. Systems providing food that can be directly consumed by nearby residents could offer many benefits for growers, consumers and the community. The availability of fresh fruits and vegetables for urban residents provides an alternative in communities and neighbourhoods where grocery stores and markets have moved out, leaving a 'food desert'. A community also dependent on food resources from distant locations is vulnerable to any unforeseen natural disasters. Growing your own produce is the ultimate way to access a food supply.

Healthy, high quality fresh foods can be produced on relatively small amounts of space in an urban environment. Gardens established on hundreds of walls, fences and pockets of abandoned land throughout the city could provide a space for urban agriculture to be introduced. Most vegetables need at least four hours of sunlight a day to successfully grow. South-facing walls and plots located close to water supplies provide appropriate settings for food cultivation. Mint, basil, chilies, lettuces, broccoli, tomatoes, brussels sprouts and melons can all be grown in restricted environments with suitable containers and fixings. In situations where food production occurs on vacant lots or other derelict strips of land, the effect of greening the neighbourhood alone is a positive outcome for all residents in terms of visual quality, sustainability and human health.

Urban agriculture provides an easily accessible locality for growing food in cities and supporting healthy communities with fresh nutritious food and new opportunities for work and recreation. Health officials under rate the satisfaction derived from tilling the soil and the benefit of mental relaxation amongst ecology to escape the burden of urban haste. Gardeners describe the activity of gardening as a foundation for efficacy, pride, self-esteem and personal satisfaction, and a self-fulfilling means to produce food for their families and the community.[38]

Researchers have identified gardening as a viable form of exercise and the gratifying expenditure of energy can reduce the risk of coronary heart disease for men and women,[39] obesity,[40] diabetes and improve glycemic control in adults and elderly men.[41] Spending more time exposed to sunlight could also reduce the risk of myocardial infarction through the protective effect of cholesterol metabolism to vitamin D.[42]

A healthy diet is imperative to our biological existence, and it is crucial for communities to work together and move public policy agendas towards a positive embrace of urban agriculture and urban planning. Connections between proponents of public health and those of urban agriculture need to be augmented with the objectives of instigating cooperative discussion, research, advocacy and practice, to improve access to healthy food for under served and vulnerable members of the population. The WHO Healthy Cities programme has recognized the benefits of urban agriculture and appealed to cities and their governments to incorporate food policies into urban plans.[43]

Community gardening is a way to increase the availability and intake of fruits and vegetables for urban residents. Gardens yield baskets full of nutritional food fit for diets of any age, and having the knowledge to grow, harvest, preserve and cook is a valuable skill. The more opportunity and experience people have in growing fresh healthy food, the more likely they are to consume it themselves. The desire of individuals to grow their own produce can be seen as a direct rejection of modern, supermarket dominated forms of food cultivation, distribution and provision. Direct encouragement will help people to make the link between their food choices and the impact on their health.

The UK government's 'Grow Your Own' campaign encourages people to set up temporary allotments and community gardens on land awaiting development, to promote neighbourhood spirit and skill sets to improve physical and mental health. New land leases are intended to be established to formalize arrangements between landowners and voluntary groups on land plots that are considered 'unused'.

The National Institute of Health lists gardening for 30–45 minutes in its recommended activities for moderate levels of exercise to combat obesity, along with biking 5 miles and walking 2 miles in 30 minutes.[44] Gardening can be a powerful tool to improve the quality of life for people with disabilities. Physical and mental fitness can be aided by the therapeutic benefits of gardening. Having the knowledge and the ability to grow vegetables can enable a move into employment, allowing someone to rebuild a life after illness or accident. The sense of achievement is often important to people whose illness has meant that they have had to drop out of things in the past. Gardening often encourages social interaction and can increase the building of confidence as well as self-esteem.

Many cities in developed countries have recognized the extensive health benefits of urban agriculture. Planning strategies have been developed to support food production within the city boundaries, focused on a strong emphasis on the social functions provided by urban agriculture. In the Netherlands, 250,000 community and allotment gardens exist across 4,000 hectares of land, with Amsterdam alone containing 350 hectares of land for urban gardens.[45] These garden spaces have been recognized for their contributions to supplying a large percentage of household vegetable needs and have contributed to community socializing, and enhancing technical growing knowledge.

The excessive use of agricultural chemicals in the growing of vegetables in China has become a grave concern for many people, prompting them to consider growing food for themselves.[46] Thousands of health conscious young professionals are joining new 'collective farms', reminiscent of Maoist-era communes. Renting plots of agricultural land in the city outskirts, the urban consumers are eager to secure a safer diet through managing the production of their own food. By bypassing the modern sophisticated food chain, the urban consumers are directly engaging in farm work themselves or commissioning other farmers to do it for them. Members of the scheme pay approximately 2,000 Yuan per year to rent a 50m2 share of farmland. One Beijing IT executive, Li Ning, says, 'It's worth the time, money and energy to grow my own vegetables ... it may be more expensive than buying vegetables from the supermarket, but those have a bad chemical taste.'[47]

38. TM Waliczek & JM Zajicek. 'School gardening: Improving environmental attitudes of children through hands-on learning', Journal of Environmental Horticulture, 1999, pp.180–184

39. R Beitz & M Doren, 'Physical activity and postmenopausal health', The Journal of the British Menopause Society, 2004, pp.70–74

40. LR Reynolds & JW Anderson, 'Practical office strategies for weight management of the obese diabetic individual', Endocrine Practice, Vol. 10, No. 2, 2004, pp.153–159

41. DM Wood, AL Brennan, BJ Philips & EH Baker, 'Effect of hyperglycaemia on glucose concentration of airways secretions', Clinical Science, 2004, pp.527–533

42. J McDougall, 'Low Vitamin D: One Sign of Sunlight Deficiency', EarthSave, Vol. 19, No. 1, 2008

43. K Morgan, 'Feeding the City: The Challenge of Urban Food Planning. International Planning Studies', Routledge, London, 2010, pp.341–348

44. 'Gardening with Allergies, Arthritis and Other Problems' [http://gardening.about.com/od/allergiesarthritis/a/Garden_Fitness.html], retrieved 2 September 2012

45. E Leeuwen, 'The Multi-Functional use of Urban Green Spaces' [ftp://zappa.ubvu.vu.nl/20090051.pdf], retrieved 1 August 2013

46. YZ Huang, 'China's Corrupt Food Chain', Food Safety in China, The New York Times, 2012 [http://topics.nytimes.com/top/news/international/countriesandterritories/china/food-safety/index.html], retrieved 2 August 2013

47. G Ng, 'Food Safety Scares Drive Some Chinese Back to Farm, 2011 [http://www.thejakartaglobe.com/asia/food-safety-scares-drive-some-chinese-back-to-the-farm/431829], retrieved 3 September 2012

Chinese authorities are increasing their efforts to improve food safety regulations and food chemistry research, after food scandals have continued to occur in the country. Milk contaminated with the industrial chemical melamine caused the deaths of six babies and the sickness of 300,000 people in 2008.[48] The scandal caused outrage in the country, and caused a huge detrimental affect on the confidence of the public food system.[49]

Farm Your Own

Keeping livestock in cities, either as a specialized enterprise or in combination with gardening and farming in an urban environment, can provide income and a source of food. Urban livestock systems exist all over the world, despite the many problems that they are perceived as creating. The ever-escalating cost of food and the questions surrounding the health of our diets is changing the attitudes of city planners and urban populations alike who do not consider cities as food producing areas. Urban consumers use more animal products than rural consumers do. Positive consideration to this sector could help to uncover the opportunities inherent in this form of livestock production in the city.

The availability of a choice of high-quality feeds such as by-products of the food processing industry, hotel refuse and kitchen waste has encouraged urban livestock systems. Concentrated feeds such as these are common in the city, a sharp contrast to the more traditional scattered fashion they are found in throughout the countryside. Goats, sheep, cows, horses, camels, chickens, rabbits, ducks, turkeys, buffaloes and pigeons can all be found living alongside people in compact city settings. In densely populated Cairo, 5% of households keep animals, primarily chickens and pigeons.[50] The extensive rearing of poultry, pigs and fish can be found in Hong Kong, Singapore, Calcutta and Dhaka.[51] Poultry, pigs and guinea pigs reared in small backyards and on rooftops reside throughout the impoverished neighbourhoods of Latin American cities such as Lima, La Paz and Mexico City.[52]

Urban fish farms can be used to regenerate a neighbourhood, and create a new source of income. In the city of Abidjan in Côte d'Ivoire, fish are fed rice bran and abattoir leftovers, and manure is used as fertilizer to produce feed. Tilapia culture in Southeast Asia is currently spreading and intensifying, demonstrating that fish protein can be grown locally. In Thailand, peri-urban enterprises use processing wastes and other inputs from cities to provide food for aquaculture farming. Raising animals in city environments only produces a fraction of the total dietary food requirements for an urban population. Urban livestock and crop farming can never produce enough food to support a huge city with an expanding population. The pollution and health risks of keeping animals in close proximity to people and the competition with other sectors for space and resources, persuades planners and policy makers to advocate that the production of food from animal origin is better shifted to larger specialized units that are located away from the city.

The role of livestock kept in urban environments is not confined to the production of food. Many people depend on their livestock for a portion of their livelihood. Small animals are particularly adaptable to restricted backyard conditions generally associated with urban habitats. Rabbits, chickens and other small pet animals are already commonly kept on balconies and in backyards throughout cities. Rearing

facing page top: Taizhou came to a stand-still to make way for the 5,000 ducks migrating to a pond one kilometre away to look for food.

facing page bottom: Nigerian men pile up dead birds to be destroyed in Kano. Thousands of chickens have been burned to try to prevent the spread of the deadly avian virus, H5N1.

137

48. Z Qian, 'Fears over tainted milk powder', Global Times, 2013 [http://www.globaltimes.cn/content/758505.shtml], retrieved 1 August 2013

49. 'China's Food Safety Scares', Bloomberg Businessweek, 2013 [http://images.businessweek.com/slideshows/2013-03-14/chinas-food-safety-scares], retrieved 1 August 2013

50+52. H Schiere et al., 'Livestock Keeping in Urbanised Areas' [http://web.idrc.ca/iicr/ev-103880-201-1-DO_TOPIC.html], retrieved 3 August 2013

51. S Jutzi, 'Livestock keeping in urban areas, FAO Animal Production and Health Division [ftp://ftp.fao.org/docrep/fao/004/y0500e/Y0500E00.pdf], retrieved 3 August 2013

small sized livestock can have positive farming credentials as they tend to require little start-up capital, are easy to sell and have the ability to reproduce quickly.

Waste Management

Waste management in urban areas is an acute problem. Existing neighbourhood waste management practices often include the use of organic waste as a feed supplement for urban livestock. Mainly consisting of goats, but also sheep and cattle, these low-carbon 'lawn mowers' are pesticide-free urban tools that can bring economic benefits to less affluent residents, who would suffer an economic loss if their supply of urban waste was reduced or eliminated by an organized waste collection and disposal strategy.

Cows and goats are useful in urban areas where there are a lot of by-products from agro industries. In the nineteenth century, urban dairies were important in areas situated around breweries. In the city of Copenhagen in Denmark herds of cows were a common sight around these buildings where their purpose was to clean up leftovers. Urban livestock systems are a potential hazard to public health. Problems such as smell, the environmental toll of increased waste and vermin, and the pollution of waterways can be the effects of keeping animals in urban environments. Keeping animals without a proper sewage system may favour mosquitoes that transmit malaria and other viral diseases, affecting both animals and people. Such viruses are more likely to spread when hygiene conditions are poor. The storage of animal foodstuffs in commercial forms of livestock keeping is prone to vermin.

In the UK, goat owners must comply with additional laws that do not apply to pets such as cats and dogs. Individualized goat identification, registration of land on which they are kept, transportation methods that are used to move the animals, and the keeping of medicine records are all required by DEFRA before a goat is allowed under a householder's supervision.[53] Since the outbreak of health scandals such as 'foot and mouth', improvements in the identification and tracing of animals have become an important part of disease control.

Similarly, regulations over the raising of chickens in urban environments are enforced in many cities, although they are often outdated and confusing. In California only six chickens may be kept on a 10,000 square foot area, whilst in Alabama holding a chicken upside down while walking down an urban street is against the law.[54]

The small-scale urban animal husbandry movement is becoming more apparent in everyday urban life. Jurisdiction is needed in order to revamp and change land-use laws to allow residents to keep their own livestock and cultivate a food supply. City dwellers are accustomed to being awakened at night by the occasional police siren or by the rumble of a landing aeroplane, yet hens are sometimes subjected to nuisance ordinances from local councils. The delightful chuckle of a hen that travels no more than a few feet is a stark contrast to the bark of a dog, and the 24-hour a day noise people make through the rattling of air conditioners and the revving of car engines in the city.

Smallest Room in the City

It is impossible to discuss food in the city, without some mention of the inherent waste management systems of the body. The culinary triangle is a concept described by anthropologist Claude Levi-Strauss and is composed of the three types of cooking: boiling, roasting and smoking, usually done to meat. For Levi-Strauss, food served as a lens through which fundamental cultural differences can be observed. Often, he notes, there is little way of reconciling different tastes; in one example serving up the story of American soldiers landing in Normandy in World War II who would burn down cheese dairies, mistaking the pungent smell of the cheese for corpses![55]

Slovenian philosopher, Slavoj Zizek proposes an altogether different, but equally enlightening, Levi-Straussian triangle, of the three basic types of toilet design in the West. By way of an 'excremental counterpoint', we see three different existential attitudes reflected in the three different toilet designs of Germany, France and England.[56] In the German toilet, the hole that removes waste is positioned at the front of the bowl giving an opportunity for reflection and inspection. The typical French toilet swiftly spirits away any waste, the hole situated far from the bowl, whilst the American and British counterpart presents a synthesis; the basin is full of water providing a view of the offering, but not to be pored over by the donor. Zizek reinterprets these toilet configurations as an intimate lens on political stance – 'German reflective thoroughness, French revolutionary hastiness, English moderate utilitarian liberalism. The reference to toilets enables us to discern the same triad in the most intimate domain of performing the excremental function: ambiguous contemplative fascination; the hasty attempt to get rid of the unpleasant excess as fast as possible; the pragmatic approach to treat the excess as an ordinary object to be disposed of in an appropriate way.'[57]

139

The apparent disparity between some legislation and 'urban sense' that occurs in cities around the world indicates that policy practitioners are not coordinating effectively across ministries and departments. A Lancet commission on 'Shaping Cities for Health' that brought together practitioners and academics across departments of University College London, highlighted the need for governments to work with a wide pool of urban stakeholders in finding effective and lasting solutions for urban health. In the case of urban food provision, as the examples in this chapter have shown, this includes engaging with the informal sector including unofficial market gardeners and even those who are participating in food production as a supplement to their formal income, such as a family keeping a chicken coop at home for eggs.

Amongst other findings, the commission also made the recommendation that in order to achieve effective progress towards urban health, local experimentation in conjunction with an assessment of practicing and decision-making processes is a necessary approach. This is especially pertinent for the development of healthy urban food practices as it is clear that systems for urban agriculture and livestock need to be developed in ways which are sensitive and responsive to the social and climatic conditions of site. Whilst lessons can be learnt from the innovative urban practices in one city, such as the mobilization of street vendors in the Philippines, proposals will always need to be refined and adapted to viably suit the identity of another.

53. 'Animal services Information', DEFRA [http://www.defra.gov.uk/food-farm/animals/sheep-goats/], retrieved 12 July 2012

54. B Finch, 'Is your backyard flock making you an outlaw?' [http://www.al.com/specialreport/mobileregister/index.ssf?outlaws.html], retrieved 12 July 2012

55. S Davis, 'The Culinary Triangle' [http://www.thesmartset.com/article/article07181301.aspx] retrieved 14 August 2011

56+57. S Zizek, 'On the Ideology of Toilets' [http://www.examiner.com/article/slavoj-zizek-1-on-the-ideology-of-toilets], retrieved 14 August 2011

Table Manners

'All right then, they would have lamb for supper. She carried it upstairs, holding the thin bone-end of it with both her hands, and as she went through the living-room, she saw him standing over by the window with his back to her, and she stopped.

"For God's sake," he said, hearing her, but not turning round. "Don't make supper for me."

At that point, Mary Maloney simply walked up behind him and without any pause she swung the big frozen leg of lamb high in the air and brought it down as hard as she could on the back of his head.'

– Roald Dahl, 'Lamb to the Slaughter', 1953

141

Our relationship to the food we have access to has been a critical influence on our physical human development. Early ancestors of human beings, Paranthropus boisei, developed enormous muscled jaws with huge back teeth to enable them to accommodate harsh climatic conditions and grind down the tough plants available at the time. Seemingly not as specialized, another ape roaming this harsh new climate, the Homo habilis, was less discerning and would track vulture activity and scavenge the remains of predator kills. A calorie and nutrient-rich meat diet meant that the Homo habilis didn't need the large intestines of the apes and earlier hominids. This freed up energy that was absorbed by the brain, allowing for the development of greater intellect. They developed tools, giving them access to the long chain fatty acids vital for brain growth and development hidden in the bone marrow of their scavenged kills. Despite their highly specialized evolutionary developments, the 'bosei' would ultimately become extinct. By contrast, Homo habilis, buoyed by their meat rich diet, and as a result their highly developed cognitive skills, would find ways to adapt and evolve around the impending Ice Age.[1]

These developments, which happened over hundreds of thousands of years, are still relevant today. Whilst the stakes may not involve the extinction of species, our physiological development, strength, cognitive capabilities and ability to fight disease, are dependent on the provision of a balanced, nourishing diet. In cities around the world, we are influenced by, adapt to and accommodate the challenges of our environments and climates through crisis and cyclical phenomena. Relative to the history of human development, we have now entered a new phase that is still in its nascent stages. As inhabitants of a globalized world, the activities of those on one side of the world can have a direct influence on those on the other. As author Jonathan Safran Foer comments, 'It's an empowering idea. The entire goliath of the food industry is driven and determined by the choices we make as the waiter gets impatient for our order or in the practicalities and whims of what we load into our shopping carts or farmers'-market bags.'[2]

This has huge implications for the global legal and policy frameworks that oversee food provision.

facing page: In San Francisco, fast-food restaurants are prevented from giving away action figures and other toys in their kid's meals unless the food meets the city's Department of Public Health nutritional requirements.

1. 'Food for thought – 3 million years ago', Science and Nature, BBC [http://www.bbc.co.uk/sn/prehistoric_life/human/human_evolution/food_for_thought1.shtml], retrieved 17 August 2012

2. JS Foer, 'Eating Animals', Little, Brown and Company, New York, 2009, p.89

Millions of years on from the trials of Homo habilis, the global food trade is only a few thousands of years old. Basic to human survival, and with commodities unique to location, food was one of the first products people were able to produce at a surplus for trade. Also a relatively new phenomenon, political boundaries necessitated the need for trade. In some cases national boundaries have resulted in some countries being unable to produce all the food supplies they need whereas others have saturated local markets.

Almost as old as the trade of food is the history of food traded against peoples' will. Agriculture in colonies was primarily focused on growing export crops for profit and sale in the colonial powers; among them sugar, tobacco, tea, coffee, cocoa and tropical fruits. After independence, many countries continued to cultivate the same crops, and with greater national control over these exports a wave of legal frameworks and policies regulating this trade was implemented.[3] Trade laws and economic policies placed tariffs on agricultural goods and stunted the returns back to the newly independent states.

The 1980s brought the theory of 'trade liberalization'. A key feature of the 'Free Trade' model is a theory of 'comparative advantage' under which countries trading across borders should specialize in foods consistent with their provision of resources, such as arable land, availability of labour and capital. These foods are then to be traded with importing countries that pay by exporting in return commodities that the reciprocal country does not produce. In theory, this system should lead to an efficient global food chain that is mutually beneficial in resources and leads to collective economic growth. However, these deals tended to favour the wealthier former colonial powers with lower or no tariffs on their commodities whilst tariff escalation was imposed on commodities produced by countries in competition with these wealthy states.[4]

The establishment of the World Trade Organization (WTO) in 1995 was a result of the culmination of a several decades of trade negotiations that had taken place under the General Agreement on Tariffs and Trade (GATT) and has been cited as a 'mark of how strongly the notion of free trade had captured the imaginations of governments'.[5] The formation of the WTO gave these trade agreements a governing body, and through the threat of trade sanctions, a system of enforcing global trade rules.

However, a failure to achieve consensus at the WTO on food and agricultural agreements would lead to regional agreements gaining strength. Regional trade agreements such as the European Economic Community (a predecessor to the EU) would also have the effect of creating markets impenetrable to poorer economies, whilst preserving established wealth, often accrued through the instruments of colonialism. Post-colonial societies are also regionally mobilized. During the 1990s, the FAO reported 15 new regional trade agreements agreed per year such as the Southern Common Market (MERCOSUR) established by Argentina, Brazil, Paraguay and Uruguay.[6]

Throughout all these global trade agreements, tariff and non-tariff barriers have been identified as the biggest obstacles to food import and exports. Tariffs are imposed for a variety of reasons. One example

facing page: Tsukiji Fish Market, Tokyo. At the time of writing, the bluefin tuna had become the latest commodity to polarize global legislatures. A ban on the harvest of the fish, highly prized by sushi connoisseurs, has been successively blocked by aggressive lobbying from the United States and Japan despite suggestions of a precipitous decline in its numbers.

3+6. C Hawkes & S Murphy, 'An overview of Global Food Trade', 2009 [http://media.wiley.com/product_data/excerpt/65/14051998/1405199865-3.pdf], retrieved 17 August 2012

4. 'Trade Liberalisation' [http://www.economicsonline.co.uk/Global_economics/Trade_liberalisation.html], retrieved 17 August 2012

5. 'The WTO: History', World trade Organization [http://www.wto.org/english/thewto_e/cwr_e/cwr_history_e.htm], retrieved 17 August 2012

is the tariff on poultry imports from Brazil set by the South African International Trade Administration Commission (ITAC). It is the ITAC's assertion that surplus poultry is exported from Brazil and sold or 'dumped' in the South African market at very low prices. To protect the local poultry market, a tariff of 62.93% on Brazilian whole chickens and 46.59% on boneless cuts has been imposed. The Brazilian Chicken Producers and Exporters Association (Ubabef) has claimed that while Brazil supplies 73% of South Africa's chicken imports, the poultry only represents 15% of all the chicken eaten in South Africa. If no agreement can be reached between the countries, the case will be referred to a WTO dispute resolution panel.[7]

The European Union Common Agricultural Policy (CAP) is another example of a regional policy with associated contentious tariffs. Initially conceived to protect food security during the Cold War, the CAP was designed to protect European producers from cheaper products available outside the EU. This was first done through subsidizing local agricultural produce, however now the policy imposes import tariffs on produce from outside the protectorate whilst simultaneously subsidizing local product. The CAP is not without controversy. The EU intervenes in surplus food production in ways many other countries deem unfair: by subsidizing the cost of export of that product at below cost price, or by storing it in the infamous EU 'food mountains' for later sale or destruction. There are cases of these exports being 'dumped', or sold at dramatically reduced cost, in poorer countries, especially in Africa, compromising the local market. The CAP has also had policies of controlling agricultural production and even paying farmers not cultivate large tracts of land.[8]

Large corporations have played as important a role as entire regions in the history of the global food trade. These corporations, from state owned or sponsored entities to private family companies, deal with phenomenal sums of capital. Four of the five biggest global grain marketing companies in the world have been in operation since the mid to late 1800s. All but one (the newcomer, Archer Daniels Midland) are privately owned family businesses. Through a system known as Foreign Direct Investment (FDI), these corporations have been able to bypass many of the tariffs by directly investing in factories in the host countries they wish to import and export from. As a result these transnational corporations (TNCs) are subject to lower barriers whilst being able to influence policy in both countries of import and export in order to secure profits.[9]

Influencing the decisions made on tariff disagreements, and policy-making at the WTO is an industry in itself. Actionaid reported in 2006 that in the EU there are 15,000 professional lobbyists based in Brussels; one for every official in the European Commission. In the EU alone, annual lobbying expenditure is estimated to be as high as €1 billion. The situation in the USA is even more extreme. In Washington DC, lobbyists outnumber US Congress lawmakers by 30 to 1.[10] These lobbyists can heavily influence the direction of the WTO's directives and food trade agreements. Actionaid reported on one group known as 'Yum! Brands' composed of a group of multinational fast food chains including KFC, Pizza Hut and Taco Bell, lobbying to influence the WTO's agriculture talks. Yum! Brands formed the US Food Trade Alliance in 2005 with food multinationals Burger King, Dominos, Dunkin' Donuts, McDonalds and Starbucks and heads the Global Alliance for Liberalized Trade in Food and Agriculture. Incorporating lobby groups from 15 countries around the world, the Global Alliance's members lobby and pressure governments, in whose countries their businesses form large parts of the economy, to relax their tariffs and open their markets through the WTO.[11]

Urban Life Under Embargo
Against this backdrop of restrictive trade policies, Havana offers a fascinating example of urban ingenuity despite being

one of the most extreme case studies of exclusion from global trade markets. The Cuban government responded to trade sanctions in the early 1960s by developing links with new allies and by maximizing internal production. An example of this move to self-sufficiency is the self-sustained agrarian framework of Havana which formally began in 1994. The Cuban government adopted a new policy, Law No. 142, to modify existing rules and regulations governing agriculture and livestock activities in urban spaces throughout the island.[12] Driven by necessity, President Fidel Castro's government granted indefinite usufruct ownership to the population to transform abandoned state-owned and private land for public cultivation.[13] The urban land-use rights fundamentally reconnected the city directly with the land and encouraged urban food production. Urban inhabitants mobilized to convert patios, rooftops and unused parking lots into productive vegetable allotments, and reared livestock in a collective effort redolent of Britain's World War II victory gardens.

Under the initiative, large state-owned sugarcane farms and agriculture enterprises were divided into 'Basic Units of Cooperation Production', small workers' production collectives to increase autonomy of governance.[14] The planning framework afforded farmers and their families greater economic responsibilities in cultivation productivity.[15] Urban food production in Havana varies in scale from individual backyard 'huertos populares', large allotments 'organiponico' by individuals and institutions, to state-owned farms operating a profit sharing scheme 'empresas estatales'. Organoponicos are the most common type of garden; made from cement blocs and discarded construction columns, cultivation takes place inside containers that act as raised beds filled with an organic matter and soil mix.[16] These small growing containers were established as a way of plugging into widespread, readily available spaces within the city, and providing a fertile growing environment in the poor quality urban soils.[17] Crop beds are generally a composite of 50% organic material (manure), 25% composted waste (rice husks and coffee bean shells) and 25% soil.

The success of the gardens was attributed to the distribution of land for food production. The power of the communist state that owned all the land in Cuba with the exception of private homes gave it the resources at its disposal that it needed to support its policies. Any citizen or entity was able to request unused lands up to 33 acres to be passed out in usufruct for 20–40 years.[18]

Due to severe shortage of fuel, sustainable food production policies were brought into practice. The land was cultivated with manual labour, and communities were introduced to organic growing principles and the reliance on locally available building resources.[19] To champion the new law, the Cuban Ministry of Agriculture initiated networks of 'extension agents',[20] consisting mainly of women from neighbourhoods to educate urban farmers in methods of permaculture, composting and the use of biological controls. This included employment of repellent plants like marigolds[21] to keep pests away since chemical pesticides were outlawed within the city. Permaculture enables the city to have a sustainable high-yielding ecosystem for urban agriculture and increased biodiversity. Co-ops were established, owned and managed by local citizens encouraging the trade of other scarce items such as seeds and tools.

State incentives allow urban food producers to sell their excess produce directly to consumers at

7. 'Brazil confronts South Africa at WTO over poultry tariffs' [http://africanfarming.net/livestock/poultry/brazil-confronts-south-africa-at-wto-over-poultry-tariffs], retrieved 17 August 2012

8. 'Common Agricultural Policy' [http://www.civitas.org.uk/eufacts/FSPOL/AG3.htm], retrieved 18 August 2012

9. C Hawkes & S Murphy, 'An overview of Global Food Trade' [http://media.wiley.com/product_data/excerpt/65/14051998/1405199865-3.pdf], retrieved 17 August 2012

10. 'Corporate Lobbying', Action Aid [http://www.actionaid.org.uk/100300/corporate_lobbying.html], retrieved 19 August 2012

11. 'Under the Influence', Action Aid [http://www.actionaid.org.uk/_content/documents/under_the_influence_final.pdf], retrieved 19 August 2012

12. 'Case study: Havana, Cuba', Future Policy [http://www.futurepolicy.org/3407.html], retrieved 21 August 2012

13+15. MG Novo & C Murphy, 'Urban Agriculture in the City of Havana: A Popular Response to a Crisis', 1999 [www.ruaf.org/book/export/html/76], retrieved 20 August 2012

14. LJ Enriquez, 'Cuba's New Agricultural Revolution: The Transformation of Food Crop Production in Contemporary Cuba', Development Report no.14, Food First Institute for Food and Development Policy, USA, 2000, p.7

16+17, 19. K Taboulchanas, 'Case Study in Urban Agriculture, Organiponicos in Cienfuegos, Cuba' [http://dp.biology.dal.ca/reports/ztaboulchanas/taboulchanasst.html#toc], retrieved 20 August 2012

18. A Fisher, 'The Exceptional Nature of Cuban Urban Agriculture', 2010 [http://civileats.com/2010/04/21/the-exceptional-nature-of-cuban-urban-agriculture/], retrieved 21 August 2012

20. RR Pinderhughes, 'Urban Agriculture in Havana, Cuba', San Francisco State University, 2000

community farmers markets rather than exclusively through the state redistribution chain.[22] Local trading of organic provisions become a real source of employment for many people and helped urban farmers to achieve parity of earning with white-collar workers. The ability to provide fresh produce with zero transportation costs reduced food prices and significantly lowered the city's carbon footprint. Today, Cuba proudly grows 90% of its fruits and vegetables, with 4 million tonnes of vegetables every year from urban allotments in Havana alone. One cooperative built on a former rubbish tip, Alamo Organiponico, now provides employment for 170 people and supplies 240 tonnes of vegetables annually.[23] The spontaneous city gardens have since fed a hungry population, and radically transformed Cuba's society, politics and the urban topography forever.

Guerrilla Gardening

Few governments have integrated urban food production as a permanent policy in their city planning similar to that of Cuba. This oversight is typical of most cities; policy makers view urban agriculture on neglected urban spaces with indifference and as an interim unlawful activity, until a more lucrative development opportunity emerges.[24] However, 'Guerrilla Gardeners' have long campaigned for legal rights to land tenure and site control for productive vegetable plots and gardens, and also beautifying the urban topography. The activity is gathering momentum amongst urbanites, made possible with the aid of websites and blogs. The militant gardeners, willing to risk legal consequences, are armed with unconventional weapons: 'seed bombs', alongside traditional watering cans, shovels, trowels and pitchforks, with which the growers remove rubbish and revitalize the soil by planting flowers, trees and edible plants.[25] The roots of illicit gardening can be traced back to New York in 1973, when the artist Liz Christy and her neighbours won a land tenure petition with the city's Housing and Preservation Department to legally recognize the 'Bowery Garden', their new community garden created from an abandoned private lot.[26]

Guerrilla gardening has cleaned up many communities and has liberated pockets of derelict and barren land in cities, and yet is perceived as an on-going public health and safety risk. Many cities' authorities are concerned with communities creating food-producing gardens on contaminated soil. Poisonous by-products from manufacturing, industrial farming, city septic systems, construction, automotive garages, laboratories, hospitals and other industries introduce potential threats to the culture of guerrilla gardening. Food production near toxic waste plants and polluted high traffic roads involves enormous health risks and has been condemned by the authorities.

Feed Yourself Operation

Urban agriculture, from the growing of plants to rearing animals, is present in almost all African cities. According to the FAO, there will be 35 million urban farmers in African cities by 2020.[27] For many on the continent, an urban garden provides a degree of food security and access to fresh produce. Surplus often provides a source of industry, especially for the vulnerable such as women-headed households, the unemployed, the elderly and people with disabilities. In Harare, Zimbabwe, the sale such of fruit and vegetables on the street is an embedded urban industry. In Harare North, novelist Brian Chikwava writes of the life of some of these vendors: 'It's the Freezits and rock buns that clinch it. That is true vendor's stuff. Sadza and fish head you can say, maybe anyone can eat that. But the Freezits and rock buns – no one have those kinds of cravings unless you was once part of it the bus-terminus-vending people.'[28]

Similarly in Accra, Ghana, urban agriculture has no legal status despite establishing itself as one of the most important informal self-sustainability activities in built-up areas. In 1972, the Acheampong Government introduced the 'Feed

left, top + bottom: The local government of Belo Horizonte initiated Municipal Law No. 6,352, an integrated policy framework for food security to reduce the strain on the city's health and social services.

21+23. S Murch, 'The Vegetable Gardeners Of Havana', Food Future, BBC News, 2009 [http://news.bbc.co.uk/1/hi/8213617.stm], retrieved 20 August 2012

22. MG Novo & C Murphy, 'Urban Agriculture in the City of Havana: A Popular Response to a Crisis', 1999 [www.ruaf.org/book/export/html/76], retrieved 20 August 2012

24. A Fisher, 'The Exceptional Nature of Cuban Urban Agriculture', 2010 [http://civileats.com/2010/04/21/the-exceptional-nature-of-cuban-urban-agriculture/], retrieved 21 August 2012

25+26. M Fraser, 'How Guerrilla Gardening Took Root', Step Up, BBC News, 2010 [http://news.bbc.co.uk/1/hi/scotland/8548005.stm], retrieved 3 September 2012

27. T Bacala, 'Urban agriculture innovations feed Sub-Saharan African cities', Media Golbal [http://blogs.worldwatch.org/nourishingtheplanet/wp-content/uploads/2011/02/Media-Global-Toni-Bacala-Urban-agriculture-innovations-feed-Africa-Daniel-Gustafson.pdf], retrieved 4 September 2012

28. B Chikwava, 'Harare North', Random House, London, 2009, p.94

Yourself Operation' (FYO), an emergency urban agriculture in response to the country's food crisis after the international community refused credit and aid to Ghana.[29] City dwellers, in Accra, of mid to high socio-economic status including government officials farmed in enclosed gardens around their homes, while peri-urban cultivation occurred on the edges of the city. The urban poor and under educated rural migrants with agricultural knowledge engaged in open-space food cultivation to sustain themselves. Open space cultivators are guerrilla gardeners who cultivate land without legal rights and access permission, typically on undeveloped community land belonging to central and municipal governments, including railways and aviation authorities, parks and university campuses.[30] Guerrilla gardening in Accra has helped contribute to the greening and management of public spaces, and reduced refuse dumping and illegal drug related activities in urban areas without costing the city.

In more recent times, Ghanaian government and officials have become increasingly positive towards urban agriculture, mostly due to socio-political and economic pressures. It worries the government to alienate voters who are not given the right to subsidize their food purchases by growing and selling their own food when Ghana's economic and unemployment situation is bad, and the cost of living is very high. Government officials, in particular, are willing to endorse a popularity vote by allowing urban food production to avoid unrest and demand for change in government even though it is technically illegal.[31]

Economic factors have been instrumental in changing the negative attitudes government officials held towards urban agriculture in Accra. The increased industrialization in the country made the government consider sustaining a ready supply of labourers.[32] The perception is that foreign investors would be more attracted to investing in a country that did not have difficulty in recruiting workers with the necessary skills to work in urban industries.[33] Similarly, easing the laws on urban agriculture helped remove responsibility from the government to support an unskilled workforce in Accra.[34] Urban agriculture allows low skilled, low salaried unemployed workers to remain in the cities. By tolerating self-sustainable urban food cultivation, the government believes that the urban workforce may not feel the realities of their exploitation and will be less willing to push for salary increases. Despite the socio-economic and environmental benefits, the Ghanaian policy makers and municipal government have yet to re-evaluate their current urban land-use planning regulations to address issues of land tenure and security to support urban agriculture.[35]

Urban Agriculture in Harare

Urban agriculture in Africa has become a highly politicized issue. There are clear benefits, and indeed whole industries, built on the foundation of this urban informal sector. However, as in any global city, when practices lack the appropriate resources or infrastructure the effects can be detrimental. The use of biocides for pest control and chemical fertilizers in food production is thought to contaminate the environment and crops. Runoff from fertilizers, herbicides and pesticides into urban rivers or streams are a significant source of water pollution and risks to aquatic life, particularly fish. In 1987, it was estimated that approximately 10,000 people died and about 400,000 suffered acutely from pesticide poisoning in developing countries.[36] Recycling waste for organic urban agriculture is a solution to many cities' waste management and can significantly reduce the use of artificial fertilizers by the uninformed.[37]

A report from Harare in 2011 highlighted the tensions that exist between the urban farmers, cultivating towards a greater degree of food security, and the local council, keen to avoid damage to infrastructure and outbreaks of disease, 'With the coming of a new growing season, all places without buildings on them are being cultivated. These include football, netball and basketball pitches, road-sides and recreational parks as well as wetlands. This has resulted in serious environmental degradation including soil erosion and siltation.'[38]

To further compound the environmental damage, there are reports of dysentery and malaria outbreaks and an increase in criminal activity as thieves utilize the high crops as hiding places. The local council, led by the Movement for Democratic Change (MDC) party, took the extreme decision to authorize the police to destroy all visible urban agriculture.[39] This was quickly attacked as a poor political decision by the Zimbabwe African National Union – Patriotic Front (Zanu (PF)) party saying that, 'banning urban agriculture is the work of enemies who want to scuttle the president's generous donations of seed and fertilizer to urban supporters of the former ruling party.'[40]

Reports like these from Harare and Accra show a situation where the space for progress on the issues of urban farming or the provision of infrastructure for these activities has been appropriated by a party political, rather than a constructive, debate. The residents of Epworth, on the city fringes of Harare, understand this history of urban political displacement. The Epworth Porta Farm community are over 4,000 people who were relocated from inner city squatter settlements in preparation for the Commonwealth Heads of Government meeting in 1999. Accommodation in Epworth was only planned to last three months. Over a decade later, residents are still waiting for their promised housing plots and in the interim have subsisted on the informal sector, cultivating crops and fishing near the camps. The land is not ideal for farming, however most of the residents came to the urban areas with agricultural knowledge from the rural areas. Epworth residents cultivate maize and sweet potatoes in their backyards and in sporadic patches of unused land.

Residents often spoke of how practising urban agriculture not only gave them a degree of food security but also connected them with a comforting aspect of rural life.

Cape Town's Food Garden

There is also evidence that urban agriculture has been actively and progressively supported by local government policy in Africa. Cape Town launched the Urban Agriculture Policy in 2007 with the aims of supporting and promoting urban agriculture 'within the context that it will not degrade the quality of life of citizens, will not impact harmfully on public health, the natural environment and will contribute to the social and economic well-being of people'.[41]

The policy actively acknowledges the positive features of urban agriculture to date in improving household food security and nutrition as well as the associated economic activity. Perhaps most importantly, the city's policy pledges to include urban agriculture as part of future development planning. For Cape Town, when considering modifications to the existing fabric of the city or proposing areas of new use, urban agriculture will be considered. The policy also pledges to include consideration for urban agriculture as part of the city's planning policies for community development and environmental health. This is to be done by supporting the frameworks for urban agriculture that already exist in providing support to community groups and individuals. There is also an emphasis on encouraging the creation of healthy,

29+30. R Asomani-Boateng, 'Urban Cultivation in Accra: An Examination of the Nature, Practices, Problems, Potentials and Urban Planning Implications', Habitat International, Vol. 26, Issue 4, December 2002, pp.591–607

31–36. K Obosu-Mensah, 'Changes to Official Attitudes to Urban Agriculture in Accra', African Studies Quarterly Vol. 6, No. 3, 2002, pp.19–32

37. R Asomani-Boateng & M Haight, 'Reusing Organic Solid Waste in Urban Farming in African Cities – A Challenge for Urban Planners', Third World Planning Review, Vol. 21, Issue 4, 1999, pp.411–428

38. 'Council, ZRP vow to ban urban agriculture', The Zimbabwean [http://www.thezimbabwean.co.uk/news/zimbabwe/54472/council-zrp-vow-to-ban.htm], retrieved 12 August 2013

39. C Pdraig & S Taylor, 'Industry and the Urban Sector in Zimbabwe's Political Economy', African Studies Quarterly 7, No. 2+3 [http://www.africa.ufl.edu/asq/v7/v7i2a3.htm], retrieved 12 August 2013

40. W Anseeuw, T Kapuya & D Saruchera, 'Zimbabwe's agricultural reconstruction: Present state, on-going projects and prospects for reinvestment', Development Planning Division Working Paper Series No. 32, 2012 [http://www.afd.fr/webdav/site/afd/groups/Agence_Afrique_du_Sud/public/Dossier%20Assia%20Sidibe/Vf%20etude%20juin%202012.pdf], retrieved 12 August 2013

41. 'Urban Agricultural Policy for The City of Cape Town', City of Cape Town, June 2007 [http://www.capetown.gov.za/en/ehd/Documents/EHD_-_Urban_Agricultural_Policy_2007_8102007113120_.pdf], retrieved 12 August 2013

sustainable practices by supporting and providing infrastructure for NGOs and private entrepreneurs.[42] This policy is already having a positive effect on Cape Town. One report from 2012 painted an exotic image of an urban Capetonian farmer, Matt Allison, saying: 'Allison was talking over the roar of traffic from Constantia Main Road. Neighbour's roofs look on indifferently over the suburban barbed wire. It's a far cry from the typical pastoral scene, but just that morning the 31-year-old small-scale farmer harvested 40 carrots, 30 radishes, 1kg of lettuce and 1kg of marrows and delivered it fresh to one of the ethical Cape Town eateries he supplies.'[43]

NGO initiatives such as Soil for Life teach Capetonians, mostly in disadvantaged township communities, how to grow food in an environmentally sustainable way. In 2008, a year after the Urban Agriculture Policy came into effect, Soil for Life moved from promoting community food gardens to a programme of advocating home food gardening.[44]

Dubbed 'Cape Town's Urban Food Garden', the Philipi Horticulture Area in Cape Town, South Africa, is a 6,000 acre area of urban farmland besieged on all sides by concrete.[45] Suburbia and the inner city surrounds this historical site which hosts a variety of activities. Despite the fact that many of the farming plots have been left vacant by owners, the produce from the farmland provides over 50% of the fresh produce consumed in the city. The land is also a critical habitat for hundreds of species of migrating birds, and also hundreds of families living in metal shacks on ten separate illegal settlements on the site.[46] Farmers on the site cultivate a variety of produce. Nazeer Ahmend Sonday, a businessman in addition to being a small-scale farmer on the site, grows tomatoes, raises chickens and sheep and uses the site to produce most of the food he needs to feed his family.[47] The site is under threat from developers seeking to capitalize on the valuable central location and is already half the size it used to be.

One of the lobbyists for progressive thinking towards urban agriculture in Cape Town, Nazeer founded the Schaapkraal Developing Farmers Association (SDFA) in partnership with the Urban Food Security Department at Cape Town University. The aims of the SDFA are to promote and encourage the activities of small-scale farmers in the city. They aim to prevent the destruction of Philippi Horticultural Area by proving its potential to improve food security within the city, protecting biodiversity and providing funding and support services for the urban farmers. They see agriculture in the city as an urban tool for steering the lives of youths born into illegal settlements in a positive direction.

This approach is also considerate of the need for the agriculture to be profitable and generate an income as well as a source of food. The SDFA seeks to create a 'culture of agriculture' where a holistic system provides land, food security, access to markets and urban environmental protection. In doing this, they see urban agriculture as a way of providing people with homes, food and income and a positive tangible physical connection with the city.

Recycling Organic Waste
In addition to generating waste which can be efficiently reused, urban agriculture has also proved to be a useful source of waste management when incorporated into the city policy.

Urban agriculture has been present in Mexico City since the days when it was known as Tenochtitlán, a sprawling urban site in Mesoamerica.[48] Urban agriculture in the city today is highly complex and advanced and has been supported in various ways by the local government. The city's agricultural output varies. Urban production is composed of family gardens, backyard milk and pork production, whereas suburban production features the growth of vegetables and flowers in backyard and kitchen gardens, greenhouses and dairy production. In the peri-urban, on the surrounding terraces, nopal plants, corn, milk and dairy production and the farming of bees and sheep is in practice. Peri-urban residents combine use of kitchen gardens with the highly efficient practice of silvopasture; a mix of forestry and grazing domesticated animals. In the city's valleys, urban farmers are engaged in livestock cultivation with amaranth and tuna (prickly pear) production in extensive greenhouses.

The local government has supported the participation of women, often the most vulnerable groups in society. Groups of mobilized women in Fraccionamineto San Blas in the northern municipality of Cuauhtitlan have formed a consumer cooperative with the aim of separating domestic waste to produce compost and vegetables on their communal site.[49]

The variety of urban agricultural activities throughout the city generates many different types of waste that are put to use. In addition, a further 725 tonnes of organic waste is produced per day from the city's metropolitan food supply depot (CEDA). This is put to good use and 90 tonnes of this waste is used to feed some 2,500 dairy cows in the east of the city which produce 37,5000 litres of milk per day. Tomato waste is used to feed approximately 50,000 pigs and remaining organic waste used to nourish urban chickens and rabbits.[50] Grass clipped by the municipality from sidewalks and traffic islands is also used as fodder for dairy stables, the manure from which is used as fertilizer for the city's crops. Some reports estimate that as much as 1,320 tonnes of manure waste is used around the city per year. Urban farmers in Mexico City only need to meet the transport costs to access this valuable feed and fertilizer as all of this waste is available from the city for free.[51]

The Urban Food Desert

These cases of ingenuity in urban agricultural policy in the global South are a stark contrast to the phenomenon of the urban 'food desert' which exists in many relatively highly economically advanced societies. First used to describe a resource impoverished urban environment in 1973, food deserts have emerged as areas of cities where cheap and nutritious food, fresh fruit and vegetables are unobtainable and requires travelling by car to supermarkets.[52] In 1997, the Independent wrote of British food deserts thus, 'Car-less residents, unable to reach out-of-town supermarkets, depend on the corner shop where prices are high, products are processed and fresh fruit and vegetables are poor or non-existent'.[53]

Largely arising out of public economic policy that has favoured investments into larger corporate food suppliers, smaller and more specialized local suppliers have been unable to match the competition and have shut down. One for-profit company in the United States, Mogro, is capitalizing on these undersupplied areas by functioning as a mobile grocer. The mobile grocer operates from a 33ft long trailer with customized refrigeration units. Ten full bays displaying 200 supermarket items supply the Native American community of Santo Domingo Pueblo, New Mexico, with fresh fruit and vegetables and other grocery items. Although a profit making entity, the company has an interest in the communities in serves. An emphasis is placed on the nutritional value of the products it supplies, as is shown by the noticeable absence of 'chips, soda or candy bars'. Mogro has also partnered with Johns Hopkins

42. 'Urban Agricultural Policy for The City of Cape Town', City of Cape Town, June 2007 [http://www.capetown.gov.za/en/ehd/Documents/EHD_-_Urban_Agricultural_Policy_2007_8102007113120_.pdf], retrieved 12 August 2013

43+44. N Botha, 'Fresh from the balcony', Mail & Guardian, 2012 [http://mg.co.za/article/2012-01-27-fresh-from-the-balcony/], retrieved 5 September 2012

45–47. 'Agriculture as a Concrete Solution: Cape Town's Food Garden' [http://blogs.worldwatch.org/nourishingtheplanet/philippi-horticulture-area-pha-cape-town-south-africa-cape-town-university-nourishing-the-planet/], retrieved 6 September 2012

48–51. H Losada, J Rivera, J Vieyra & J Cortes, 'The Role of Urban Agriculture in Waste Management in Mexico City', Urban Agriculture Magazine, No. 23, April 2010 [http://www.ruaf.org/sites/default/files/UAM23%20mexico%20city%20pag40-41.pdf], retrieved 4 September 2012

52+53. 'What is a food desert?' [http://www.fooddeserts.org/images/whatisfd.html], retrieved 21 September 2012

University to host community cooking classes and events and sees the business as 'a model for filling in the gaps that make food deserts – access to healthy affordable food.'

Soup Kitchens

For the urban homeless, even living in a city abundant with shops supplying food can be as much of a struggle as life in the food desert. Homelessness is an issue facing many inner city environments. Countless people are often forced onto the streets unable to assemble the resources they need to escape poverty. Most homeless people are concerned with the basic principles of survival, and spend the large percentage of their time hunting for shelter, clothing and most importantly, food. 'Soup kitchen' projects have existed in several cities for many years in order to help provide these basic needs in an earnest attempt to help the vulnerable people who knock on their doors.

A soup kitchen is a meal centre and a place where food is offered to the hungry for free or at a reasonably low price.[54] It is a 'no condition service' providing an unconditional food supply, though usually located in lower-income neighbourhoods. Staffed by volunteer organizations, such as community or church groups, soup kitchens run alongside official government initiatives, and are a resource for the homeless, elderly, lonely and poor, providing free hot meals, clothes and toiletries, whilst creating a sense of belonging and community.

In London, up to 100 people gather at Westminster Cathedral every evening to receive free soup, sandwiches, clothes and even sleeping bags. Westminster Cathedral has become well known as a place to congregate to get free sustenance from volunteers. In 2011, controversial proposals for a ban on this practice and rough sleeping in a part of inner city London sparked a political row. Westminster City Council is seeking to pass a bylaw that will outlaw soup kitchens from operating in a designated area around the Cathedral.[55] Labour councillors have attacked the proposal as 'cold-hearted and callous' but the council says soup kitchens maintain and encourage homelessness in the area.[56]

Westminster Council claims that giving out free food encourages people to stay on the streets. The council also argues that local businesses are affected by the scheme, as they have to deal with littering, violence and disorder as a result of large numbers of people gathering in the area for the soup kitchen. Daniel Astaire is a member of the conservative Council who believes the plans should be put into place, 'The problem is that there are too many people here at night who are coming for the soup runs, and the soup runs we think do not best serve the needs of really vulnerable homeless people ... there is no reason for anybody to be living rough on the streets of Westminster, but soup runs merely encourage that.'[57]

The Council wants people to move into the allocated building spaces and use the services that they offer rather than use the soup kitchens. They believe that homeless people will receive better access to health services, food supplies and water, and will be more likely to be reconnected with the structure of former lives and be helped with housing issues to ultimately get themselves off the streets. Soup runs have a bad press as they are seen as sustaining people on the streets, rather than providing actual

facing page top: Westminster Cathedral in London has become well known as a place to congregate to get free sustenance from volunteers. However, Westminster City Council is seeking to pass a bylaw to ban soup kitchens from operating around the Cathedral.

facing page bottom: In New York, the Relief Bus outreach consists of two former school buses customized into mobile food centres to help the poor and homeless.

54. 'Services', The Pavement [http://www.thepavement.org.uk/services.php?facility=&service=13&city=1], retrieved 22 September 2012

55+56. 'Plans to ban soup runs near Westminster Cathedral', BBC News, 2011 [http://www.bbc.co.uk/news/uk-england-london-12594397], retrieved 4 August 2011

57. 'Council wants to stop soup run for homeless' [http://www.youtube.com/watch?v=TEMnBGKMl64], retrieved 4 August 2011

help. However, many members of the community argue that giving someone food is a gateway to talking and giving them advice and support. David Coombe is an organizer for 'Street Souls': 'It is mean spirited to say that the most needy of people in our society cannot have free soup and sandwiches – there is such a need and it is inhumane not to allow it. It is a draconian legislation that they are trying to pass through ... we are out here twice a month looking after a hundred people and what we do is unfortunately a necessary thing.'

Like many, Coombe believes that tending to the most needy members of the community is a duty of care and that everybody should be helping them in whatever way they possibly can. Great prejudice surrounds homeless people and many people stereotype them as drug addicts or alcoholics. In many cases a homeless person is a productive citizen who just needs to be given a chance. Street Souls carried out a small census on the people they were feeding. Of an informal study of 37 people, Street Souls found only one person who would commit to spending a night in provided accommodation.[58]

At a time when economic struggle is leading an array of 'cuts' that are being applied across a lot of services, the criminalization of volunteers who fill gaps in services would appear to be misguided. Homeless Day Centres are struggling with funding, and hostels are closing, rendering few options available to a homeless person. Soup kitchens are about poverty and people who do not have much in the way of networks. While people are sympathetic to the idea that volunteers could be relinquishing their generosity to better use in other areas, many believe that losing soup kitchens is simply the wrong approach to the issue.

There is great urgency for cities to reform existing planning law and policies relating to urban food production and integrate food security into the national planning policy. Food production in cities has a strategic role for developing sustainable, healthy and productive urban habitats. The global food system will experience an unprecedented confluence of pressures, as the global population will increase to over 9 billion by 2050.[59] Two-thirds, or 6 billion will live in cities.[60] The intense demographic shift and rapid urbanization of arable land may lead to an overall drop in agricultural production of 20 to 40%, depending on the severity and length of natural global disasters and regional conflicts. Simultaneously, food export restrictions by food-producing nations,[61] and access to sustainable energy and water are further inhibiting affordable food. Wheat and rice prices have continuously soared globally, affecting the most important stable food source for a large part of the world's population, forcing the social classes into food insecurity.

The global crisis of increases in food prices has caused political and economical instability alongside social unrest in both poor and developed nations. Public displays of protest and anger occurred in over 60 countries during 2009.[62] Riots in Algiers in 2011 were widely perceived as based on deep frustrations with the ruling elite over concerns in the doubling of prices of flour, cooking oil and sugar in the space of six months.[63] Simultaneously, millions of hectares of agricultural land in developing countries are being bought by rich governments and corporations in an effort to secure long-term food supply interests. Rising food prices are fuelling charges of new colonialism.[64] A strategic national and city-planning framework with integrated food production policies could prove an important response to anticipated food shortages, while providing a number of economic, social and health benefits.

Food security is critical in community regeneration both at a local and national scale. The fundamental goal of any

planning framework is to ensure residents access at all times to affordable, high-quality food. Inner city residents on low incomes need better access to quality food retail outlets.[65] Currently, planning policies for town, district and city centres in the UK permit the loss of food shops to other non-retail uses such as estate agents, banks, pubs and take-aways. By splitting retail into two separate use classes, namely food retailing and non-food retailing, planning permission would therefore be required for changing a grocery to other retail use. A national size limit on floor space on all retail premises would also prevent large food retail developments dominating town centres that could potentially undermine small shops and create local monopolies. The amalgamation of small shops (200–250m2) to create a larger store or supermarket, and development of restaurant chains within a centre or neighbourhood should not be permitted in cities. Allocating sites for markets in all local centres would help to promote diversity of food access.[66]

155

Most urban inhabitants live in a cash economy; the mentality has led people to buy their food rather than to grow it. This dependency on purchasing, especially of imported food, has made them extremely vulnerable.[67] For new cities, housing developments can be planned to integrate agriculture at the scale of landscape; buildings can be used to terraform the natural topography, be surfaced in growing media and orientated to receive sunlight. Alternatively, new housing must include space for off-site allotments provision, designed and located consciously to facilitate the maximum opportunities for the potential of growing food. Community growing initiatives should be thoughtfully encouraged as a planning concern. The management of food consumption and waste must be factored in to the design and considerations of new-build housing developments and flat conversions by providing space for separate waste storage. The kitchen should provide space to store food, encourage cooking and promote a healthier, more wholesome lifestyle.

The lack of consideration of food systems in the planning frameworks of cities has become a serious worldwide issue of the twenty-first century. Food is vital for human life, and its production in cities must be given equal attention as the traditional concerns of urban development policies for housing, transport, air, water and economic development within communities.[68] Ultimately, in order for life in cities to be sustainable, all aspects of food including its growing, production and processing, distribution and retail, consumption and waste should become the priority of new planning policies to regulate the future demands of rapid urbanization.

58. 'Westminster Bans Soup Runs' [http://www.youtube.com/watch?v=_jxLcqVbo0A], retrieved 4 August 2011

59. 'The Future of Food and Farming: Challenges and choices for global sustainability', The Foresight Report, The Government Office for Science, London, 2011, p.9

60. 'Human Settlements', United Nations [http://www.un.org/en/globalissues/humansettlements/], retrieved 7 August 2011

61. 'Asian States Feel Rice Pinch', BBC News, 2008 [http://news.bbc.co.uk/1/hi/world/south_asia/7324596.stm], retrieved 7 August 2011

62+64. K Morgan, 'Feeding The City: The Challenge of Urban Food Planning', International Planning Studies, Vol. 14, No. 4, November 2009, p.430

63. 'Fresh Riot Break Out in Algerian Capital Algiers', BBC News Africa, 2011 [http://www.bbc.co.uk/news/world-africa-12134307], retrieved 4 June 2012

65+68. K Pothukuchi & JL Kaufman, 'The Food System: A Stranger to the Planning Field', Journal of the American Planning Association, Vol. 66, No. 2, 2000, p.7

66. E Cox et al, 'Re-imagining The High Street: Escape from Clone Town Britain', New Economics Foundation, London, 2010

67. G Dyer, 'The Future of Food Riots', 2011 [http://www.commondreams.org/view/2011/01/10-1], retrieved 8 August 2011

Fast Food

'London was once a city of smells and I can map my life there through them ... I must have a knack for smells because my next move was to Bermondsey, close to the Sarson's factory on Tanner Road (which, as the name suggests, had once smelled even worse). When the wind blew in the right direction, you didn't need to put vinegar on your chips: the air did it for you. Somehow the ubiquitous tang was rather comforting. You could always find your way home in the dark.'

– Carolyn Steel, 'Hungry City', 2008

Globally, more than enough food is produced to adequately satisfy the nutritional demand of the world's population. Thus, the chronic problem of international food shortages is one of distribution. At any time of the year, in cities all over the world, fresh foods can be found irrespective of whether they are in season or not. Whether it's Alphonso mangoes from India or avocados from Peru, food retailers today can source foods from anywhere to satisfy the eclectic demands of an urban food culture. The globalization of the food economy has been aided by the coincidental growth of food transportation over the last 50 years. The international transportation of food is reliant on a number of infrastructural and technological developments that have prolonged the lifetime of organic foods and enabled them to be conveyed over great distances. These modern advances have permitted a greater distance between where foods are grown and where they are eventually consumed which has had a profound effect on patterns of consumption and production.

The geographical detachment of the primary production of food from the location of its eventual consumption has led to the emergence of a general trend according to the economic principals of the global food economy. Whilst the agricultural production of food is increasingly relocating to developing countries and regions where land and labour are cheap, the distribution of food to wealthy economies, where it can be sold at a high unitary cost, has simultaneously increased. As a result, countries that are net exporters are generally becoming specialized in terms of the things they are producing. Ecuador for example, despite a population of just 15 million people, 0.2% of the global population, is responsible for producing 5 million tonnes of bananas each year, which is 10% of the bananas eaten world wide. At the same time, countries that are net importers of food are becoming less and less dependent on their own agricultural economy. America is reliant upon imports to contribute over 60% of its domestic food supply.[1]

Whilst the unrelenting rise of food transportation may offer economic efficiency and occasionally, energy efficiency by allowing the most successful primary industries to access international markets, it is

facing page: At train stations in Tokyo and inside Shinkansen trains travelling between Japanese cities, there are food vending machines and mobile trolley services offering 'Ekiben' (train station lunch) made with local produce of the departure station.

1. S Smith, 'Fairtrade Bananas: A Global Assessment of Impact', Institute of Development Studies [http://www.fairtrade.org.uk/includes/documents/cm_docs/2011/F/Fairtrade%20in%20the%20Banana%20Sector_IDS%20Final%20Report%20December%202011.pdf], retrieved 12 January 2012

also a huge contributor to global greenhouse emissions, reliant on an exorbitant consumption of non-renewable resources and a enabler of the social exploitation of a vulnerable workforce. Furthermore, a recent study by the UN has revealed that the further foods have travelled, the more their vitamin and mineral content deteriorates. The global food system is responsible for 30% of all global emissions, the majority of which are incurred by the transportation of food.[2] 'Food miles' is the common term for the distances travelled by foods from fields to forks and has become an important social parameter influencing consumer culture. Understanding our foods in terms of the distances they have travelled is critical to equating our food with its impact on climate change as well as its effects on air pollution and traffic congestion.

Whilst food miles do significantly contribute to global carbon emissions and climate change, they can be an unreliable indicator when evaluating the energy efficiency and environmental impact of food economies. Growing green beans in Kenya is a manual and labour intensive industry that uses organic fertilizers and low-tech irrigation methods. As well as producing high yields of beans in an energy efficient and environmentally friendly way, agricultural industries such as this are a very significant employer of under-privileged people in the developing world. In stark contrast, European and North American green bean production is reliant on oil-based fertilizers and diesel burning tractors. It is hence the case that, although green beans from Kenya must be packaged and shipped to foreign food economies, they often have a smaller carbon footprint than green beans produced locally.

Food miles almost exclusively refer to the distances travelled by food from their country of origin to the supermarket where they are sold, and forget the miles travelled by consumers. A recent study of Britain's food economy revealed that almost half of its food miles came from vehicles going to and from the shops. The average British family drives 136 miles a year to buy food.[3] By driving to buy shopping, the average UK consumer emits more carbon than is emitted by transporting the food to the UK in the first place. The Department for the Environment, Food and Rural Affairs (DEFRA) has calculated the cost of food miles to be £9 billion a year to the UK, which is more than the total contribution of the agricultural sector.

To reduce food miles without comprehension of the environmental opportunity cost of alternative supply lines would be detrimental to the global food economy. The notion of food miles should instead be used to encourage the reduction of food miles incurred by consumers and to economize all existing international supply lines. Whilst farmers markets support local agricultural economies and are environmentally responsible in terms of the impact of their agricultural production and transportation, as there are so few of them, especially in cities, they are responsible for many food miles by the consumer.

From a social and environmental perspective, much of the transportation of foods is unjust and immoral. Many of the world's poorest countries have the largest primary agricultural industries relative to their size, yet, despite the volume of food they produce, they suffer from chronic under nourishment as most of the food they produce is exported. Commercial food transportation is insensitive to food shortages and malnourishment. Instead, what little food aid there is, is provided by non-profit organizations such

facing page: The state-run Xin Fa Di Agricultural Wholesale Market in Beijing is one of the world's largest with over 80,000 regional and international traders.

159

2. D Carrington & J Vidal, 'Global food system must be transformed "on industrial revolution scale"', The Guardian, 24 January 2011

3. A Smith, P Watkiss & G Tweddle, 'The Validity of Food Miles as an Indicator of Sustainable Development', DEFRA, 2005 [http://archive.defra.gov.uk/evidence/economics/foodfarm/reports/documents/foodmile.pdf], retrieved 5 January 2012

as The Red Cross and UNICEF. The economic and political forces on the global food economy have encouraged richer economies to become reliant on imports, poorer economies to be reliant on exports and the entire system to be reliant on international transportation. This universal reliance on transport places all cities in a vulnerable situation as it ties them all to the unstable and ill-fated non-renewable resource economies of oil and gas.

Special Delivery

In one of the world's biggest and busiest cities, the pace of life is so fast that even eating can be a challenge. But as globalization radically reshapes India's cities, there is one labour-intensive tradition that refuses to surrender to economic pressure. The 'Dabbawallas' of Mumbai and Karachi deliver home cooked lunches to staff at their desks working in urban office developments in a unique procedure, which continues a tradition a century old.

Established in 1890, this system was created by Mahadeo Havaji Bachche who travelled along with hundreds of others to the northern capital of Maharashtra desperately seeking work. Bachche soon realized that for those people who were fortunate enough to actually have jobs, lunch posed quite a challenge. The scarcity of restaurants and cafés in the then British ruled Bombay, simply made lunch a rather anticlimactic respite.

Eager to satisfy the disappointed appetites of hundreds of workers, Bachche looked at the alternative sources. Inviting workers' families to cook a simple meal of rice, dhal and curry, he proposed an organized home delivery service to send family made meals to the workplace. The method has remained much the same to date. Mumbai has an estimated 5,000 'Tiffin' carriers who deliver approximately 175,000 lunch boxes each day.[4] The Dabbawalla (dabba derived from the colonial term 'Tiffin dabba' meaning light meal and walla referring to the male carrier) refers to a colour code on each of the Tiffin boxes used to denote owner, work address and floor. Rather than succumbing to the temptations of new restaurants and cafés, urbanites still prefer to use the service infrastructure acknowledged as one of the most reliable supply chains in the world with only an average of 3.4 errors per one million deliveries.[5]

Indeed, a similar approach is applied to the commodity of milk. India is the largest producer and consumer of cattle and buffalo milk in the world, and commonly delivers the commodity in metal containers, usually on a bicycle, in a system fashionably reminiscent of the Dabbawalla.[6]

The Milkman

In the UK, the milkman has heralded the British morning for more than a century. The appeal of fresh milk delivered daily has overcome the reliably inclement British weather and the rationing of two world wars. Milkmen have provided a convenience, and the eyes and ears of the early mornings for many people and local communities. The dairy business has developed with the need for mass produced milk as towns have expanded.

Alongside the increase of refrigeration and private car use, shopping habits were changing by the 1960s.

facing page from top left clockwise: Food delivery services in Ipoh and New York, and the Dabbawallas of Mumbai and Karachi.

4. 'Tiffin Carriers for Royal Wedding', BBC News [http://news.bbc.co.uk/1/hi/world/south_asia/4425345.stm], retrieved 5 January 2012

5. S Rai, 'In India, Lunch Survives Globalization', The New York Times, 29 May 2007

6. D Sahni, 'A New Luxury for Mumbai's Rich: Fresh Milk', The Wall Street Journal India [http://blogs.wsj.com/indiarealtime/2011/05/24/a-new-luxury-product-for-mumbais-rich-fresh-milk/], retrieved 7 February 2012

Supermarkets wanted customers to shop more often than once a week and focused on milk and bread sales to bring customers through the doors more regularly. By the mid-70s an increasing volume of fresh milk was being purchased from convenience stores, newsagents and garage forecourts.

Supermarkets put pressure on the traditional markets of local farmers and the neighbourhood butchers, bakers and milkmen. These companies typically offered lower prices and one-stop shopping, by having the financial reserves to weather price wars and economic downturns, often driving small firms out of business. Changes in buying habits forced the British milkman to reinvent his role.

A Global Vending Machine

The last 50 years have seen major shifts in the way that people buy their food. Fifty years ago most people bought their food from markets or specialist food shops, such as greengrocers, butchers, fishmongers and bakers. In the UK, approximately £76 billion is spent on groceries each year, and more than 80% of this goes to supermarkets.[7] Supermarkets have become huge businesses and their dominance is killing the diversity of the high street. 'Asda Walmart' is now the world's largest company by turnover,[8] while Tesco takes one in every seven pounds spent in the UK.[9] This change in food retailing has had many impacts on the environment.

A recent survey of all supermarkets estimated that, including car parking, supermarkets now cover a land area of 24.5 square miles, or the equivalent of 15,000 football pitches in the UK alone.[10] Supermarkets generate thousands of car journeys. Recent work for DEFRA (the Department for Environment, Food and Rural Affairs), suggests that car use for food shopping results in costs to society of more than £3.5 billion per year, from traffic emissions, noise, accidents and congestion.[11]

Traffic congestion also occurs on a larger scale as the distribution systems used by supermarkets generate large amounts of traffic. Over the last decade, the distance that food travels before it reaches shoppers has increased. Supermarkets continue to distribute the vast majority of their goods by road freight. In a report compiling the response of nine of the UK's top supermarket chains to a detailed questionnaire on their environmental performance, only three supermarkets claimed that they used rail transport, which only accounted for less than 4% of their total freight mileage.[12] It was also calculated that the lorries of the nine supermarket chains travelled an approximate total of 670 million miles per year.[13] This is equivalent to nearly four return trips to the moon every day. Such volumes of traffic produce large quantities of climate changing emissions.

Food travels further than any other type of good.[14] Imports of fresh produce are increasingly occurring via air transport. Food now accounts for 13% (by weight) of air freighted goods, and this is increasing rapidly.[15] A dedicated road into Heathrow Airport was built to facilitate the smooth handling of 140,000 tonnes of fresh food produce per year.[16] Tropical fruit imported by plane uses over 30 times more energy per kilo than home-grown apples.[17] Further, around one in ten car journeys in the UK are for food shopping,[18] and it has been estimated that the carbon dioxide emissions generated by people driving their food shopping home could equal those generated by the commercial transportation of food within the UK.[19] Consumer decisions on specific choices of food and transport can have an important effect on the environment. As a result, buyers can lessen their environmental impact by avoiding large supermarkets.

Online shopping could be more environmentally friendly than driving to the shops. Assessing the environmental effects of delivery logistics, a new survey conducted by the 'Logistics Research Centre' at Heriot-Watt University in Edinburgh, indicates that on average, having goods delivered to your home by a package delivery company generates considerably less carbon dioxide than making a specific trip to the shops to buy the same item.[20] The assessment discovered that a typical van-based home delivery produced approximately 181g CO_2, compared with 4,274g CO_2 for an average trip to the shops by car, and an average bus trip by a shopper producing 1,265g CO_2.[21] The research found that when a customer drives to the shops and buys fewer than 24 small items per trip or travels by bus and buys fewer than seven items, home delivery proved to be more environmentally friendly.[22] The results imply that the potential of home delivery may be the green future of our grocery shopping.

Posh Pleasures

Ocado is a British online-based retailer specializing in groceries. Operating from a purpose-built 'picking' centre, the supermarket is unusually based purely online without any physical shops or networks of stores. Consumers register online and choose products on their computers before having them delivered by a fleet of vans that inform customers of their purchase arrivals via a text message to their mobile phones.[23]

Teams of energy consultants at Greenstone Carbon Management have analysed the carbon emissions of a typical bricks and mortar supermarket versus the operations of Ocado using a carbon audit testing system, and actually verified the concept as the greenest option. This is possible because of the design of traditional food stores themselves. Large shops and supermarkets have massive open chillers keeping food at the right temperature, bright lights to make the food look visually appealing and heating to make it a comfortable environment for people to walk around and purchase items in. These processes use vast amounts of energy.

Greenstone Carbon Management claims Ocado drastically cuts its carbon footprint by purchasing energy efficient refrigeration systems, and allowing its customers to see when delivery vans will already be in the neighbourhood online, cutting down on food distribution miles.[24] Ocado also collects and recycles customers' unwanted plastic bags, sources biodiesel for fuel such as vegetable fats produced by UK growers, and offers recipes to beat food waste on its website. Expensive moves adopted by the retailer to become greener before they are forced to by law or public opinion, has made Ocado a popular supermarket alternative. With a service that extends to approximately 70% of the UK,[25] Ocado could perhaps offer a uniquely innovative and greener substitute to the traditional grocery shopping system, by offering a network that is simple and more accurate. Ordering from the sofa could now not be seen as a 'posh pleasure', but as the most environmentally friendly way of food distribution.

Food Information Technologies

Greenling is the first and largest fresh organic and local grocery delivery service in Texas.[26] By using technology to shorten the supply chain that food typically endures, they aim to make it easier for consumers to access fresh, local produce through the delivery of 'Community Supported Agriculture'

7. 'The Economic Position of the Agri-Food Sector: Quarterly Analysis – Winter 2004/05', DEFRA [http://archive.defra.gov.uk/evidence/economics/foodfarm/reports/afq/AFBWinter04.pdf], retrieved 8 February 2012

8. 'CIO 100 ASDA', CIO [http://www.cio.co.uk/cio100/asda/4143/], retrieved 8 February 2012

9. A Ramsay, '10 facts about Tescos' [http://brightgreenscotland.org/index.php/2011/04/10-facts-about-tesco/], retrieved 10 February 2012

10, 12+13. 'How to ... oppose a supermarket planning application: A short guide', Friends of the Earth, 2005 [http://www.foe.co.uk/resource/briefings/campaigning_against_supermarkets.pdf], retrieved 10 February 2012

11. A Smith, P Watkiss & G Tweddle, 'The Validity of Food Miles as an Indicator of Sustainable Development', DEFRA, 2005 [http://archive.defra.gov.uk/evidence/economics/foodfarm/reports/documents/foodmile.pdf], retrieved 10 February 2012

14,15+19. T Garnett, 'Wise Moves, Exploring the relationship between food, transport and CO2, Transport 2000 Trust, 2003 [http://www.thepep.org/ClearingHouse/docfiles/wise_moves.pdf], retrieved 12 February 2012

16. R Bridger, 'Freshly Flown In?', The Jellied Eel, Issue 18, Autumn 2007, p.10 [http://www.sustainweb.org/pdf/LFL_News18_lowres.pdf], retrieved 12 February 2012

17. 'Tescos' [http://www.tescopoly.org/index.php?option=com_view&id=353&Itemid=97], retrieved 12 February 2012

18. 'Commuting fact sheet', Department for Transport [http://www2.dft.gov.uk/pgr/statistics/datatablespublications/nts/factsheets/commuting.pdf], retrieved 6 August 2013

20–22. 'Online shopping "better for environment"' [http://www.netimperative.com/news/2009/march/online-shopping-2018better-for-environment2019], retrieved 12 February 2012

(CSA) boxes. CSA consists of a neighbourhood of individuals who honour support to a local farming operation where the growers and consumers share the risks and benefits of the food production. CSA usually consists of a system of weekly deliveries or collections of vegetables and fruit, in a vegetable box scheme.

The structure of CSA focuses on transparency in the food production system. A whole season's budget for producing a specified wide array of products for a set number of weeks a year, alongside a common-pricing system where producers and consumers discuss and democratically agree to price, based on the acceptance of the budget, is typically employed. CSA pledges a risk and reward agreement, whereby the consumers receive what the farmers grow even with the sudden change in behaviour of seasonal growing.

A distinctive feature of CSA is the method of marketing and distribution. Shares of food are usually provided weekly with collections or deliveries occurring on a designated day and time. CSA subscribers often live in towns and cities. Local drop-off locations, convenient to a number of members, are organized. The advantage of the close consumer–producer relationship is increased freshness of the produce because it does not have to be shipped long distances. The close proximity of the farm to the members also helps the environment by reducing pollution caused by transporting the produce.

A system such as CSA has the potential to use information technology to innovate the way food is sourced, consumed and interacted with. This provides the ability to start organizations such as Greenling and in similar respects, Ocado. Websites can connect local consumers with farmers and communicate their demand, so producers can focus on farming. From the comfort of their home, customers can see what the farmers are growing and directly order the food they need by picking and choosing their own selections. Commercial farms often use technology to develop chemicals and pesticides to grow produce faster and in larger quantities. In a modern counter-reaction to this ethic, technology is now being used to make more healthy food available to a wider audience rather than just the rich few, with ultra low transportation costs and effect on environment.

Great Yarmouth and Waveney Mobile Food Store
In an area identified as having one of the lowest rates of fruit and vegetable consumption in the UK alongside high levels of unemployment, a council initiative has established a new way of providing healthy food produce to a needy population.[27] The 'Mobile Food Store' is a project set up by the organization 'Community Connections' and the Great Yarmouth and Waveney National Health Service (NHS) in East Anglia. Supplied with fruit and vegetables from a merchant in the nearby city of Norwich at wholesale prices, a grocery van travels between deprived areas in Great Yarmouth and Waveney offering fresh produce, and healthy choices for the community at wholesale prices. The van travels a regular route around the area, and residents are able to find out when the van will be in a street near them by referencing a timetable posted online.

The Mobile Food Store is a personalized approach to changing the behaviour of local residents by providing access to healthy food at competitive prices. Customers are invited to climb aboard the mobile food van to select the goods they would like to buy themselves. Health trainers, who sell the produce and give advice on recipe ideas and information on how to store and cook food, whilst offering tasting sessions, deliver the service.

With the health of the community at the core of the programme, the NHS of Great Yarmouth and Waveney used geo-demographic information to determine the best route for the mobile fruit and vegetable store. Maps were created to show where people who were most at risk of a heart attack or a stroke, and those who were registered with diabetes, lived. Additionally, more detailed maps were made by 'Experian', a credit information group who used their 'Mosaic' data system to analyse population types and show where those people most likely to eat less than one portion of fruit and vegetable per day lived and worked. The data was then used to target the postcodes and households, producing a travel route for the mobile food store, with special 'healthy start vouchers' distributed to vulnerable members of the community.

Meals on Wheels

In many cities throughout the world there are elderly people who are homebound and unable to shop or prepare meals for themselves. Unfortunately, this is a problem that grows every year with the increase of the elderly population. The fastest growing sector of the UK population is made up of those over the age of 65, who often suffer from chronic disease or disability.[28] 'Meals on Wheels' is a service that prepares and delivers thousands of nutritious meals a day to elderly people who depend on the service. The programme meets the nutritional and special needs of the elderly in order to help them maintain their independent lifestyles.

The benefit of the meals on wheels programme is not only that they feed homebound elderly people in the community, but they deliver companionship as well. Someone knocking on the front door every day can be extremely comforting to lonely individuals, making them feel that they are more a part of the outside world. Daily interaction with volunteers and staff drivers helps combat loneliness and reduces isolation. The service also provides early opportunities for intervention should an elderly person become ill or injured. Through partnerships with local businesses and churches, a coordinated effort ensures that vulnerable members of the community are cared for and never face the threat of hunger.

Elderly people want to be at home and food is one of the most important services that keep them there in their homes. By delivering the food to them Meals on Wheels enables that elderly person to stay where they want to be, out of elderly people's institutions and in their own home.

The mobile food service improves the quality of life for a lot of people. The service had a major role during the Blitz when thousands of homes and their kitchens were destroyed, often depriving families of the facility to cook. The Meals on Wheels scheme, serviced by the Women's Volunteer Service for Civil Defence, provided cooked food to families who would not otherwise have had access to a hot and nutritious meal.

Pavement Restaurants

Tokyo's Yatai mobile food bars bring local food to the urban streets, laden with ramen, noodles, soup and sweet potato. In a mechanical system that unfolds from a cycle drawn cart, these mini restaurants permeate the streets with their rich aromas and themed recordings, which alert passersby to the freshly

23. 'Start Webshop', Ocado [http://www.ocado.com/webshop/startWebshop.do], retrieved 15 February 2012

24. 'Welcome to Ocado', Ocado Media [http://www.youtube.com/watch?v=5pKwGvTEBf0], retrieved 16 March 2012

25. 'Ocado plans new capacity as sales rises 25%', BBC News, 2011 [http://www.bbc.co.uk/news/business-12646610], retrieved 16 March 2012

26. 'Greenling' [http://ideacomm2011.wikispaces.com/Greenling], retrieved 20 March 2012

27. 'Strategic Plan – NHS Great Yarmouth and Waveney 2009-14', NHS, 2010 [http://www.gywpct.nhs.uk/_store/documents/agendaitem7a-7b-strategic-plan-and-financial-strategy.pdf], retrieved 15 April 2012

28. 'Office for National Statistics' [http://www.statistics.gov.uk/cci/nugget.asp?id=949], retrieved 1 August 2013

cooked food, that is hot and ready to be served. The local menu in the Yatai changes by season. Spring brings fava beans and white, green, and purple asparagus. Summer sees lily flower bulbs, bamboo shoots and long slender cobs of baby corn that are commonly steamed by the kerb. Small groups of businessmen and students gather around the trailers, creating a temporary eating space to consume the food on offer and exchange light conversation.

The practice of the portable food stall has existed over centuries. At sushi stalls, for example, sushi was not so much a meal as a snack, and customers would stand at counters while the sushi-maker sat inside, preparing orders. Ironically, this is the reverse of what is common today, where the sushi chef generally works standing up while the customers are seated. The sushi bar arrangement where chef and customer are in close interaction is unmistakably a legacy of the mobile Yatai kitchen.

The ice cream van is a classic British depiction of urban life, as quintessential as fish and chips, and Sunday roast dinners. Children and adults alike go into a frenzy when they hear the sound of playground melodies echoing around neighbourhood streets. Potential customers gather around ice cream vans and create a socially orientated physical space. This increase in social gathering can give a neighbourhood a subtle sense of community.

Mobile food vendors attract foot traffic to commercial districts, which increases retail sales and creates a more vibrant retail business environment. By offering low-cost, culturally diverse foods for people on the go, they typically complement, rather than compete with 'sit-down' restaurants and give people more reasons to frequent local shopping areas. Mobile food vendors can bring positive activity to a street and add a festive, people-orientated feel to an environment that helps to improve public safety. Vendors provide a window into many diverse cultures, and can introduce people to new foods and to the pleasures of spending time in the public space of the city.

Transportation Methods
A low price often neglects fair and humane food transport, however Japanese sushi enthusiasts have a proposal that uses an alternative medicine of antiquity. Sushi chef Toshiro Urabe guarantees his fish are as fresh as alive by using acupuncture to humanely pacify the aquatic vertebrate before slicing and dicing, but the technique has caught on with fish transporters and restaurants looking to reduce costs.

After a fish is caught, it is put to sleep using acupuncture needles so it becomes less active. This enables double the quantities of fish to be packed into portable tanks. This procedure technically reduces the carbon footprint of fresh fish and also halves delivery costs. Consumers are safe in the knowledge that no tranquilizing chemicals were used in the process that could harm the taste of their fresh plate of sashimi. Shifting scale from global food transport to local food distribution, it is difficult to imagine how the drovers transported their turkeys, geese, pigs and horses along the streets of historical London. The pattering of booted goosefeet and thrum of iron cattle shoes were familiar sounds en route to Smithfield meat market.

Traders no longer walk with their livestock to the markets within day's proximity of each other. Droving's demise came during the nineteenth century as it was inadequate compared to a growing rail infrastructure and the industrial revolution in agricultural practice. Modern capitalism and cost effective transportation of food have since eliminated livestock from our streets, leaving droving in its memory.

left top: The Damnoen Saduak Floating Market, near Bangkok is a well-established point of trade for fresh, locally cultivated produce that takes place on a waterway.

left bottom: Transient pavement restaurants in Seoul and Tokyo permeate the urban streets with rich aromas of local food.

167

Primitive modes of food transport do live on. The 'Damnoen Saduak Floating Market', in Thailand, is a well-established point of trade and exchange for fresh, locally cultivated produce that takes place on a waterway. The land around the canal beyond the densely populated banks is particularly fertile. Local agricultural workers excavated over 200 tributary canals to irrigate their farmland whilst simultaneously functioning as an effective transport infrastructure.[29] Local farmhands float their produce to market in the neighbouring provinces and Bangkok. The inland rivers and canals are a sustainable centre of commerce but now heavily reliant on the support of tourism as roads pave their way to the towns and villages for carbon intensive, vehicular food transport to dominate.

Mobile kitchens are no new phenomenon on the streets of LA, but since Chef Rag Choi stepped on board the 'Kogi BBQ' truck, street food has experienced a well-deserved revival. Consumers travel as far as 30 miles to join the long queues outside the elusive truck and patiently wait to sample Choi's Korean adaptation of the Mexican taco. In the UK, mobile canteens did not assume popularity until the World War II. A mobile canteen would be deployed at remote theatres of war, providing hot food, tea, cigarettes, conversation and news on the wireless to soldiers in need of a morale booster.[30]

Business Class

Long distance food delivery has existed throughout history. A meal from abroad is a glimpse into a place, its culture, its people, what and when they eat, how they source their food, and the gastronomic rituals they observe. People have always wanted to taste what the world has to offer. The sensory overload of sugars and spices enticed an era of discovery and long distance food transport that has existed since ancient times. Without these invaluable commodities, food remained bland and often unpalatable. The Spice Islands of Indonesia, India and east Africa's Malabar were major sources of cloves, cassia, coriander, nutmeg, mace and others. India and its fortunate geographic location became the centre of the world spice trade, accepting ship imports from the Spice Islands that continued onwards by sea to the Middle East where Arab traders traded with Venetian and Italian vessels, before stock reached Europe.

From the ninth century, Venice and Genoa became powerful trading states to Western Europe, accumulating wealth as merchant classes and cities developed after feudal austerity. Wars were waged to control lucrative spice routes and the valuable trading commodities imbued with mystery and exoticism. To secure Middle Eastern control of the spice trade, the source remained classified and merchants would recount manufactured tales of mystery and peril to deter inquisitive European buyers. The tactic was partly successful until Marco Polo publicized his expedition along the Silk Road and his sighting of spice plantations, inspiring the dawn of a European Age of Discovery.[31]

Preceding the Ottoman takeover of Byzantine Constantinople in 1453, Western Europeans, keen to avoid extortionate taxes, set sail on a voyage to circumnavigate Africa via the Cape of Good Hope. Vasco Da Gama, the Portuguese explorer and navigator, was the first to succeed in 1498, undercutting the Middle East and opening routes for direct European trade with the East. Incidentally, the Cape of Good Hope is a unique example of the enduring impact of the early trade routes. In the seventeenth century, the

facing page top: In the ninth century, Venice was a powerful spice trading state between Europe and Asia, accumulating wealth as merchant classes and cities developed after feudal austerity.

facing page bottom: Cape Town is a unique example of the enduring impact of the early trade routes. In the seventeenth century, the Dutch East India Company settlers established a wealth of imported fruit plantations including grapes, citrus and other species; a legacy that has had a lasting influence on the society, economy and the urban development of the region.

29. 'Damnoen Saduak Floating Market' [http://www.asiatravel.com/floating.html], retrieved 15 March 2012

30. 'Your Mobile Canteen in Action' [http://www.vads.ac.uk], retrieved 15 March 2012

31. J Turner, 'Spice: The History of a Temptation', HarperCollins, New York, 2004

Dutch East India Company settlers established a wealth of imported fruit plantations including grapes, citrus and other species; a legacy that has had a lasting influence on the society, economy and the urban development of the region.[32]

European ignorance of and isolation from the cosmopolitan, intellectual and commercial life of Asia was abruptly ended as the spice trade began to flourish. The Western merchant classes used spices as a new form of commercial credit to purchase new flavours and weapons. This allowed the first great corporations, and the crucial components of future capitalist operating systems, to spread their trading networks across the seven seas and make the world a significantly smaller and less bewildering place in the sixteenth century. Now termed the 'small world' network, these early spice traders would be the first pioneers of the globalized, highly connected world we live in today.

Early trade also presented some unexpected contributions to the local food markets. Sago, a white powdery starch used to make a milky pudding similar to tapioca, was initially put to use as a packing material protecting delicate chinaware during the turbulent journeys of the sea cargo trade. Initially imported in vast quantities as an early form of polystyrene, the material later proved doubly profitable as it could be sold as a foodstuff at the other end of the journey![33]

Early Food Hubs
Cities continually evolve and adapt their food infrastructure systems to meet economic obligations. London's Docklands, formerly part of the Port of London and once the largest port in the world, experienced significant functional and formal modifications in response to the rise and fall of the shipping industry. The West India Dockyard on the Isle of Dogs officially opened on 27 August 1802, to secure and accept the import and export of goods with the West Indies. A 20ft high wall to prevent the theft of goods, a commonplace occurrence at the crowded docks upriver, encircled the docks to protect profits. Georgian warehouses were designed and built in accordance with the commodities they were to stock, and came to represent physical urban manifestations of the food trade.

The English architect George Gwilt and his son were appointed to design and construct 10 warehouses each with dimensions 224ft by 114ft, 40ft apart with five 8ft tall stories for sugar in the eighteenth century.[34] At that time, designs that extended greater than 8ft in height were reduced, commonly under the instruction of leading London wharfinger Edward Ogle. Attempting to build a warehouse for casks of sugar, or 'hogsheads' as they were known, Gwilt and his son were told that their stock was too heavy to be stacked higher than 8ft. Warehouse basement vaults commonly stored rum and attics usually stored lighter goods.

Since the advent of the shipping container, shipping at London's Docklands declined from 1960 to cease trading in 1980. The demise of the docks at the Isle of Dogs led to another urban transfiguration as part of the Docklands scheme and the developments of Canary Wharf. Finance, not food, now dictates the urban aesthetics of the docks. Building codes in response to efficient office space planning now dictate storey heights, not sugar hogsheads.

Sea Change
Transporting commodities, particularly by ship, can rearrange native ecosystems and food chains. As the global exchange of commodities prospers, catastrophic environmental damage along the logistical network of trade routes is inevitable.

The Bosphorus Strait is a geological water channel separating the European and the Asian parts of Istanbul lying between the Black Sea and the Sea of Marmara. Although the Bosphorus Strait is a difficult body of water to navigate due to its treacherous currents, it is one of the heaviest sea-traffic regions in the world. The volume of traffic in the Bosphorus is five times heavier than the traffic in the Panama Canal.[35] As Turkey's portal to Russia, the Strait suffers the passage of approximately 1 cargo ship every 10 minutes along its 19 miles.[36]

The passage of ships from distant shores and continents has caused irreversible damage to the marine environment due to the discharge of contaminated ballast water. The pollution in the Sea of Marmara is also threatening many living species and having a knock on effect on the potential of fishing in the area. One example is the emergence of the predatory ctenophore, Mnemiopsis Leidyi, native to estuaries of North America that is now being seen in the Turkish straits. The animals are thought to have been introduced to the waters by passing cargo ships. The Ctenophore specie populations exploded in the Black Sea during the 1980s with a biomass that peaked 450 million tonnes.[37] Confirming scientific concerns, local anchovy fisheries consequently collapsed. The additional discharge of oil and chemicals through ship ballast has contributed to a fishing reduction 1/60th of previous numbers.[38]

Think Global, Act Local

Governments around the world try to safeguard their nations' commercial interests in global agricultural trade, protecting farmers and the value of their produce by imposing taxes on imports and imposing import restrictions. A colossal immoral disproportion in global food trade is caused by the US and EU subsidies and leads to the inevitable collapse of smallholder farms. The Common Agricultural Policy (CAP) encouraged agricultural production across Europe by supporting farmers with monetary subsidies after chronic food shortages and a weak agricultural sector following the World War II. Fortunate European financial resources have put developing economies at a subsequent disadvantage. The CAP often causes over production, inadvertently lowering the value of produce on the global market. Farmers less fortunate in receiving subsidies struggle to turn a profit on the competitive market and must compete with the price of surplus produce when it is imported into their local economy.

Global food trade and transport policies fail to differentiate between poor and rich agricultural economies and societies as part of the immoral paradox that favours an increase in returns from developed economies at home whilst sowing seeds of misery and inequality for the economically disadvantaged abroad.[39] Only large farm holders applying the economies of scale have a chance to negotiate bureaucracy from Brussels and infiltrate a defence system of strict EU quality standards.

Given the economics of the food trade, farmers who grow food for export are often using land they might instead use to feed themselves, without getting adequate compensation for this sacrifice. Food bearing the Fairtrade signature offers the consumer a guarantee that the farmer of a developing nation has received a fair deal, and has been given a chance to escape poverty. The policy protects the close social connection between grower and eater over a long distance, to ensure that the eater is helping the local community to improve its livelihood. The Fairtrade Foundation is 'the independent non-profit organisation that licenses the use of the FAIRTRADE mark on products in the UK in accordance with

171

32. S Pooley, 'Jan van Riebeeck as Pioneering Explorer and Conservator of Natural Resources at the Cape of Good Hope (1652–62)', Environment and History, Vol. 15, No. 1, 2009, pp.3–31

33. J Wordie, Review of 'Merchants of Canton and Macao', Sunday Morning Post, 2011

34. H Hobhouse, 'The West India Docks: The buildings: warehouses', Survey of London: Vol. 43+44: 'Poplar, Blackwall and Isle of Dogs', 1994, pp. 284–300 [http://www.british-history. ac.uk/source.aspx?pubid=369], retrieved 15 August 2013

35. A Paul, 'Kanal Istanbul – three minute wonder' [http:// www.sundayszaman.com/ sunday/columnistDetail_ newsId=242751&columnistId=69], retrieved 8 July 2012

36+38. A Rodriguez, 'The Bosporus: Environment vs. Economy', 2003, p.5–7 [http://www.stanford.edu/ class/e297a/The%20Bosporus.pdf], retrieved 8 July 2012

37. 'Anglers Are in Dire Straits Along Istanbul's Bosphurus' [www. tourismandaviation.com], retrieved 8 July 2012

39. 'Truth or Consequences', Oxfam Briefing Paper 81, Oxfam International [http://www.oxfam.org/sites/www. oxfam.org/files/truth.pdf], retrieved 10 July 2012

internationally agreed Fairtrade standards'.[40]

The international standard ensures global trade favours the poor and disadvantaged to guarantee equality and the sustainable development for farmers and agricultural communities alike. Fairtrade agreements often require that the producer receives a price for their commodity that is a certain percentage higher than the price on the world market, or that the farmer and farm worker have access to health and education benefits as well as the right to organize into unions and cooperatives.

Producers are entitled to receive an agreed price for their produce to cover the costs of production and a decent standard of living whilst the Fairtrade organization guarantees buyers of Fairtrade produce pay a fair price and contributes to an additional Fairtrade premium. The premium is an additional subsidy to be invested in the future of the farm and its local community, providing improved education and healthcare, clean water supplies, waste recycling or help to improve the standard of their crops.

For those who can afford it, the long distance food system offers unprecedented and unparalleled choice. But the global vending machine often displaces local cuisines, varieties and agriculture. Products enduring long-term transport and storage depend on preservatives and additives, and encounter endless opportunities for contamination on their long journey from farm to fork. People everywhere depend increasingly on food from distant sources. The reason is partly location, as fewer people live near food production centres. Perhaps more importantly, advances in technology that allow longer storage and more distant (and less costly) shipping have encouraged the food system to sprawl out of control.

Of course, it is not enough to simply look at the 'food mileage' of a single meal. There are even cases where an imported product has a lower embodied carbon footprint than the equivalent locally produced. A detailed study by Lincoln University in 2006 showed how the energy required producing lamb in the UK is four times as high as to produce the equivalent quality of meat in New Zealand.[41] Although a key factor, examples like this show our food cannot simply be judged on its transportation costs, and as British food critic Jay Raynor writes, this would be missing the big picture.[42] Instead, as the chapters of this book have shown, we are duty bound to examine how our food systems engage with the complex social, political and cultural variables that are woven together and underpin today's burgeoning cities.

facing page: Anglers trailing their lines into the waters over Galata Bridge, Istanbul. The passage of ships into the Bosphorus Strait from distant shores and continents has caused irreversible damage to the marine environment due to the discharge of contaminated ballast water.

173

40. 'Fairtrade Foundation' [www.fairtrade.org.uk], retrieved 1 August 2013

41. C Saunders, A Barber & G Taylor, 'Food Miles – Comparative Energy/Emissions, Performance of New Zealand's Agriculture Industry', Agribusiness & Economics Research Unit, Lincoln University, Research Report 285, 2006, p.86

42. J Rayner, 'Why worrying about food miles is missing the point', The Guardian, 2013 [http://www.guardian.co.uk/lifeandstyle/2013/may/26/worrying-about-food-miles-missing-point], retrieved 1 August 2013

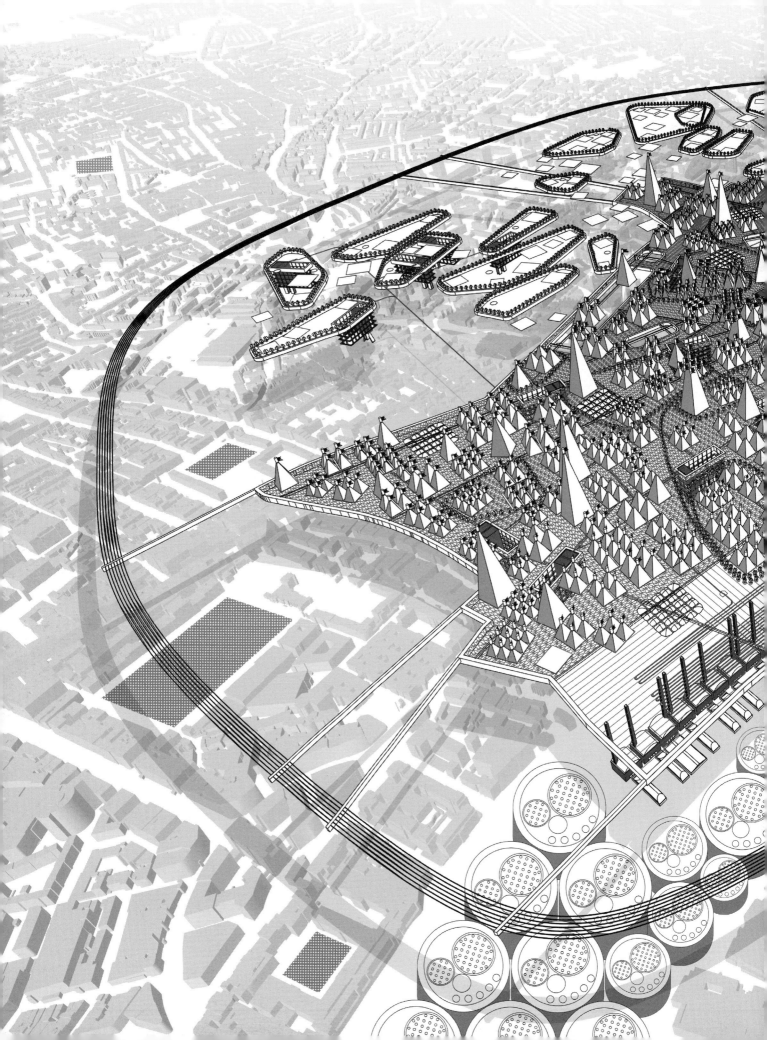

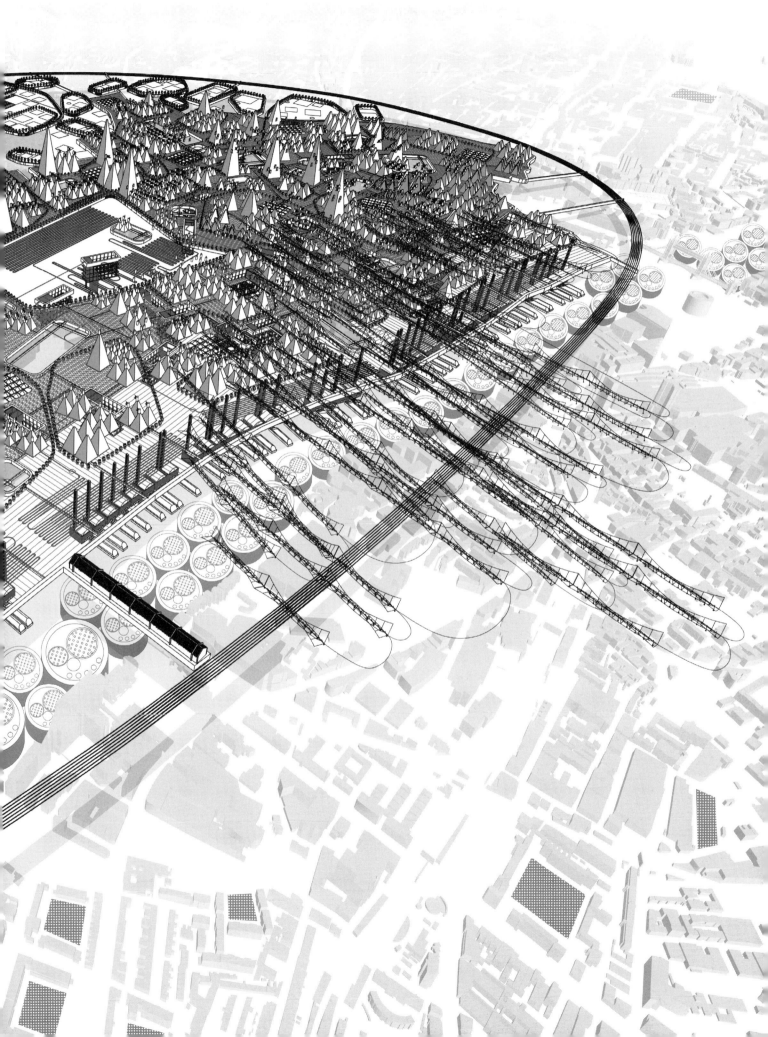

A Manifesto

INVITATION TO JOIN THE FOOD PARLIAMENT OF LONDON

London is at its best when the bonds between people are strong and when the onus of civic responsibility is manifestly clear. Today, the challenges facing London are monumental and multitudinous. Our economy is overwhelmed by debt and our economic systems are anachronistic and riddled with flaws that fuel social inequality and prevent social mobility. Our environment is ravaged by the inexorable and catastrophic effects of climate change, catalysed by the profligate attitudes of a society accustomed to overconsumption and wastefulness. Our society has become frayed by chronic hardship and injustice and disenfranchised by ineffective governments that have persistently failed to bring about change in spite of the innumerable promises made.

Former governments have attempted to change the fortunes of our nation's capital via the perpetual manipulation of the same old tired economic mechanisms of adjustment and through the introduction of countless abortive social programmes. Instead, The Food Parliament proposes a dramatic and all-encompassing restructuring of our economy and a radical realigning our social and environmental principles.

Food will cease to be regarded simply as sustenance. It will no longer be that which we buy in supermarkets and eat at dinner tables with unconscious regularity. Instead it will become the primary social capital at the very heart of our economy and our society. Planting, growing, harvesting, cooking and eating will become the core mechanisms that drive London's economy, protect its environment and secure its long-term health and prosperity. Yes, this is ambitious. Yes, this is revolutionary. Yes, this will require lots of hard work from every member of society.

Indeed, how could we successfully achieve such a radical transformation without universal support and participation? How could we energize tomorrow's generation without each of us taking responsibility for themselves and their community today? How could we believe that our efforts would be rewarded unless we believe in each other, in our society and in our government? By investing in food we are sumultaneuously investing in our society, the welfare of our environment, our physical health and wellbeing and our sense of civil responsibility. The most important investment made however, is in you and your commitment, passion and involvement. Only collectively, can we hope to eradicate debt. Only collectively, can we achieve self-sufficiency and guarantee our food security. Only collectively, can we mend our broken society. Only collectively, can we rediscover our faith in government.

So our invitation today is this: to join the Food Parliament of London and march together in taking London on the road to recovery.

CHANGE THE ECONOMY

The vaults of the regional bank Credito Emiliano hold a pungent gold prized by gourmands around the world – 17,000 tonnes of Parmesan cheese. The bank accepts Parmesan as collateral for loans, helping it to keep financing cheese makers in northern Italy even during the recession since World War II.[1]

How can we regain control of our wealth? How are we going to get back to work? What can we do to ensure a sustainable future and social stability? These are questions the Food Parliament will answer. The time has come to secure alternatives to the repeating collapse of our capital economy.

Food is money. The garden is made of money. Everyone will have the opportunity to exercise influence over food and finance. **We can grow a fortune by cultivating a new green economic model, for a fair and balanced sustainable future.** We are empowered to influence the economy of the Food Parliament. No more endless red tape, no more useless quangos, no more finance built on debt, no more unsustainable consumer borrowing and no more artificial blooms of wealth.

The Food Parliament is a sovereign state open for business. Help us to rebuild our nation. If we all contribute by trading locally within our constituencies and by investing in a homegrown green wealth, we can rebuild social cohesion and put an end to the dole queue. London's population is on the rise, so it is vital that we radically reform the City of London to improve its urban efficiency and maximize its potential to propagate wealth.

We are citizens of the 'anthropocene'; a new geological epoch brought about by irreversible human induced climatic change.[2] The worst droughts since records began exist alongside the worst floods on record. Failing crops and starving livestock are now more common than ever before. Time is slipping away minute by minute, barrel by barrel, and a dream treaty to halt climate change looks ... dreamy. We have the science yet politics mire any real change. World leaders are effectively condemning future generations to the misery of environmental change.

So what are we going to do about it? The UK is well equipped with a skilled workforce in the energy industry and has a strong, high tech manufacturing sector. The Food Parliament will support local green energy enterprise by balancing new and traditional technologies to grow a sustainable fertile economy. As a nation, we will restore our biodiversity, reduce our food carbon footprint and end our reliance upon carbon intensive energy.

We need to go green and our parliament makes it easy for you. **A user centred approach will build relationships and improve levels of trust to boost individual and collective recovery capital.** For the first time, Londoners will have six clear standards against which we can judge the success of our new notion of wealth. The Food Parliament will actively promote local, sustainable and immediate policies for building a green economy and put security back into our food.

Cultivating A New Food Economy

The problems we face with respect to soil fertility, biodiversity, food quality and local economies are not primarily problems of technology. They are problems of finance. In a financial system organized to optimize the efficient use of capital, we should not be surprised to end up with cheapened food, millions of acres of GMO corn, billions of food miles, dying Main Streets, kids who think food comes from a supermarket and obesity epidemics side by side with persistent hunger.[3]

We are left vulnerable and suffering in the aftermath of economic misery. Along with the barrage of job losses, home repossessions reached a 14-year all time high with 46,000 repossessed in 2009.[4] Bankers are still making their loot with extortionate handouts; RBS has been saved with £20 billion of public money yet paid staff £1 billion in bonuses.[5] It is time to put a stop to their game of Russian roulette. We cannot continue to punish the nation's savers who, under the current monetary system, see nil returns on account balances.

We propose an alternative, where we can come together with a new mindset, a new religion to secure a green national grid for a sustainable distribution of wealth. We will invest our food in the Food Parliament – a bank insured for a secure and sustainable wealth.

At the Food Parliament, we bring the economy back down to earth and return ecology to the City of London. Our localist approach is based on a belief in common sense and shared accountability for the propagation of wealth, and its role in stemming the loss of biodiversity. Waste, an inevitable by-product of our city's wealth, rejoins the Food Parliament lifecycle to meet our energy demands. The Lord Mayor champions the parliamentary green national grid. Each of his anaerobic digesters trade organic waste for energy and compost, supporting local farmhands and our economy.

Governments talk green and yet the UK relies on getting more of its energy from fossil fuels than it did in 1997. Rather than wasting time defending the status quo, the new Food Parliament acts on a local, green micro-economy to drive the proposed notion of wealth and deliver its zero carbon target.

So who does the work? We all do. The outmoded squabble between big versus small state ends here. We should not rely on a top-down authoritarian power to change an economic religion. **We will cut the networks of patronage along the corridors of Whitehall and encourage your talent and innovation to give London a new lease of life.** The green economy requires the collective strength and activism of a community empowered. We are looking for entrepreneurs and innovators who are prepared to take risks. It only needs a little social creativity for us to reap the benefits of the seeds we sow.

Westminster Hall is a sight to behold, transforming London's skyline into a flotilla of glass pyramidal greenhouses. Each greenhouse floats directly above London's existing streets and landmarks. The new infrastructure safeguards our city whilst providing a central banking landscape; the catalyst propagates and cultivates local sustainable capital.

The budget in the Food Parliament is directly related to the size of the harvest. The bigger the harvest, the bigger the budget. No more hidden figures and no more bureaucracy. **Our budget is there for all to see and trust.** The Red Briefcase, a series of giant bulging timber barns, bellow up in the good years and contract after a low harvest for all to see. You can judge when and where we invest the fruits of our labour. Trust and transparency are key to the economic growth of London and the value of Parliament in nurturing the food culture.

So how does the Food Parliament work? Public taxes, but not as you know it. You control what you pay by the amount you grow. It will be clear-cut. You can grow your own taxes and deposit them with your visiting MP in return for a 'Victory Pie' – parliament's services include health, nutrition, education and general well being in our constituencies without having to rely on glum central bureaucracy.

Some people say 'devolved power is only a disguise for more job cuts'. We say 'devolved power is only a tool to engage society and cultivate more green jobs'. The Food Parliament opens its 'Goose-Guard-Parade' to a variety of new employment opportunities, from our glasshouse cleaners at Westminster Hall to our dieticians at the bakeries.

Your vote counts. You can control your wealth and what we grow. Each time you meet one of your MPs campaigning, you can make your voice heard and literally taste the change. MPs take the voice of constituencies back to parliament for real change in response to socio-economic policies and public services.

A Green National Insurance Policy

Our green banking system for the new parliament will see an end to boom and bust. Every cabbage saved is a cabbage earned. We value the hard work of all our constituents and members of parliament. Together, the green national insurance can secure a prosperous food economy, protect the environment and create employment opportunities.

Food is the greatest resource of our green national insurance policy. We can all collaborate in cultivation to protect the natural resources on which agriculture depends – soil and water. We want to nurture and tap into the broad range of community assets. There is a wealth of knowledge and expertise waiting to be unearthed to ensure social capital and food security right here on our doorstep.

For the Food Parliament, the practice of equal opportunities is mandatory in urban agriculture activities to save our ecology and restore our civic pride. The popularity of the garden has seen a growing resurgence in recent years and as the urbanites flock to the allotments, waiting lists extend into the decades.

We understand how important it is for you to find a tranquil spot to relax and unwind in the city. That is exactly what we tailor in the Food Parliament – the roof tops of the City of London, directly below Westminster Hall, have been transformed into a wetland habitat. Repeating fishponds rest on the city skyline and all our constituents are welcome to pick a spot and try their hand at angling. With the bounty of fish and frogs on offer, you're bound to get lucky and catch dinner fresh from its source. It takes a little patience, but we've got plenty of time.

The Food Parliament calls upon the city to share in the wealth that we cultivate together. Six hundred and forty-six MPs act as travelling banquets delivering feasts to communities around the country. Chefs, nutritionists and farmers use makeshift street hawkers and portable furniture to bring gastronomic pre-election rallies to you – the people parliament serves. Our hot 'Victory Pies', plucked from the cloaks of your MPs, will spread knowledge, nourishment and good fortune with fellow constituents and support communities that feel economically and socially excluded.

The Food Parliament ensures a continuous buoyant economy. Each of our glass pyramids at Westminster Hall will deliver a substantial harvest each year. Vacant urban structures left to rack and ruin, are converted into new banking Libraries for archiving recipes, seeds, food and preservation techniques. The new infrastructure is buried under heaps of soil, forming natural refrigerators. At subterranean level, we can deposit our food wealth in giant urban ice freezers. **So 'grab a shovel' and let us dig society's very own economic safety net.**

The green national insurance policy protects more than just food. It secures our ecological wealth by reducing crime on our streets, greenhouse gas emissions, providing green in our city and fresh air on our streets, and natural daylight through our windows. Your Food Parliament ensures collective as well as individual wealth by helping civic enterprise take root.

The Food Parliament has one clear planning policy in mind – to turn as much of the city over to bio-diverse green plots as possible. It is our duty to protect and restore our natural environment. Existing green spaces are protected and extended, introducing new wildlife corridors and biodiversity to every street and park in London. With vehicles gone, the silence is golden and the air is fresh. Wild deer graze in the city parks whilst vegetables flourish in our gardens, windowsills and on our streets. In a society driven by work, leisure is big business. So why not return to the garden for a living and enhance your natural environment?

But with all this reform how do we ensure our constituents receive the best service at the best value? Simple. The City of London can measure all services by the six service charters developed in consultation with community-led commissioning – where local constituents survey their own requirements before procuring services to fulfil them. We are open and accountable to the board of trustees at the 'Table of the House' or at worst 'Mr Speaker'.

The Food Parliament is ready for the demographic shift, ensuring employment opportunities for every generation. We all have the chance to grow our economy and get the 1.48 million people claiming job seeker's allowance back to work and feeding the growing populace. One in five young people are currently unable to find a job, leaving a generation undervalued and without the skills required to take over our nation's workforce.[6] We invite parliament's voluntary social mentors and entrepreneurs to share their vital skills and knowledge with society, offering a new way forward for youth services. If we do not act now, vital skills with regard to

food production and home economics will be lost to society forever. Constituents of the third age will be assigned a group of young apprentices and share with them their nutritional knowledge and manual skills, tackling an accelerating obesity epidemic. The mentors constitute the advisory board, securing a cohesive Food Parliament to sustain the new notion of wealth through generations. We want to give our elders the dignity they deserve, so they can independently lead the nation, encourage physical, social and mental wellbeing and enable them to achieve financial independence.

The job opportunities are endless. Everyone will benefit from economic growth. Farming apprenticeships have an essential role in securing our nation's food security and getting people growing again, eliminating unemployment and ending child poverty. Your Food Parliament creates a new industry for employment, calling all – social workers, nutritionists, laboratory assistants, food bankers, bakers, chefs and MPs.

SOW FOR SUSTAINABILITY

Lets grow a greener, fairer and sustainable wealth for our nation, minimizing our reliance on food imports and the supermarket monopolies. We only need to change our mindset from state sponging to state contribution and have a little more patience. You the citizen will become a local farmhand, cultivating the one thing that brings all cultures together – food. This way we all contribute to our wealth, social wellbeing and even the environment.

Severe food shortage during two World Wars proved how vulnerable an import dependent nation could be. Agricultural interventions increased home-grown production and the communal effort for self-sufficiency. Farmers maximized their output, converting grazing pastures into wheat and potato fields, maximizing energy per acre. 'Dig for victory' was much more than propaganda, wartime food production considered nutrition, waste control and consumption, which has since been forgotten as globalization paves our cities. Heathrow, the world's busiest airport, is symbolic of the transition. Beneath the runways lie a history of agriculture and a patchwork of fields that once fed the City of London. Globalization is now a far cry from Caesar's Camp on Hounslow Heath, Heathrow, which in 1723 was enclosed ready to be cultivated.

Government and corporate bosses are long overdue a reality check. It is clear that only we can pull their heads out of the clouds and take action. An energy crunch is looming, threatening our national food security. We currently rely on oil to secure our economy and social wellbeing. Supplies are running out faster than anyone ever predicted and production could peak in the next 10 years.[7] The worldwide demand for carbon rich black oil will see endless price rises in the food we consume.

UK food supplies are taken for granted. We have conveniently ignored the point of origin of our supermarket supplies. Since the industrial revolution, food imports have always been a crucial element of Britain's food supply. Agricultural price spikes of 2007/8 raised some serious questions about UK food security and signalled events to come. This cannot be ethical. **We will construct local modes of food supply to ensure equality and confidence in food with provenance.**

Our prophecy may not appear so extreme in comparison to a wartime crisis, but we need to face our food security head on before it is too late. The Icelandic ash cloud was both shocking and unsettling for the global food supply chain. UK airspace was cleared and food imports were halted. We at the Food Parliament do not wish to rely on supermarkets to secure our food security in the event of crisis. However, it is certainly not practical to sever all our food trade routes.

A nation's food security must rely on a contingency plan that protects food supply during periods of natural disaster and the risk of contamination or disease epidemics. It is inconceivable to demand a UK food chain which is completely self-sufficient, or promote any sense of nationalism. Maintaining trade routes between nations can make up any domestic supply shortages. This may sound comforting but the Food Parliament does not cherish an overriding faith in trade imports that are vulnerable to the effects of climate change and oil deficits.

To begin to alleviate some of the issues which implicate UK food consumption, the UK government has already published strategies in 'Food 2030' as part of the DEFRA (Department for Environment and Rural Affairs) organization, setting out the vision of how the food system should look in 2030.[8] We offer to facilitate and exceled such policies on the scale required to make an adequate difference to London's food security. As consumers in the city, we have the opportunity to take responsibility for the food that we eat and to secure a wealth that is not reserved for the bank accounts of the supermarkets.

The Food Parliament ends the illogical boomerang trade that sees the UK importing 22,000 tonnes of potatoes from Egypt and exporting 27,000 tonnes in the opposite direction.[9] **We will build a regional economy that favours local enterprise with mutual traditions, creating responsive services that empower citizens and communities to meet their ambitions.** The quality of the Food Parliament's produce is displayed on our streets, windowsills and at the pyramidal glasshouses of Westminster Hall. We are all entitled to see the source of our food and exchange it locally and openly at a competitive price.

Restore Nature's Civil Liberties

Too many cities have lost touch with the pace and turn of the seasons. Globalization drains the Earth of its natural resources and science modifies the speed of food production. Historically 'time is money', so it is no surprise that technology has been brought in to tamper with Mother Nature. The Food Parliament is just not willing to play this dangerous game.

The consumer is not the only victim of product severance; the food itself has been dislocated from the reality of its natural source to hastily fill the shopping aisles. Supermarkets stock generous quantities of produce all year round yet we rarely ask how it gets there when it is not in season. Eating non-indigenous fruit and vegetables throughout the year comes at a considerable cost to the environment. We rack-up substantial food miles from importing our food, while much of our consumption requires high-energy artificial conditions to produce. At the Food Parliament, we celebrate seasonal food when it is fresh and tastes its best.

The Food Parliament lives and breathes with the turn of the seasons. Big Ben, the new parliamentary border, just inside the Goose-Guard-Parade, is a densely planted seasonal orchard. Varying colours indicate the exact time of year and season. The fruit harvest is used to make food-dye to colour the water of London's canals accordingly. The canal, like silent church bells informs the entire city about sowing, growing and harvest seasons.

Glass pyramids float over the City of London, propagating the wealth of parliament. Rather than dislocating agriculture from our city, a communal symbiotic dialogue provides a sustainable set of shared services between parliament and constituents. The Food Parliament provides the surface area to enhance the natural environment and secure wealth right in the centre of London.

We share the privilege of London with the red deer that graze in our local parks and on green droving lanes. Nature's civil liberty is restored and we can all return to the natural principles of a food cycle. Living alongside nature's wildlife is more helpful than you might think. We can safeguard endangered species, re-establish biodiversity and in return, the red deer bring green infrastructure back to the City of London. With your confidence we will set the sleighs in motion.

Agribusiness is big business. At present, control over our food is no longer in our hands or even the hands of the farmers, but a handful of massive corporations that have monopolized the industry. 'Food, Inc.', directed by Robert Kenner, brought us the chilling reality of food production. The commercial spin that packages the food we consume usually presents a pastoral image of its source, which could not be further from the truth. Industrial food production has put public health, animal welfare, workers' rights and the environment at the bottom of its list of priorities whilst shareholder profits remain firmly at the top. The law currently sits in defence of corporate monopolies that prevent competition from small-scale producers. Instead of one-sided investment we offer fair and balanced support for local farming entrepreneurs with community-based land distribution and civil services.

The Food Parliament abolishes spin-doctors and immoral sources of production. We have been duped for long enough by season-less supermarkets, sterile pit stops conveniently servicing our 'impatient' lifestyles. Our parliament has nothing to disguise – we can watch the wealth grow right in front of our eyes. Together we can fight back against globalization and corporate bosses to restore green civil liberties and sustainability of the local. As details emerge about industrial food production, we are beginning to search for ethical alternatives.

Organic foods cultivated with a respect for nature have seen a renaissance. Positive news, but with a price tag of 10–40% more than standard produce,[10] it is simply unaffordable for low-income families. So how will it be affordable? The Food Parliament prioritizes food in its sustainable economy. We can provide nutrition and healthy diet for all constituents at an affordable exchange. Yes, we can trade the food we grow at home, eat with the seasons, as well as respecting nature's civil liberties.

As well as action, we must continue to reform by communicating and debating about current issues that affect parliament's new notion of wealth. The famous Woolsack, reserved only for the Lord Chancellor, no longer fulfils its duty in our modern society. Instead, you oversee the Food Parliament and sit on the Woolsack, urban scale scarlet cushions for you to picnic on and debate current issues. It is time we take environmental and civic responsibility seriously.

CHANGE PARLIAMENT

We will take back control. We will clean and green our parliament. Our MPs return to the constituents they serve, campaigning for the new notion of wealth.

A living, breathing, Food Parliament requires radical political reform and your MPs cannot do this alone. We want you, the constituents to be the mechanism and power behind the new Food Parliament. MPs have lost touch with their constituencies, caring more for who they are and their ministerial perks rather than whom they serve and what they campaign for. Together we will put an end to MP expense scandals and the public tax payments that subsidize gardeners, mole catchers, moat clearing and duck houses.[11] The cost was far greater than expense claims, loss of your trust and faith was the biggest loss to politics.

Now let us draw a line under the grovelling of the untrustworthy that has escalated into a shameful 'my shirt is hairier than yours' competition.[12] We will restore some self-respect in parliament, work for your trust, strip waste and devolve power to your community. At the Food Parliament, MPs do not just talk but act, campaigning locally, to deliver their 'Victory Pies'. Our MPs are a local and accountable provision of democracy to make sure your voice is acknowledged as part of a simple network of provision. Change is coming and we will share the wealth of knowledge, health and nutrition together with neighbouring constituencies.

Clean and Green Parliament

The Food Parliament is transparent. Westminster's glass pyramids display the wealth of the nation. Seeing really is believing. Parliament is shrouded in dirt. Scandal after scandal the dirt thickens. It is time for a clean, so cleaning is exactly what we will do. There will be no hiding place for politics in parliament. 'Mr Speaker', the 'temperamental cloud' is charged with administering bad weather to sustain transparency and restore order. Spots of dirt or unruly behaviour are dealt with by a downpour. The honourable arrangement will be watching and listening and the months that follow will vindicate your trust. **You have never known a parliament so clean.**

A clean parliament requires a green infrastructure. The UK Carbon Transition Plan has set out targets of what the economy needs to do to combat climate change; agriculture is to reduce emissions by the equivalent of 3 million tonnes of CO_2 by 2020.[13] It is easy to register with our bikes and deer carriage schemes, a carbon neutral transport.

We put our faith in the new green religion for a sustainable economy. Parliament invests in a local ecological footprint and local consumerism, rather than globalism and a nonsensical food carbon footprint. The new policies enable us to grow a green and fertile economy, bringing our agricultural history back to the City of London and restoring our civic pride.

Our energy principles:
– Procure incentives to go green
– Trade our low carbon energy
– Develop local heating networks using biogas
– Invest in renewable energy technologies
– Cultivate a closed sustainable system for waste recycling
– Encourage constituent stakeholders in local renewable energy projects

Together we have a big voice so let it be heard; you are the 'Queen' of our city. We want our Food Parliament to return to the centre of social and political equality. If we can mutually support our city and help restore democracy, civil liberties will return to every constituency and every household.

We trust your common sense – and together we can recoup civil liberties back from big government and big supermarket monopolies. With a clean and green parliament, the city's voice can again be heard without fear of being overshadowed by closet scandals. **Let us tell it straight and cut the bureaucracy; this is a new agenda for smart politics.**

Make Parliament More Local
Rosemary Street • Herbal Hill Gardens • Saffron Hill • Camomile Street • Poultry • Lime Street • Fish Street Hill • Pudding Lane • Salt Tower • Ginger Apartments • Eden Street • Apple Tree Yard

Local food production has generally disappeared from London's high streets but its history still lingers in the street names. Yes, there is food on the streets – and it is certainly worthy of the bins it misses. Gone are our local fresh staples that littered every corner shop. Gone are the bakeries that filled the air with the aroma of fresh bread and the sweetness of treacle sponge.

The Food Parliament comes to the streets of London with fresh produce. Fast food grease is exchanged for fresh fruit and vegetables, contributing to the new notion of wealth. We can roll out the green carpet in your community. Parliament's bakeries, one for each of the 32 of London boroughs, line the river Thames. Like a Melton Mowbray pork pie on baking day, the Food Parliament's 'Victory Pies' fill the air with a heavenly whiff of hot buttery pastry, prompting an automatic association with the sovereign state and our food standards. Nobody can resist a visit to the bakery. The artisan dieticians at the bakeries will invest their hearts into each order and once again the love for food disseminates through the city. Now food is back on the streets, we can re-engage with street life, have neighbourly exchange of food, and discuss parliament's current affairs with our community. Local areas will be free from the pressures of overly prescriptive central government.

The permanent 'Goose-Guard-Parade' marks the territory of Westminster Hall, but our MPs take parliament to every local constituency beyond the City of London, campaigning for the new notion of wealth. **On the corner of every park and square, MPs listen to their local constituents.** They will trust and take your concerns very seriously, without any formal barriers, to provide a responsive, relevant and efficient service. Grab a chair from under their cloak, enjoy a delicious 'Victory Pie' and whinge to your MP about your sufferings or suggest ideas for London. Parliament will be tailored to our personal needs; so let your voice be heard.

The old parliament cost the British taxpayer £500 million a year, a figure which has doubled since 1997.[14] **Together we will stop the gravy train in government.** With all our hard work, the Food Parliament can cater for all our wealth, and no one will go hungry again.

After the binge on state welfare, we are looking toward innovative service reforms to cure our hangover. You can rely on the Food Parliament to strengthen support for your front line services. No more endless red tape and bureaucracy to be passed on through continuous layers of government. Power is devolved from management to co-operative enterprise, entrepreneurial green business development and welfare services. Like other religions, the Food Parliament has a board of trustees at the 'Table of the House', the altar for the city where you are invited for a feast. On this table trustees do not just talk, but listen and act.

There is nothing more irritating than listening to our Ministers harp on about cutting costs whilst being chauffeur driven in their Mercedes, claiming food subsidies and waiting to claim their gold plated pension. It is only fair we all feel the pinch during leaner years and share the wealth of parliament equally amongst constituencies during eras of prosperity. A mutual, self-sustaining support network for our constituents will develop socio-economic relations and construct cohesive, independent communities in parliament.

The Food Parliament delivers zero carbon emissions and contributes to the UK's commitment to cut greenhouse gas emissions 20% by 2020. We do not want the burden of irreversible environmental damage to be on our heads and we must lead the world toward radical, sustainable interventions.

Together, as a society, we can reconsider the pace of globalization. Heathrow operations, contributed 2.31 million tonnes of CO2 in 2009.[15] London's transport infrastructure is under intolerable strain and exhausts 34% of London's energy demands.[16] In the last two decades, food transport in the UK has increased by around 30% with the average distance travelled increased by nearly 60%.[17] We can reduce the food carbon footprint through local urban agriculture, right on our own doorstep. What better incentive to go green, than to cultivate your own money and recycle energy for a living?

Car ownership is expected to increase from about 2.25 million in 1991 to 2.7 million in 2011.[18] The Food Parliament is a car-free zone – no more vehicles to choke the city with toxins. **We are actively seeking planning alternatives for our city if we are able to rebalance energy demands.** First, London's main roads will welcome the return of drovers with their herds of deer. Second, London's secondary roads, beyond the sovereign state of parliament, are subject to unavoidable vehicular traffic,

The Food Parliament bikes will give you the freedom to ride our streets travelling at a speed that helps restore nature's rhythm in the city. Why not hop on the bike every day or two and get your shopping fresh whilst keeping your body active. Sometimes you may need to transport produce and at other times, it may be wise travel as a group. So why not take a deer carriage to your destination, towed by our local deer? These porters of the Food Parliament are given the right of passage to trot along designated droving lanes as part of a sustainable infrastructure for London.

CHANGE SOCIETY
Society is on the slippery slope of decline. Gone are the days when we would exchange with our neighbour a cup of sugar for some butter. The state money pot that so many of us have come to rely on has run out. So we need a new approach: we need to find an even keel, support our Nutritional Health Service, raise food education standards, create more green jobs and tackle urban poverty.

Social wellbeing starts at home and can help bring healthy family values back to households, and our families back to our communities, and our communities back to parliament. Social security is not a peripheral condition of the Food Parliament; it is the golden thread running throughout the sovereign state. Together we have to dispel the culture of fear, loneliness and unhappiness. Urban agriculture, the premise of our Food Parliament, gives everybody the chance to get back involved in society.

Our constituents of the Food Parliament cultivate energy, natural ecosystems, civic justice and the city's wealth. Each governs the need for carbon sequestration, wildlife habitats, raw materials and biomass. The redistribution of power will enable us to take an active role in our community, helping to cultivate the new notion of wealth. The Food Parliament believes devolving socioeconomic responsibilities to the constituents, increases productivity of the city and stronger social cohesion. With trust and confidence we will heal our disfunctional society.

Food can bring all of us together, irrespective of background or race. In the UK, we have taken food supply for granted and are plagued with overindulgent, rather than deficient food consumption. The convenience of supermarket retail and minute meals has distorted the reality of food supply chains and the value of nutritional consumption. We will change our wasteful habits by introducing green infrastructure reform, renewable energy, waste recycling and water harvesting. We can make real changes to mass attitudes concerning climate change.

Cultivate Green Communities
The Food Parliament cultivates social action, helping community social enterprises to deliver public services. We have an appetite to make green changes, and if we work together we can all make a substantial difference.

Let us cultivate our communities and cities as a society and tackle the root problems of social discourse. Rather than handing out record numbers of ASBOs, otherwise known as 'the badge of honour',[19] we offer new youth employment opportunities. The Food Parliament is behind you every step of the way on the cycle path to social recovery. We promote a sense of belonging in the community. You are the key to social and environmental recovery. It is not all about empowering the constituencies; the new parliament is a catalyst for economic, environmental and social recovery.

Each autumn, the 'State Opening of Parliament by the Queen' marks much more than the beginning of harvest season. It is an annual festivity celebrating all the hard work and commitment that you and your local constituencies have contributed to make the Food Parliament a success. Let us use this opportunity to encourage wider participation. There is no better setting for our festival than underneath the temporary regal canopy, which trails along the orchard avenues, turning golden yellow in November.

'Waste not want not' is the recurring mantra of the Food Parliament. We want every constituent to be reminded of this wartime favourite. Food waste currently costs UK consumers £10.2 billion a year and when production, transportation and storage are factored in, it is responsible for 5% of the UK's greenhouse gas emissions.[20]

We appeal for your commitment to achieve a zero carbon parliament and London. The Food Parliament is way ahead of the game. The closed sustainable system eliminates food packaging and recycles organic waste as part of a perpetual motion machine. At the bakeries, a zero waste policy will ensure every edible morsel of food is used in each recipe, regardless of its original shape or size.

We will recycle all our organic waste by feeding the Lord Mayor in exchange for bio-energy and compost that contribute to our energy demands and the soil's fertility. We will even recover and recycle waste from our green infrastructure. Animal droppings are collected from the droving lanes by voluntary teams of dedicated 'pooper scoopers', to yield a rich source of compost. Sewage, another unavoidable vital waste resource of the food cycle has until now been dumped out at sea. We direct sewage along the green national grid to the Lord Mayor. The Solid Clarifier separates water from solids, a provider of bio-energy and fertilizer. Local reed beds filter the water before use to irrigate the agricultural land.

The Food Parliament exploits the UK's all-year-round wet weather to meet the increase in agriculture demands for 'liquid gold'. Rainwater and air moisture are harvested and stored in the fleet of Victoria Towers, the highest points in Parliament. Rooftops below Westminster Hall earnestly capture displaced surface water to fill the fishponds. Even 'Mr Speaker' takes part in the water conservation effort. The honourable 'temperamental cloud' will be busy harvesting the morning mist from parks, before choosing to shower the parliamentary infrastructure.

The Food Parliament proudly develops leading technology to co-exist alongside traditional agricultural methods for a fertile food economy. Opaque photovoltaics carpet the glass surface of Westminster Hall, hovering above the city, silently harvesting solar energy whilst the wealth grows below in turn with the seasons. The Victoria Towers are multipurpose water and energy assimilators – the turbine and dynamo at the base of each tower will harvest wind energy.

Common agriculture is energy intensive. The Food Parliament invests renewable energies in food production, but favours labour intensive agriculture without carbon intensive equipment. We must feel remorse over industrial farming and toxic fertilizers that destroyed our rivers and wildlife habitats. We should feel betrayed by breathing petrol-fumed air. We can stop this now and put the city back on an even keel with nature.

Raise Food and Health Awareness
Research indicates that while 93% of British children aged 7–15 know how to play computer games, only 54% can boil an egg.[21]

It is not uncommon for children to consider the supermarket as the sole food manufacturer, as education with regard to the grower and food production has fallen by the way side. The displacement of today's curriculum is evidently a factor behind the childhood obesity epidemic.

The National Child Measurement Programme has recorded alarming childhood obesity results. By year six, 31.6% of children are overweight or obese and childhood obesity is more prevalent in London than anywhere else in England and Wales. 11.3% of four- and five-year-olds and a huge 20.8% of 10- and 11-year-olds have a severe weight problem.[22] Decades of inaction, cheap food and a food education deficit have left our children's health paying the price of excess weight.

The time has come to raise food education standards and urban agriculture is the tool. The nutritional and health benefits are clear. One ambassador using his notoriety to educate children with practical food and cooking skills is 2010's TED prizewinner, Jamie Oliver. His wish 'for your help to create a strong, sustainable movement to educate every child about food, inspire families to cook again and empower people everywhere to fight obesity',[23] has caught considerable attention. The Food Parliament offers tax relief to local community enterprises that focus on food education and the national curriculum will shift toward the things that matter: urban farming, food, nutrition, health and green science.

An increase in demand for hot nutritional school dinners marks the success of Jamie Oliver's campaign to get kids eating healthily again. 'Now is the time to move up a gear'[24] and extend the success to radical new possibilities. Every child is entitled to food education and your Food Parliament will provide it. Society's youth can contribute by helping cultivate the land and foraging for food directly from the soil. We can rediscover the meaning of hand to mouth existence and take back control of the food we consume. Cookery lessons are a valuable part of our national curriculum and we will entrust our children to prepare the nation's 'Victory Pies'.

The MPs distribute our knowledge and education standards as well as social and ecological ideas to local constituencies. Consider your MP as your local welfare worker campaigning for the new notion of wealth and its endless health benefits. The 'Victory Pies' disseminate knowledge, nutrition and civil liberties of the Food Parliament. Just what the doctor ordered.

The Food Parliament re-evaluates our relationship with food. Although we do not propose a complete U-turn toward the primitive lifestyle of hunter-gather societies, we can return animals to the city. **Deer hunting will return to the social and seasonal food calendar.** Hunting has a history that dates back to hunter-gatherer societies of the Palaeolithic, long before the dawn of agriculture. In fact, reindeer 'may well be the species of single greatest importance in the entire anthropological literature on hunting'[25] and continues to be of vital importance to the lives of families in North America and Eurasia. The hunt gives us the opportunity to reconnect with the source of our food in a local environment. We want to restore mankind's natural bond with society and nature when hunting and gathering food.

Let's reject the poor quality, highly processed portion of meat, high in cholesterol that we are consistently served on the high street. Parliament's deer will provide a visible source of local protein that is of high quality and low in cholesterol. Every constituent will have the option to feast on their share of nutritious provender wrapped in the butter pastry of your 'Victory Pies'.

Back the Nutritional Health Service (NHS)
We back the NHS reform to focus on prevention and cause of nutritional, mental and social health problems in later life. Together we will cultivate a national grid of food that will provide a backbone for our service.

Malnutrition may not catch as many headlines as an obesity epidemic but it certainly rings the same alarm bells. A poor diet costs the NHS £13 billion a year according to the British Association for Parenteral and Enternal Nutrition, more than double the cost of obesity.[26] More than 3 million people are living at a high risk of malnutrition, which is associated with a range of socio-economic factors. If we do not act now that burden is set to rise. If we really are what we eat lets 'grab a shovel' and show our support for the Nutritional Health Service. **The Food Parliament gives us all the chance to cultivate a healthy, balanced and nutritional diet.** Your support for the Nutritional Health Service will relieve the financial burden of treatment and instead invest in prevention and education.

Our levels of fitness are dropping. Our kids are turning to excessive indoor gaming rather than outdoor activities. We are in danger of nurturing a generation of social introverts. Video gaming has been linked with low self-esteem, mental health issues, behavioural problems and in some cases this has resulted in bullying and even game inspired murder.[27] The Food Parliament realigns the balance between digital media and the benefits of social, physical activities. If we work together to change our cultural mindset, we can encourage our kids out of their bedrooms and into the garden alongside friends and family.

The UK government recommends that adults should aim to do at least 30 minutes of moderate intensity activity on five or more days a week and young people to do 60 minutes everyday.[28] A labour intensive approach means we could easily do more. **We have the opportunity to cultivate our wealth whilst getting fit and healthy right here in our local communities.** Physical activity can halve the risk of developing many major illnesses, and substantially reduce the risk of premature death, so there is every incentive to take part.

Education is the principle service of the NHS. The new curriculum educates in vital subjects to avert dietary and nutritional health complications in later life. Core subjects include home economics, animal husbandry, agriculture, agribusiness and biology. Our whole-person approach does not rely heavily on state investment. On the existing surface area, an urban paraphernalia is waiting to be adapted and cultivated.

ANNUAL NATIONAL 'FOOD PARLIAMENT DAY'
We will launch an annual national 'Food Parliament Day' to mark the new urban wealth and the successful revitalization of London. The 'Food Parliament Day' will celebrate the work of each and everyone; our efforts to construct a new urban ecology and to encourage more citizens to actively participate in our gastro-revolution.

We will work to ensure that the 'Food Parliament Day' is an event without equal! To each citizen a Victory Pie; a slice of the ideals of the new sustainable city helping to bring about a shift in attitude towards a positive and rewarding urban life.

Making the 'Food Parliament Day' a success will require a concentrated national effort. We are committed to making a whole-government effort, and we appeal for your contributions. The Food Parliament will ensure, at all levels and on all cylinders, that the day is a mass participation event. **We need <u>you</u> to make the Food Parliament a sustainable reality.**

notes:

1. A Migliaccio & F Rotondi, 'Parmesan as Collateral for Bank Loans', New York Times, 2009

2. 'Welcome to the Anthropocene' [http://www.anthropocene.info/en/anthropocene], retrieved 14 August 2013

3. W Tasch,'Inquiries into the Nature of Slow Money', Chelsea Green Publishing, White River Junction, VT, 2008, p.xvii

4. 'Home repossessions hit 14 year high' [http://news.bbc.co.uk/1/hi/business/8510077.stm], retrieved 14 August 2013

5. B Brady & D Randall, 'Backlash over bankers bonuses' [http://www.independent.co.uk/news/uk/politics/backlash-over-bankers-bonuses-1604034.html], retrieved 14 August 2013

6. 'Get Britain Working', Conservative Manifesto, 2010, p.15

7. S Connor, 'Warning: Oil supplies are running out fast' [http://www.independent.co.uk/news/science/warning-oil-supplies-are-running-out-fast-1766585.html], retrieved 14 August 2013

8. L Jessop, 'Food 2030: the UK's national food strategy' [http://sd.defra.gov.uk/2010/01/food-2030/], retrieved 14 August 2013

9. A Simms, V Johnson, J Smith & S Mitchell. 'The Consumption Explosion: The Third UK Independence Day Report', NEF, London, 2009, p.4

10. CK Winter & SF Davis, 'Organic Foods', Journal of Food Science, 71(9):R117–R124, 2006

11. P Viggers, 'MPs Expenses' [http://www.telegraph.co.uk/news/newstopics/mps-expenses/5380178.html], retrieved 14 September 2012

12. A Widdecombe, 'My Shirt's Hairier Than Yours', Nick Robinson's Newslog [http://www.bbc.co.uk/blogs/nickrobinson/2009/05/my_shirts_hairi.html], retrieved 20 July 2012

13. 'Food Strategy 2030', DEFRA, 2010, p.12

14. 'David Cameron on Cutting the Cost of Politics', Conservative Party [http://www.youtube.com/watch?v=5dRfO-EOOW0], retrieved 20 July 2012

15. 'LHR Climate Change Brochure', Heathrow Airport, 2010, p.1 [www.heathrowairport.com/.../Heathrow/Heathrow%20downloads/.../LHR_Climate_brochure.pdf], retrieved 20 July 2012

16–18, 21. J Petts, 'Urban Agriculture in London', Series on Urban Food Security, Case Study 2, WHO, 2001, pp.2–3

19. G Owen, 'Asbos don't work because thugs think they're cool' [http://www.dailymail.co.uk/news/article-379615.html], retrieved 12 July 2012

20. O Paterson, 'Food Waste' [https://www.gov.uk/government/policies/reducing-and-managing-waste/supporting-pages/food-waste], retrieved 14 August 2013

22. S Boseley, 'Obesity rates start badly and get worse' [http://www.guardian.co.uk/society/2008/feb/22/children.health], retrieved 8 March 2010

23. Ted Prize [http://www.tedprize.org/jamie-oliver/], retrieved 8 May 2010

24. D Campbell, 'Jamie Oliver calls for more funding to back school meals revolution' [http://www.guardian.co.uk/education/2010/jul/08/jamie-oliver-school-meals], retrieved 14 August 2013

25. ES Burch, Jr., 'The Caribou/Wild Reindeer as a Human Resource', American Antiquity, Vol. 37, No. 3, July1972, pp.339–368

26. 'Combating Malnutrition: Recommendations for Action' [http://www.bapen.org.uk/res_press_rel42.html], retrieved 14 August 2010

27. M DeLisi, C Anderson et al., 'Violent video games are a risk factor for criminal behavior' [http://www.news.iastate.edu/news/2013/03/26/violentvideogames#sthash.XqB3PKBb.dpuf], retrieved 14 August 2013

28. 'Benefits of Exercise' [http://hcd2.bupa.co.uk/fact_sheets/html/exercise.html], retrieved 14 August 2013

183

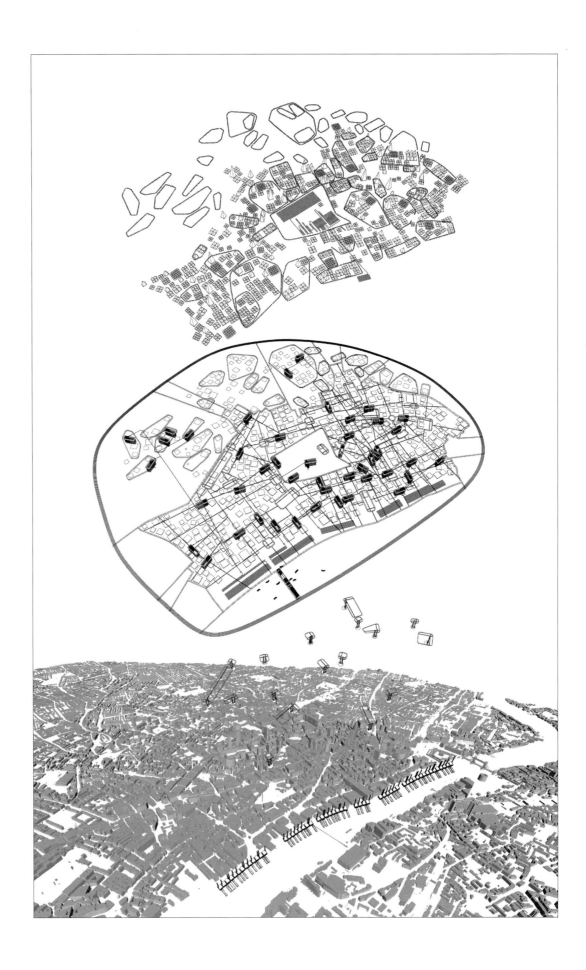

The Food Parliament

'Parliament examines what the Government of the United Kingdom is doing, makes new laws, holds the power to set taxes and debates the issues of the day. The business of Parliament takes place in two Houses: the House of Commons and the House of Lords in the Palace of Westminster, more commonly known as the Houses of Parliament. Today, the Palace of Westminster covers eight acres (32,400m2). It contains around 1,100 rooms, 100 staircases and 4,800 metres of passageways. From the Victoria Tower at the south end to the Clock Tower at the north, the building is nearly 300 metres long. Over the course of nearly a thousand years of history, the architecture has transformed from royal residence to the home of a modern democracy and has continually evolved, sometimes by design, sometimes through accident or attack.'

– www.parliament.uk, 2014

The Food Parliament is the fictional supreme food legislative body for London and its territories. Reimagined here as a landlocked sovereign city-state, it has an area of approximately 3.15km2 over-laid onto the existing city. As a secondary infrastructure,[1] the Food Parliament functions as a holistic ecology: an environmental strategy and food system that is self-perpetuating yet engaged in a symbiotic dialogue with contemporary London below. The main territory of the Food Parliament sits 100m above sea level and traces the outline of the historic City of London,[2] defined by the defensive London Wall built around AD 43 by the Romans to enclose Londinium.[3] Twenty-eight new vertical service-circulation cores, a network of appropriated satellite parks, disused sites and streets named after influential food sources constitute the extension of the infrastructure into the city.

The Food Parliament enjoys similar privileges to that of the City of London with a singular relationship with the Crown, and possessing a unique political status as a communal city. The formally unorthodox, collaborative parliamentary components promote the advantages of decentralization and independence. The Food Parliament has three main pledges: to promote the city as the world's leading international centre of excellence for food sovereignty; to facilitate local communities and individuals in the cultivation, processing and distribution of food within the city; and to disseminate the new notion of wealth.

The functionaries of the United Kingdom's supreme legislative body are transfigured into tectonic analogs responsible for tabling and implementing the new acts of parliament. Each tectonic analog, steered by Erskine May's 'Parliamentary Practice',[4] uses spatial relationships to reframe the spaces of food consumption and production, analysed through historical precedent, function and form. The characters are not human, but anthropomorphic totems that perform duties running in parallel to their

1. The speculative multi-use infrastructure of the Food Parliament also evokes the spirit of unbuilt utopian projects from previous decades, such as Buckminster Fuller's domed-over city project, published in 'Utopia or Oblivion: The Prospects for Humanity' (1969), which outlines a provocative blueprint for the future in which the needs of all humanity are met.

2. 'The City of London' [http://www.cityoflondon.gov.uk/about-the-city/history-and-heritage/Pages/the-city-history.aspx], retrieved 26 August 2013

3. 'History and Research: London Wall' [http://www.english-heritage.org.uk/daysout/properties/london-wall/history-and-research/], retrieved 26 August 2013

4. M Jack, 'Erskine May's Parliamentary Practice', 24th Edition, LexisNexis Butterworths, London, 2012

real world flesh-and-blood counterparts. There are 646 Members of Parliament (MPs) regulating the city and responding to the manifold problems created by urbanization. Victoria Towers are water harvesters, the Red Briefcase is a food repository, and 10 Downing Street an urban scarecrow.[5] Simultaneously, the historical and geographical resources of early urban tectonics of London are appropriated to fuel the processes of the second city. The River Thames collects urban organic waste and feeds it back into the agriculture above, instigating a waste-free cycle.

The Food Parliament propagates sustainable capital as part of the new economic model and is the support mechanism for transparency in local and national food governance. The city's green micro-economy is rooted in the earth and the environment, establishing equality and shared accountability for the propagation of wealth. The Food Parliament is premised on the adoption of food as the local currency standard of London. Food is a commodity that is in increasingly short supply in the real world. World agricultural production has declined with severe natural global disasters and rapid urbanization of arable land. The rural is becoming urbanized through the migration of urban and peri-urban areas, and the appropriation of the rural for the burgeoning city. Simultaneously, food-producing nations are imposing food export restrictions, and constrained access to sustainable energy and water are further inhibiting affordable food. Given the failures of our debt-based monetary system, the fragility and unsustainable nature of our agricultural practices, and the social exploitation orchestrated by vast unregulated corporations, a reserve currency backed by the tangible asset of food, although improbable, is not illogical.

With the Food Parliament comes a new green religion. The green ascription is protecting more than just food; it secures ecological and social wealth for the city by expanding the commonly received notion of wealth to include fresh air and water, natural daylight, green space and reduction of greenhouse gas emissions. Urban sprawl and old building stock are synonymous with climate change issues including air pollution from transport and the relentless increase in energy consumption, resulting in negative health impacts. The new infrastructure of the Food Parliament sets out an optimum environment for the city below to prevent the problem of increasing summer air-conditioning and winter heating. The innovative renewable energy technologies of the city silently coexist alongside nature, harvesting solar, wind, bio and hydro energies, and recycle organic municipal waste for urban agriculture. Zero carbon deer-pulled carriages have replaced all London buses and taxis. In the past, London has failed to address the issue of energy consumption, as well as its food sourcing.

Food cultivation, a typical oversight for most cities, is now at the heart of all urban planning and urban health initiatives in London. The Food Parliament has adapted city laws to address issues of land security and tenure, and declared indefinite free rights to cultivate food on disused private sites and vacant municipal land. The new micro-economy invites the English arcadia back into London; wildlife corridors and bio-diversity traverse car-free municipalities. The infrastructure of the Food Parliament accommodates the welcome return of locally grown food in London. Land is legitimately appropriated for bio-diverse green allotments of urban agriculture, and wild deer graze in public parks in a campaign to restore nature's civil liberties. Urban kitchens and bakeries will only source food within a 10 mile radius. Consumerism is no longer the sterile, cursory experience redolent of supermarket aisles – streets are alive with trade, gastronomy and ecology. The wetland habitat from the River Thames has migrated onto the city's undulating rooftops, harvesting fresh rainwater for aquaculture and irrigation within repeated fish ponds perched on the skyline. Historically, the distribution of provisions to modern cities is tenuous, relying on transport and storage mechanisms that are taken for granted but nonetheless vulnerable to natural and manmade disasters. Here, local fresh food is distributed along a green national grid without the historical overriding reliance on extensive food miles.

The second city acts as both a catalyst and support network for a safe, nutritious and life enhancing diet that is agro-ecological, through social inclusivity, community and personal empowerment. Socio-economic responsibilities are devolved amongst London's constituents with a user-centred approach, developing social relationships and trust through local food production to boost individual and collective recovery capital. Social enterprises nurturing food provenance and safety empower communities. The 'third age' are no longer sidelined in demographic state policy – pensioners are invited to mentor a new generation of cultivators with their invaluable food related knowledge and experience. Food support partnerships may appear modest in scale but they play a vital role in stimulating the perceptual shift in how city dwellers think about and procure meals. The Food Parliament can demonstrate spatial phenomenology in the city, stimulating our eyes, ears, noses, minds and tongues – vision made real, social capital that can be tasted.

The Green National Insurance Policy promotes sustainable vegetable cultivation and animal husbandry to protect food and social security. London's inhabitants have come together to cultivate using the new infrastructure; and convert patios, rooftops and unused parking lots into productive vegetable allotments and reared livestock in a collective effort redolent of the World War II victory gardens. Civic enterprises are taking root with employment opportunities for every generation disseminating knowledge and life skills to cultivate collective and individual wealth. Co-ops are established, owned and managed by local communities encouraging renewable energy ecosystems in the food cultivation chain, providing substantial cost savings and healthy revenue.

The Food Parliament firmly believes in 'prevention rather than cure', and has invested in a local food distribution system and nutritious diet plan. Through the Nutritional Health Service, the second city communicates with its constituencies by employing gastronomic festivities, and disseminating nourishment and knowledge on wellbeing. The service also educates urban cultivators in methods of permaculture, composting and the use of biological controls. Permaculture enables the city to have a sustainable high-yielding ecosystem and increased biodiversity. The vertical allotments transform London's skyline,[6] providing city dwellers with a 'green health centre' to rediscover the meaning of hand to mouth existence. The popularity of the garden rekindles mankind's natural bond with food, nature and society, offsetting contemporary introverted pursuits in digital media with real time.

The Food Parliament, a fertile plain over London busied by pollinating insects, and studded with lush agriculture, is a provocation. The physical absurdity of the proposal intends to raise serious questions about the priorities of our governing bodies and to engage individuals with issues of food sovereignty and climate change. However, the principles that underly its premise and the justification for its existence, in some form or other, are both real and urgent. Food is the driver for the restructuring of employment, education, transport, health, communities and the justice system, re-evaluating how the city functions as a political and spatial sustainable entity. The Food Parliament ensures its constituents the freedom to exercise their new green religion, cultivating a green notion of wealth – the city is ready for the future.

5. The use of symbolism and narrative structure is similar to John Hejduk's 'Victims' (1986), applying architectonic forms to combine fiction with architecture, 'spinning a narrative in which it is no longer possible to tell what is being designed: the habitat or the inhabitants, the structure or the institution'.

6. The Food Parliament drew architectonic inspiration from the imaginary London skyline of 'A Tribute to Sir Christopher Wren' (1838) by Charles Robert Cockerell, which brought together Wren's major buildings into one vast urban landscape.

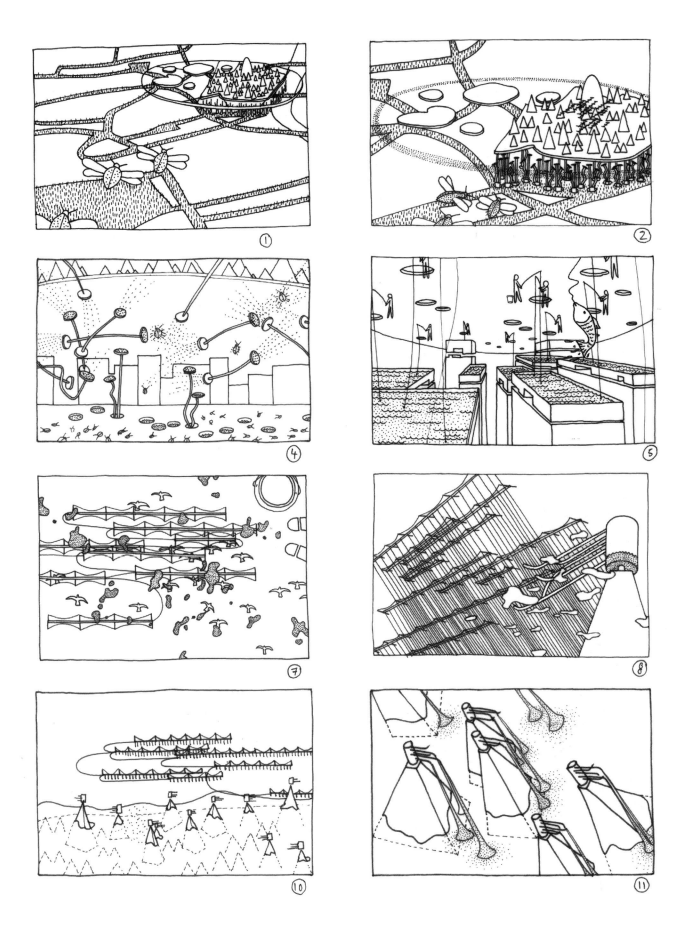

The Food Parliament Storyboard

1. View from the Hampstead Heath looking towards the square mile and the new parliament hovering over the city.
2. Upon approaching the new parliament one notices a fence of giant hairpins. This is the Ministry of Defence protecting the crop from pests.
3. When not in combat these guardians rest upright in a puddle of organic pesticide soaking up liquid pest killer.

189

4. At the first sign of bugs, they propel themselves up and through centrifugal force squirt out a spray of organic pesticide.
5. A view beyond the Ministry of Defence, in-between the roof-scape of the old city and the crystal landscape above. Roofs of the office towers are clad in huge fish tanks forming a blue carpet. Holes, strategically placed in the Westminster Hall, allow people to fish from these ponds.
6. Mr Speaker, who is eager to keep the Parliament clean.

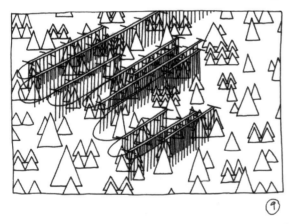

7. Mr Speaker presides over the house like an angry black cloud. Responsible for maintaining order, he may punish members who break the rules of the House. The Speaker resides in the Parliamentary estate, within Big Ben and is therefore on the lookout for offenders.
8. Often cleaning up after misbehaving MPs.
9. Like a giant urban-scaled scrubber he makes sure the Westminster hall sparkles and shines at all times.

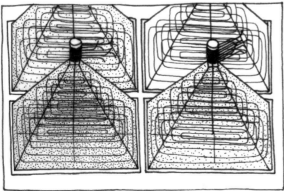

10. After the rain: A misty landscape punctured by the crystal pyramids.
11. MPs sitting atop the pyramids harvest the rain. The flags suck up the misty fog.
12. The water which is stored in big drums is then injected into the pyramids for irrigation.

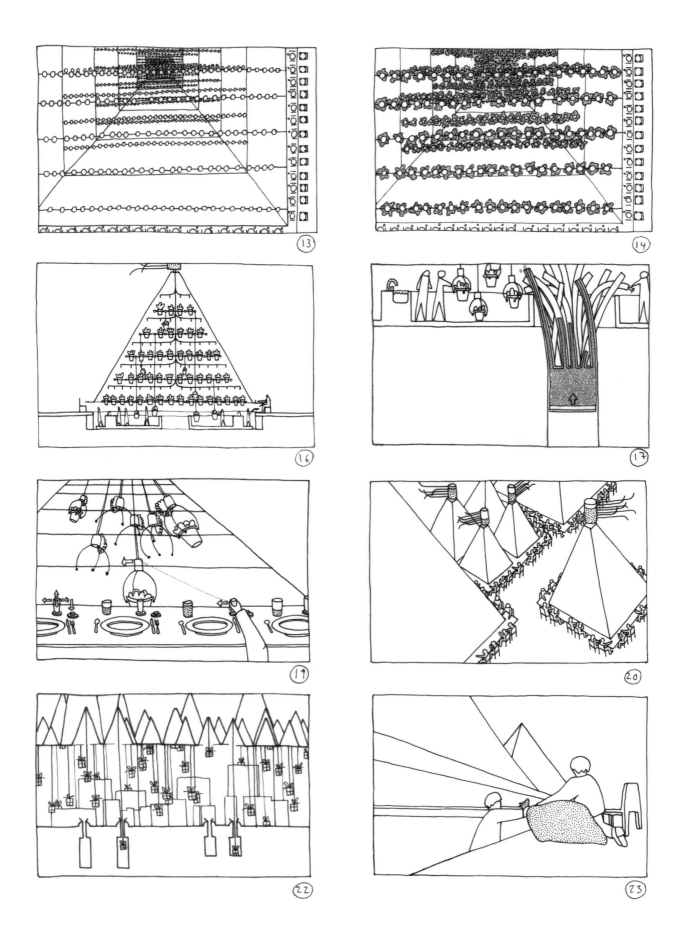

13

14

16

17

19

20

22

23

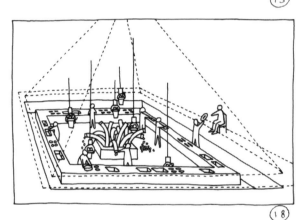

13. Looking up into one of the many greenhouse pyramids. Plant-pots are suspended on fine wires allowing sunlight to pass through to all plants and the city below.
14. As time passes plants grow.
15. Harvest time.

16. Fully grown fruit plants are lowered into the local pyramid kitchens.
17. Victoria Towers bring back fresh vegetables from the London suburbs for use in the Pyramid Kitchens.
18. The Pyramid kitchen. The Victoria Towers' bristles pierce the kitchen floor and form a central vegetable tree. Food is served under the table.

19. Alongside cutlery and plates you will find an 'arcade' claw control unit to pick your food of choice from the Pyramid and lower it into the kitchen.
20. Lunchtime: people gather around the Pyramids for lunch.
21. Uncooked fresh foods are wrapped into parcels ...

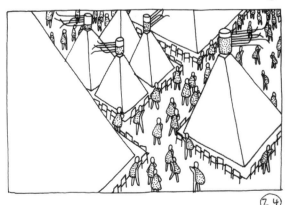

22. ... and lowered into deep wells/natural refrigerators where they will keep fresh for use in the near future.
23. All restaurant customers are required to pay for their meal by labour. They are passed a sack of food that needs to be processed for preservation and storage in the Red Briefcases.
24. 'Heigh-ho, heigh-ho, it's off to work we go ...'

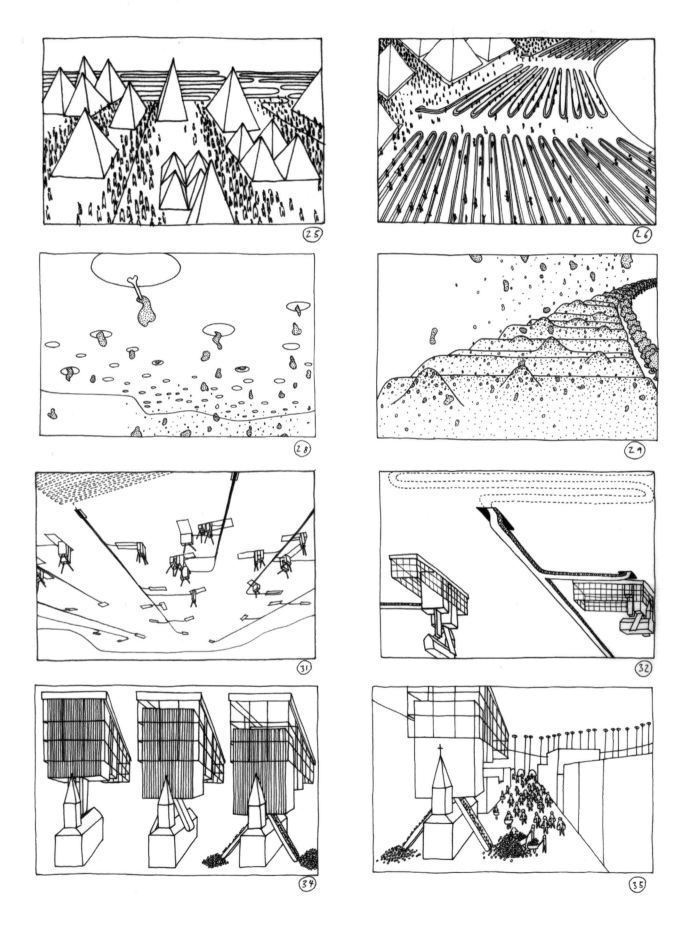

25. 'Whistles' ... Hordes of people carrying masses of fresh food to the Table of the House at the south edge of the parliament.

26. People arriving at the Table and taking their position in this conveyor table landscape.

27. At work on the Table, separating the wheat from the chaff.

28. Whatever isn't good enough for the Red Briefcase gets dropped into the Lord Major. This is the scene shortly after a weekday community lunch. What looks like snowy landscape is a carefully orchestrated recycling process.

29. The Lord Mayor, flowing underneath the Table of the House is the compost river that serves the whole of London with fertilizer all year round.

30. The Table of the House going underground.

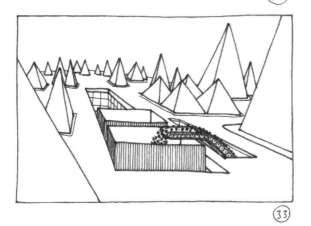

31. The underground network of tables transporting the processed food to the Treasury for safekeeping through the new parliamentary year.

32. The Treasury and the Red Briefcases are located right above the many churches in the City of London, giving them a presence in the new Parliament.

33. Close up of table emerging from the glass landscape and spilling its contents into the Red Briefcase.

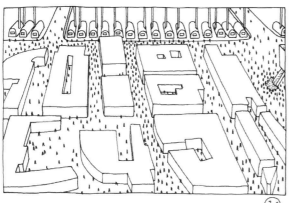

34. As a Red Briefcase swallows the budget for the following year, it slowly lowers itself into the volume of the existing city. Hovering above, two arms hug the church. Eventually when the briefcase is full, the surplus food is spilled into the streets of the Square Mile.

35. The Bakers from the Ministry of Health are quick to realize that the Treasury is being generous. They load their wheelbarrows with the food.

36. Bakers out hunting for ingredients for their pies.

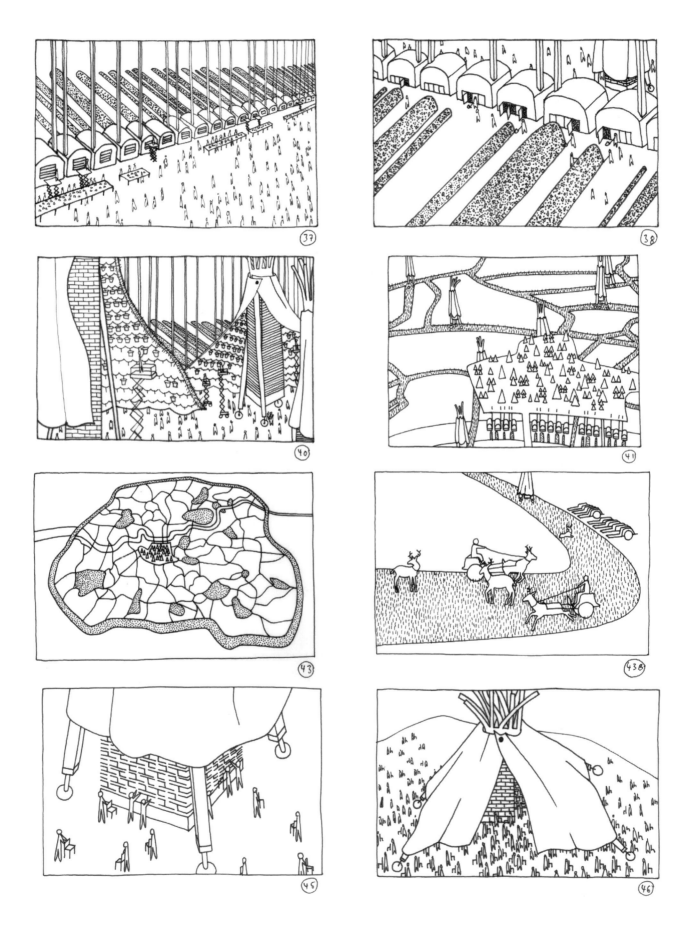

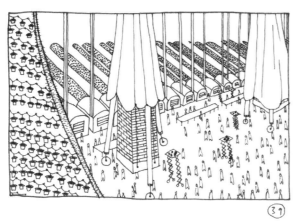

37. The Ministry of Health located at the edge of the Parliament. Health Ministers preparing pies on the mile-long table.

38. Ministers at work burning rubbish to power the huge pie-baking ovens. Rubbish piles stretch like a tail behind the pie-ovens and form an urban sized barcode indicating the pie-turnover of the Ministry of Health and thus the overall wellbeing of the Parliament.

39. Victoria Towers arrive to collect the baked pies for delivery to all.

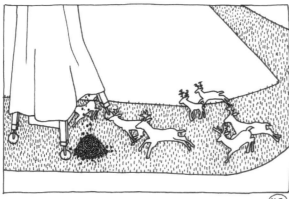

40. The cloak of the rook is being lined with thousands of pies.

41. Lined to the brim with pies, the Towers begin their journey into the depths of London.

42. Along the way they come across the deer that graze on the Regal Canopy.

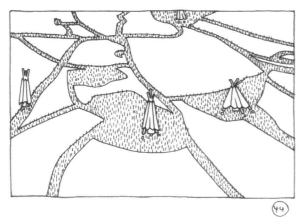

43. The Regal Canopy is a green grazing lace that stretches as far as the M25. This is the main transport route for Londoners. As hundreds of thousands of trained deer are grazing these streets, you only need to hook your carriage to one of them and it will take you anywhere. The rooks also travel on the Regal Canopy.

44. In time, the towers reach their destinations.

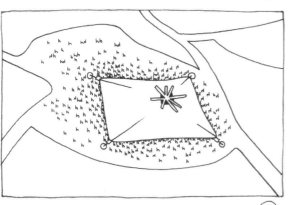

45. People stream into the parks for a communal pie-feast. The main structure of the rook is formed of layers upon layers of chairs. People help themselves to a chair by simply pulling it out of the chair-brick-wall.

46. As more and more people come, brick by brick is taken away and the rook shrinks.

47. Eventually, as all chairs are taken and spread around the park, the rook is no more than a canopy lined with tasty pies.

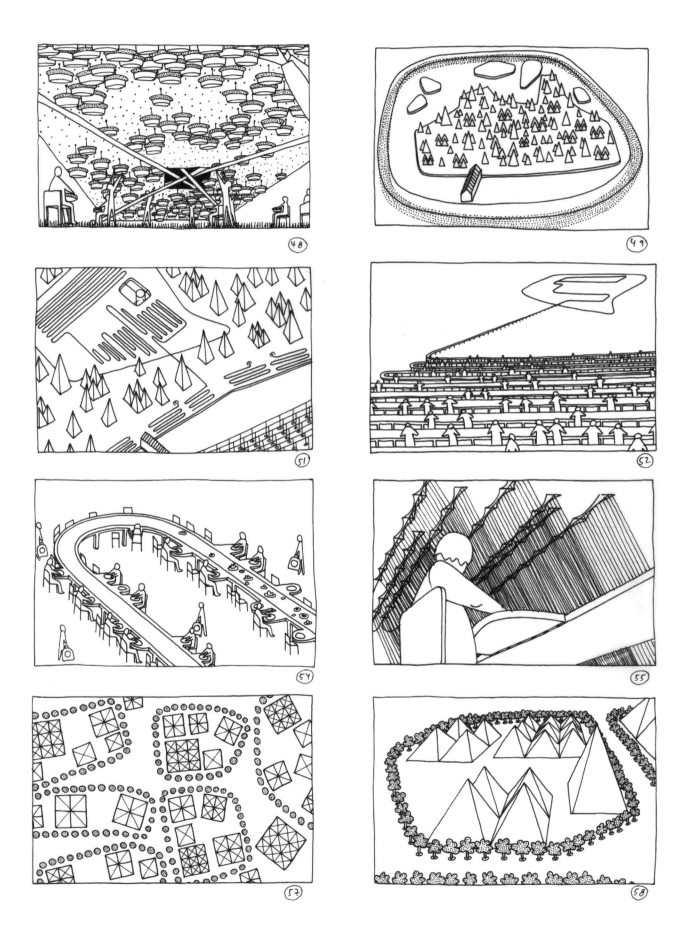

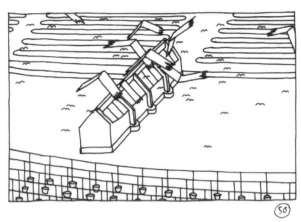

48. All help themselves to a pie – fish pie, chicken and mushroom pie, corned beef pie, cottage pie, pork pie, steak and kidney pie, bacon, egg pie, butter pie ... and venison ones.

49. Meanwhile back in the Parliament: Big Ben is bright red: a sign that election time is looming.

50. The Prime Minister is trying hard to keep the Parliament clean. Like giant eagles, his 23 Cabinet Ministers flutter and flap above the Westminster Hall trying to scare the pigeons away.

51. The Houses of Parliament are getting ready for the crucial debate.

52. The Lords are preparing meals for the MPs.

53. The House of Commons: in the foreground are the seats of the opposition parties fiercely attacking the seats of the government in the distance.

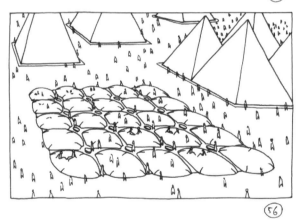

54. The MPs arrive, hook their dine-cases to the table and get ready for a heated dinner.

55. Mr Speaker is watching, thundering down on any misbehaving MPs.

56. In the meantime the people are picnicking on Woolsack, and debating how to cast the vote ...

57. ... while enjoying the new wealth of the city.

57. Admiring the lush agriculture.

58. Enjoying the new wealth of the city.

59. ... more to come.

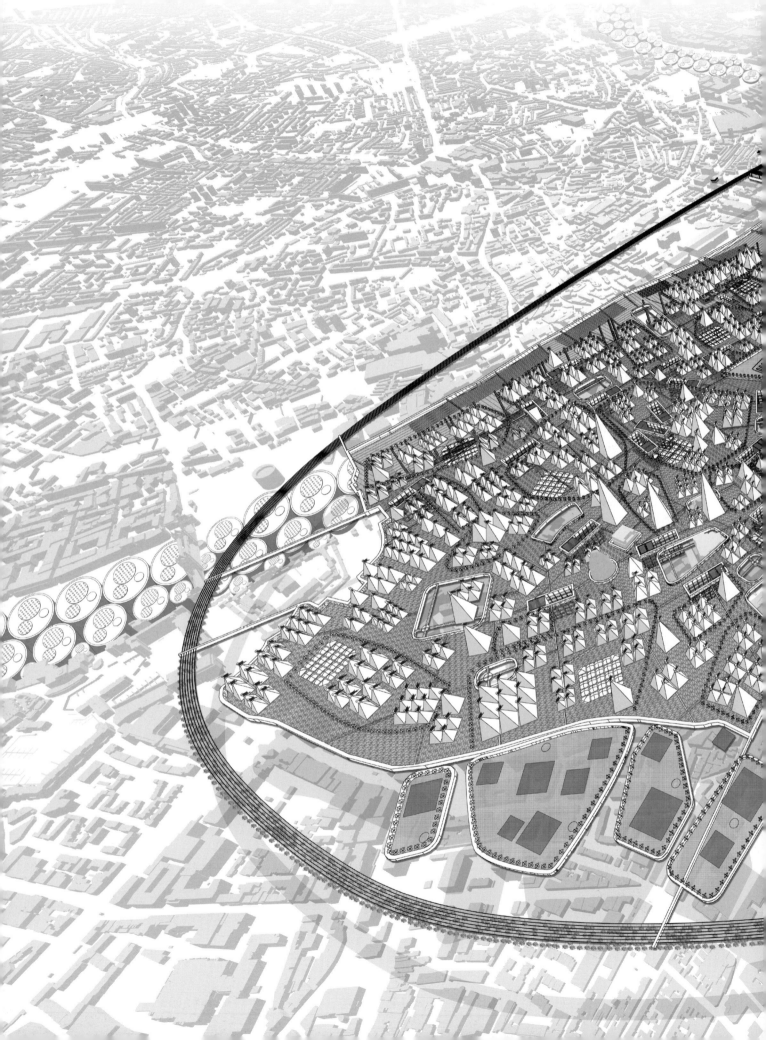

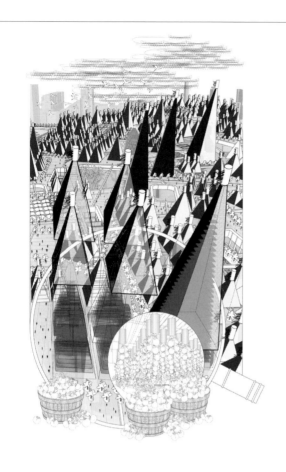

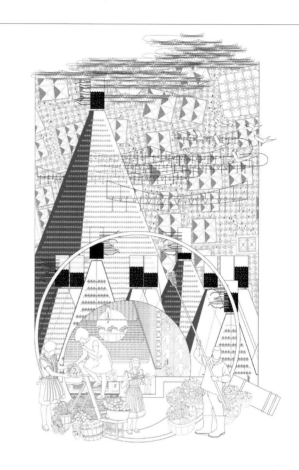

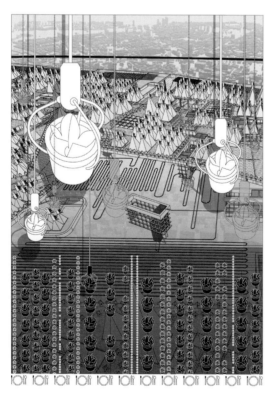

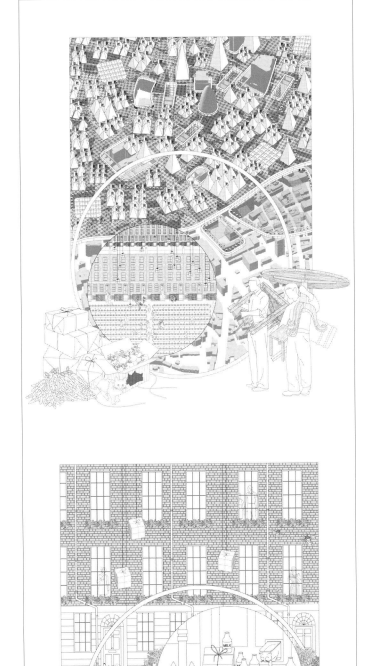

facing page left: Pledge 1 – The Food Parliament aims to promote the city as the world's leading international centre of excellence for food security.

facing page right: Pledge 2 – The Food Parliament aims to facilitate local communities and individuals in cultivation, processing and distribution of food within the city.

left: Pledge 3 – The Food Parliament aims to disseminate the new notion of wealth.

The Food Parliament – The redefinition and creation of new urban paraphernalia and allegories of sustainability for London:

– The Queen
– 10 Downing Street
– Westminster Hall
– The Blue Carpet
– The Victoria Towers
– The Department of Health
– The Lord Mayor
– Mr Speaker
– The Table of the House
– MPs
– The Regal Canopy
– Big Ben
– The Red Briefcase
– The Woolsack
– The Red Lines
– The Ministry of Defence
– The Parliament Library
– The Ministry of Transport

The Queen

'The Queen is the Head of State of the United Kingdom and oversees a further fifteen Commonwealth realms.'[1]

The constituents, in their entirety, comprise the head of the sovereign state of the Food Parliament. Power is fully devolved amongst the individual constituents, all employed in the pursuit of food sovereignty: cultivators, social workers, bakers, chefs, dieticians, scientists, laboratory assistants and food bankers. Shared responsibility and accountability underpins the society, empowering the population as a whole.

203

facing page: Street celebrations after the harvest across London.

left: From within the Gherkin, constituents celebrate the new urban wealth that takes into account food security, physical and social wellbeing, waste and energy management, and community empowerment.

1. Her Majesty the Queen [http://www.royal.gov.uk/HMTheQueen/HMTheQueen.aspx], retrieved 1 August 2013

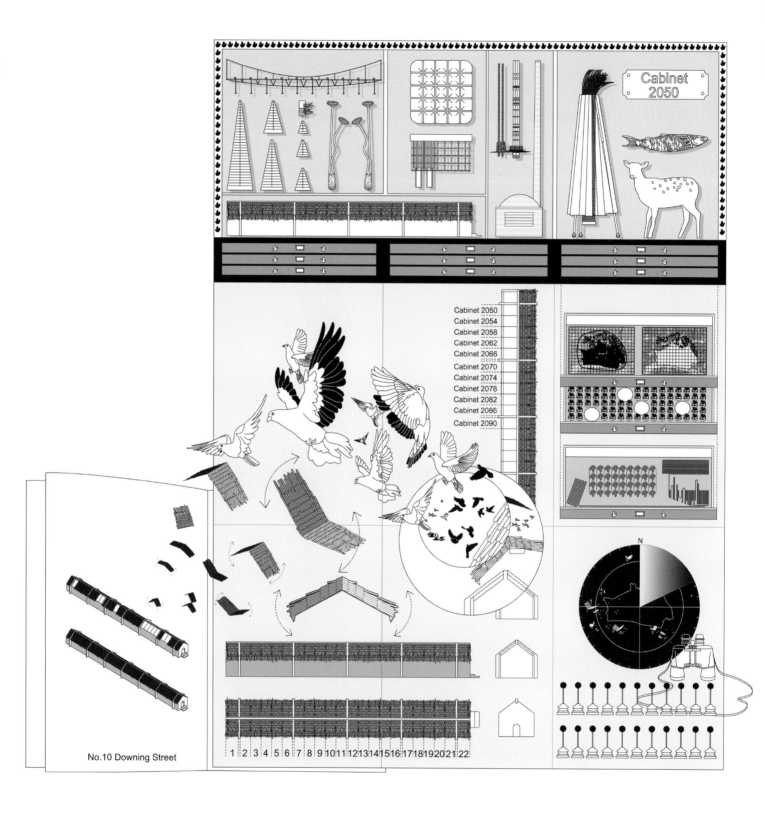

Cabinet 2050

Cabinet 2050
Cabinet 2054
Cabinet 2058
Cabinet 2062
Cabinet 2066
Cabinet 2070
Cabinet 2074
Cabinet 2078
Cabinet 2082
Cabinet 2086
Cabinet 2090

N

No.10 Downing Street

1 2 3 4 5 6 7 8 9 10 11 12 13 14 15 16 17 18 19 20 21 22

10 Downing Street

'Instantly recognisable around the world for its iconic black door on which sits two humble white numbers, 10 Downing Street is the official residence of the Prime Minister of the United Kingdom.'

The city's urban scarecrow, number 10 is presented as a vernacular structure branching 250m from the southern perimeter of Westminster Hall. A steeply pitched, couple roof reduces outward thrust and the risk of overturning. Roof rafters rest courtesy of birdsmouth joints over supporting wall plates. Timber roof boards span between the roof rafters and are clad with slate shingles. The roof is split into 23 sections – each performing the role of a Cabinet Minister of Parliament. Ministers can swiftly leap into action and take flight from the supporting wall plates to collectively watch over Parliamentary proceedings. Each rafter is hinged at the ridge board allowing the roof and shingles to flap and remain in flight. Their activity wards off controversial airborne activity that is in contempt of Parliament. Inside 10 Downing Street is the Parliamentary archive. Shelved cabinets, fronted with secure glazed doors, line the internal walls. Each shelf is stocked with a record of Parliamentary developments to protect and improve the public service of the office.

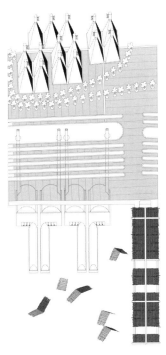

facing page: The Components Manual of 10 Downing Street.

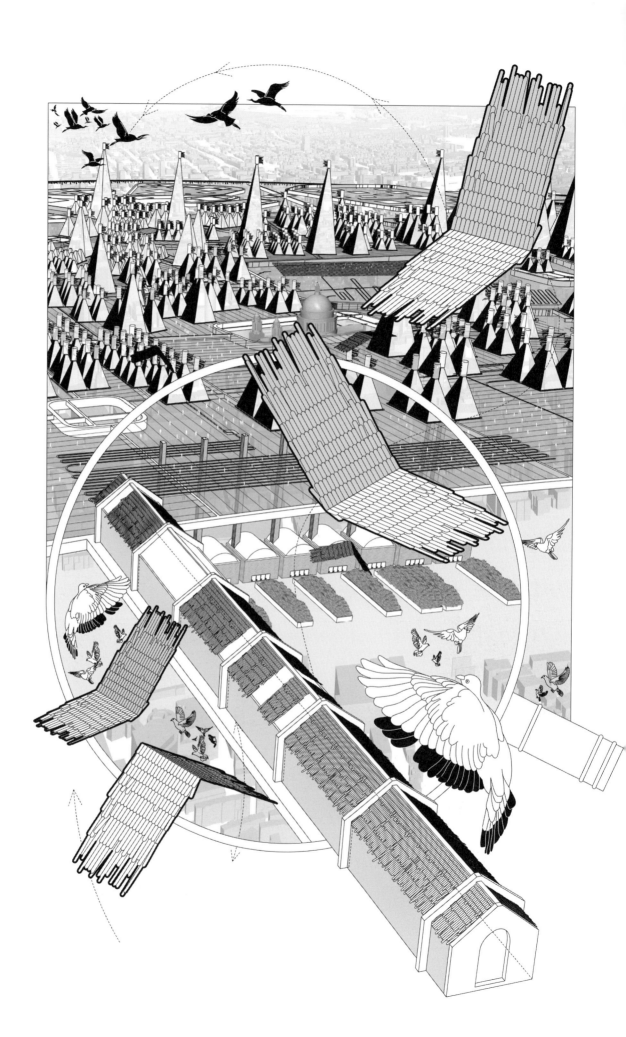

facing page: All 23 Cabinet
Members working together as urban
scarecrows, fighting off the persistent
flying rats!

left: A visit to the Parliamentary Food
Archive at 10 Downing Street to view
the Components Manual. In
the Manual (inspired by Erskine May's
'Parliamentary Practice'), the tectonic
analogs describe the protocols and
their daily functioning within the new
Food Parliament.

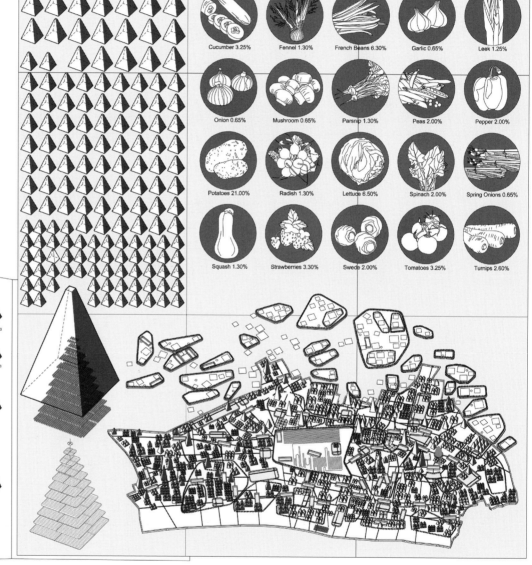

Asparagus 3.25% Beetroot 2.60% Broccoli 3.25% Brussels sprouts 3.25% Cabbage 8.10%

Carrot 6.50% Celery 1.30% Califlower 5.25% Corn 3.25% Courgette 2.00%

Cucumber 3.25% Fennel 1.30% French Beans 6.30% Garlic 0.65% Leek 1.25%

Onion 0.65% Mushroom 0.65% Parsnip 1.30% Peas 2.00% Pepper 2.00%

Potatoes 21.00% Radish 1.30% Lettuce 6.50% Spinach 2.00% Spring Onions 0.65%

Squash 1.30% Strawberries 3.30% Swede 2.00% Tomatoes 3.25% Turnips 2.60%

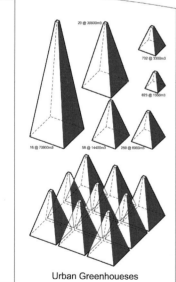

20 @ 30600m3
702 @ 3300m3
623 @ 1350m3
16 @ 70900m3
58 @ 14400m3
259 @ 6000m3

Urban Greenhoueses

Westminster Hall

'Westminster Hall is the oldest chamber of the British Parliamentary system. For over 900 years, the Hall has sheltered the growth of the United Kingdom's Parliamentary institutions, from the law courts, government offices and Parliament itself.'[2]

Westminster Hall is manifest as a 3.15km2 horizontal glass surface area over-laid onto the existing City of London. The glass surface area supports an armada of pyramidal glasshouse laboratories. The glasshouses propagate food for Parliament. Each party of glasshouses, parted by the 'red lines', propagate food voted for by the constituents and each individual glasshouse is a laboratory for organic food production. Vegetables are grown in a series of hydroponic cups positioned in an efficient stepped, pyramidal arrangement for improved sunlight access. Vegetable roots float in nutrient rich water to maximize yield per square metre. Westminster Hall is the largest and most technically advanced greenhouse in the world, providing year round nutritious produce with provenance. Anti-bandit, laminated float glass has been cut, drilled and edgeworked to construct apertures in the glass surface, naturally ventilating the streets below. The glass, certified fire resistant, complies with Smart Standards and building codes through intumescent layers applied during manufacture. A carpet of semi-opaque thin film photovoltaics finish the glass surface and harvest solar energy, contributing to the city's green national grid. The semi-opaque film is an effective environmental control feature, reducing the risk of excessive solar gain beneath Westminster Hall. Each horizontal panel of glass is fitted to a structurally rigid steel frame with a 1.5 degree minimum fall. The frame has a provision of movement joints to mitigate stress from environmental loads. Rainwater falls to oversized glass, gutter-like reservoirs around the perimeter of each pyramid glasshouse. The oversized gutters store rainwater to irrigate the crops grown in each glass pyramid. Laboratory assistants inside each glasshouse monitor growth and add organic nutrients to the rainwater. The nutrient rich water is then pumped to the hydroponic cups. To avoid the incidence of flooding or overloading, additional overflow gutters connect with downpipes to direct excess rainwater to a 'Blue Carpet'.

209

facing page: The Components Manual of the pyramidal greenhouses on Westminster Hall.

2. 'Westminster Hall' [http://www. Parliament.uk/about/living-heritage/ building/palace/westminsterhall/], retrieved 1 August 2013

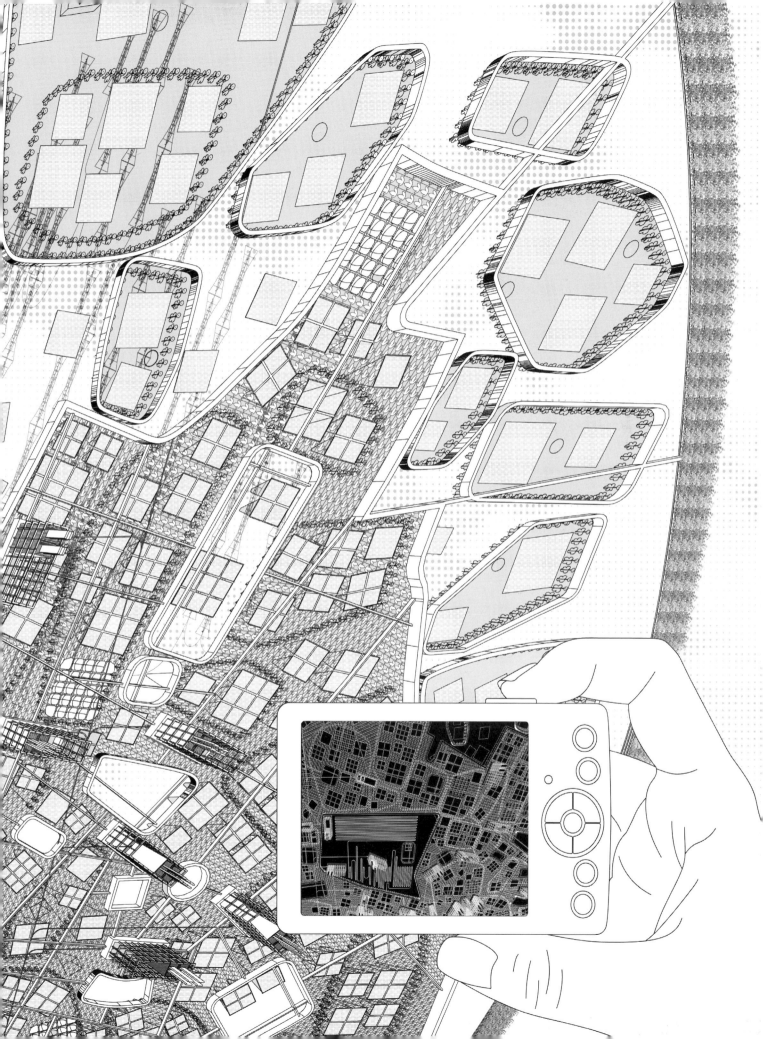

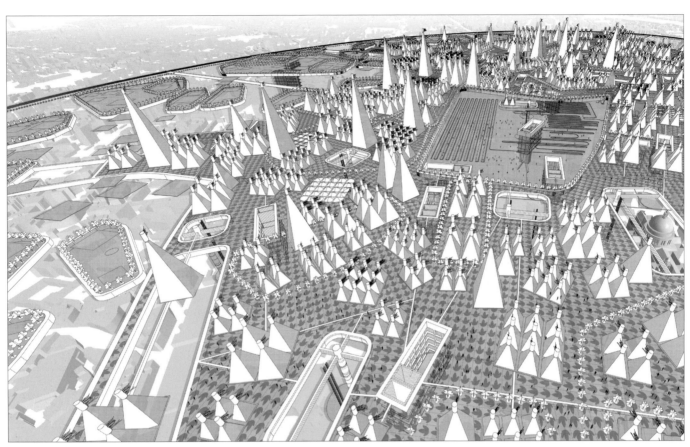

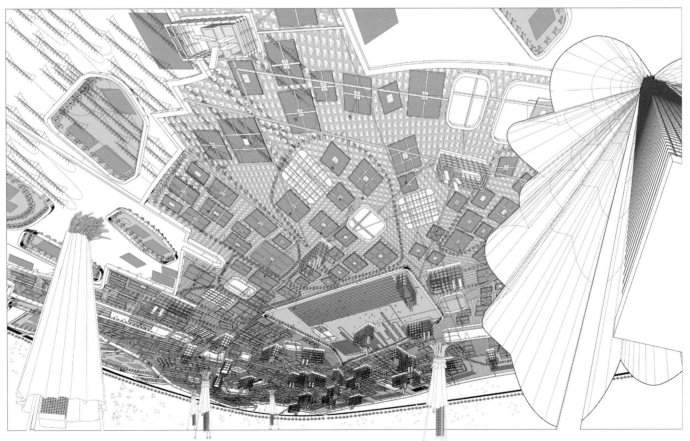

the food parliament

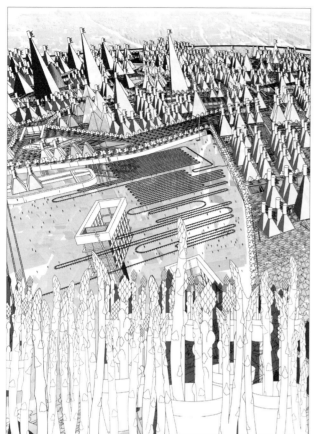

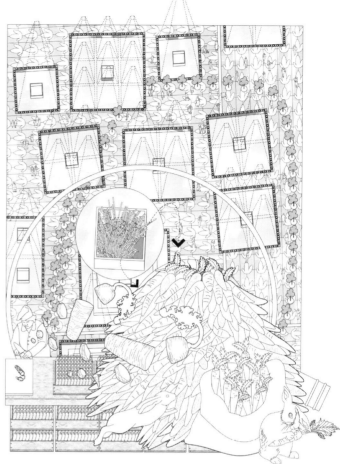

previous pages: Recording the new 'inhabitable' sky above London.

facing page top: The 3.15km2 Westminster Hall with an armada of pyramidal glasshouse laboratories over-laid onto London.

facing page bottom: Westminster Hall viewed from street level.

top left: The asparagus is ready to harvest before it becomes woody!

top right: Community kitchens prepare the 'food security and social wellbeing' pies for the Department of Health.

bottom: A great natural carbon absorber – the tomato greenhouses help lower the carbon content of London.

following pages: Vegetable yields from pyramidal glasshouse laboratories on Westminster Hall.

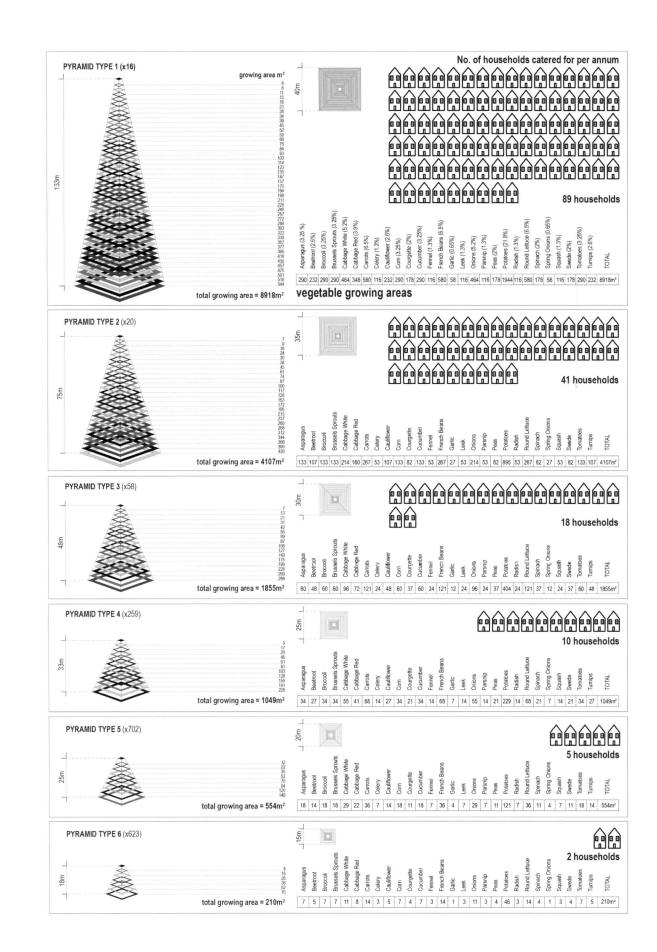

Example growing specifications and estimated yields per annum
(Yields are estimated from data obtained from 'The Ministry of Food' by Jane Fearnley-Whittingstall (Hodder & Stoughton, 2010) and are based on an allotment size of 2.4m x 4m)

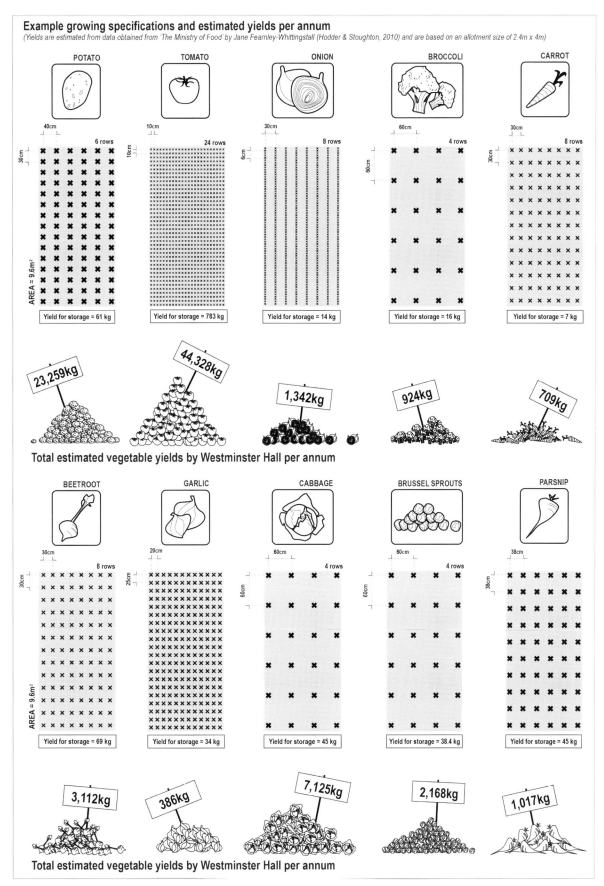

POTATO
40cm | 6 rows
30cm | AREA = 9.6m²
Yield for storage = 61 kg

TOMATO
10cm | 24 rows
10cm
Yield for storage = 783 kg

ONION
30cm | 8 rows
6cm
Yield for storage = 14 kg

BROCCOLI
60cm | 4 rows
60cm
Yield for storage = 16 kg

CARROT
30cm | 8 rows
30cm
Yield for storage = 7 kg

23,259kg

44,328kg

1,342kg

924kg

709kg

Total estimated vegetable yields by Westminster Hall per annum

BEETROOT
30cm | 8 rows
30cm | AREA = 9.6m²
Yield for storage = 69 kg

GARLIC
20cm
25cm
Yield for storage = 34 kg

CABBAGE
60cm | 4 rows
60cm
Yield for storage = 45 kg

BRUSSEL SPROUTS
60cm | 4 rows
60cm
Yield for storage = 38.4 kg

PARSNIP
38cm
38cm
Yield for storage = 45 kg

3,112kg

386kg

7,125kg

2,168kg

1,017kg

Total estimated vegetable yields by Westminster Hall per annum

217

218

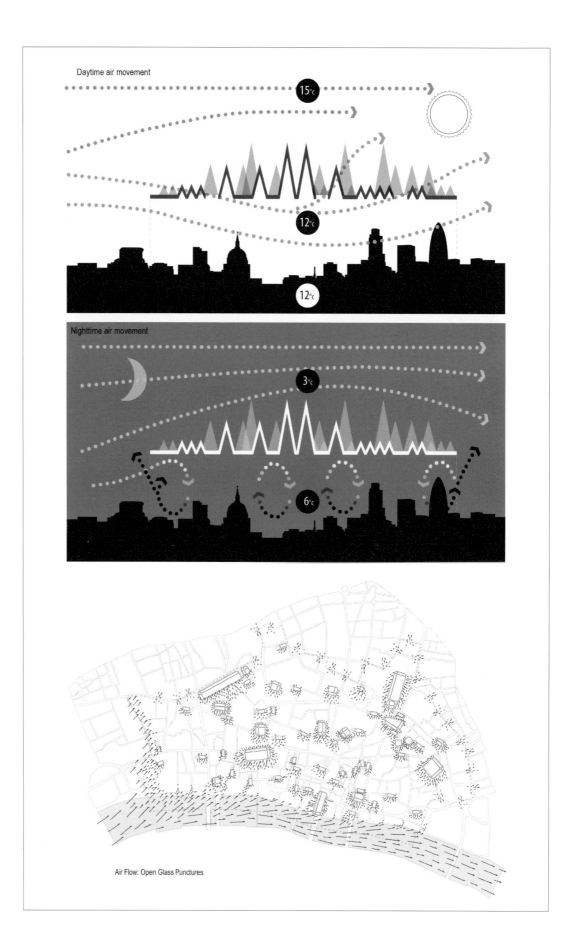

Daytime air movement

15°c

12°c

12°c

Nighttime air movement

3°c

6°c

Air Flow: Open Glass Punctures

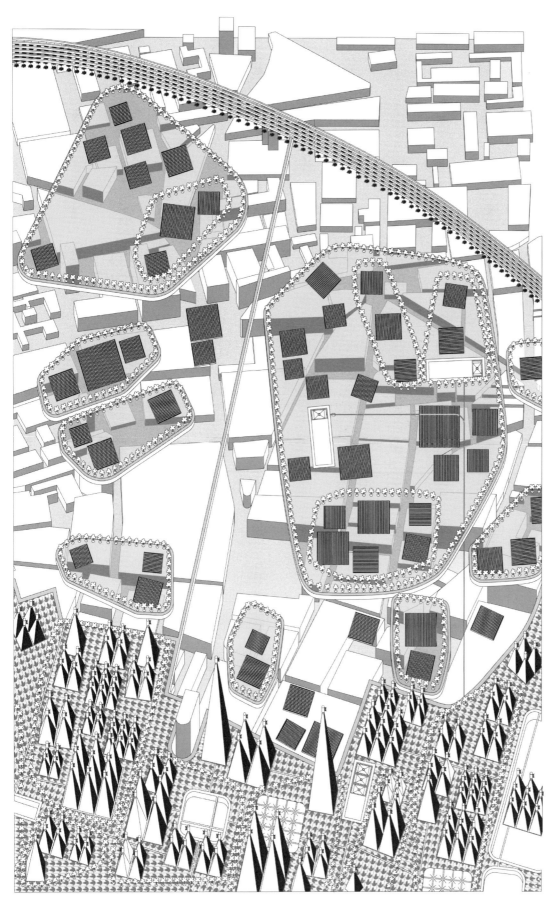

facing page: Natural Ventilation and Air Permeability. Westminster Hall plays a major role in maintaining acceptable thermal comfort and improving energy performance. The adjustable openings control flow rates which tweak the city's core temperature. Prevailing winds are guided around and over the Parliament's structure, trapping air beneath it. At a localized scale, convection occurs naturally, creating sufficient air changes.

left: Light and Solar Shading. Using seasonal vegetation as a solar shade allows the plants to naturally develop leaves in the summer to provide shade whilst shedding leaves in winter for maximum light transmission. Furthermore, the vegetation can filter air pollutants, mask noise and have a calming psychological effect.

Semi-translucent solar cells on the surface of Westminster Hall help reduce the daylight factor in summer conditions. During winter, the cells rotate a few millimetres, acting as louvres, positioning themselves to reduce shading. Energy harvested from the solar cells is stored in the Lord Mayor, similar to car batteries which store and release energy on demand. In winter, the artificial lights mounted on the underside of Westminster Hall illuminate the city from above; thousands of light pixels form the newly lit sky.

The Blue Carpet

'On the State Opening of Parliament, a blue carpet is rolled out in the Royal Gallery. At every opening, the Yeomen of the Guard flank its sides.'[3]

The 'Blue Carpet' is no longer reserved for the State Opening of Parliament, and instead performs year round as the fisheries of the Food Parliament. Fishponds are positioned atop the flat roofs of London's existing building stock beneath Westminster Hall. A series of steel footings span and reinforce existing roof decks to underpin the additional considerable load. Open top, toughened glass containers rest on the supporting footings and are filled with rainwater collected from the surface of Westminster Hall. Rooftop aquaculture acts as a superimposed asset to the environmental responsibility of existing building stock. The insulating body of water mediates the internal building temperature. Westminster Hall's semi-opaque glass panels protect the ponds from direct sunlight and temperature fluctuations. The 'Blue Carpet' is rolled out across the skyline, bearing a wetland wildlife habitat for the City of London. An alternative community of Yeomen, constituent anglers are free to line the aperture perimeters of Westminster Hall and send their lines down, catching fish fresh from its source as a healthy alternative to red meat.

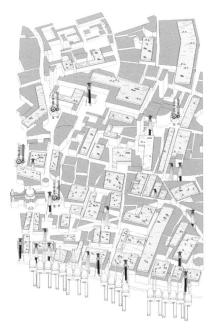

facing page: The Blue Carpet on the roofs of existing buildings in London.

following pages: Fishing on the Blue Carpet – fish & chips for dinner!

3. 'The Houses of Parliament Tour – 2006' [http://golondon.about.com/od/augustannualevents/fr/parliamreview.html], retrieved 1 August 2013

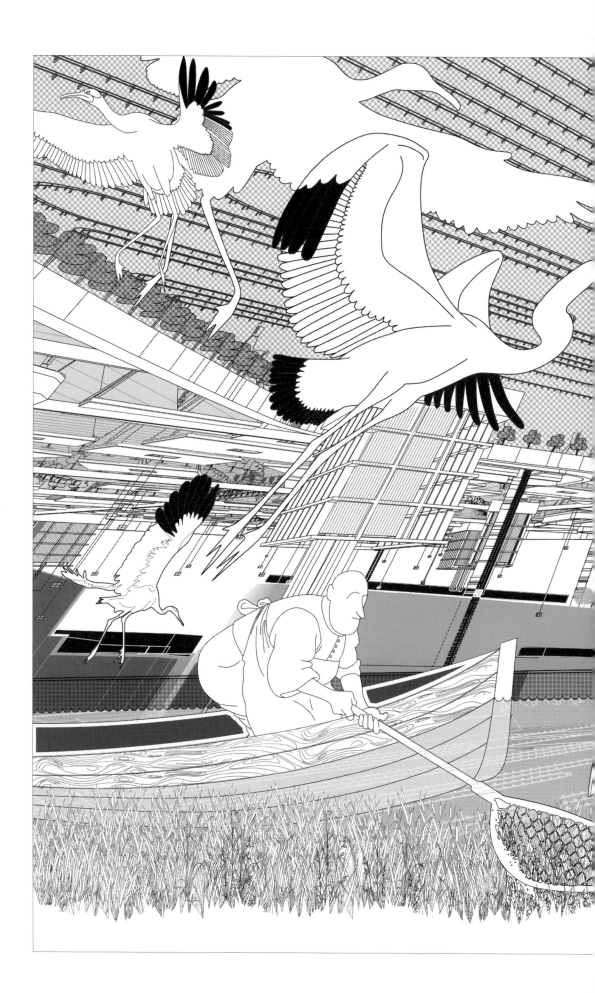

224

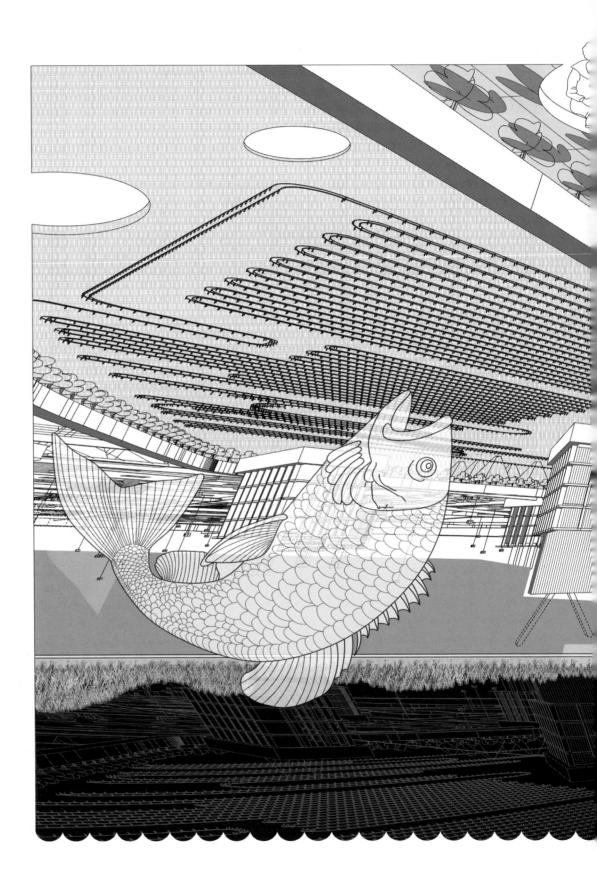

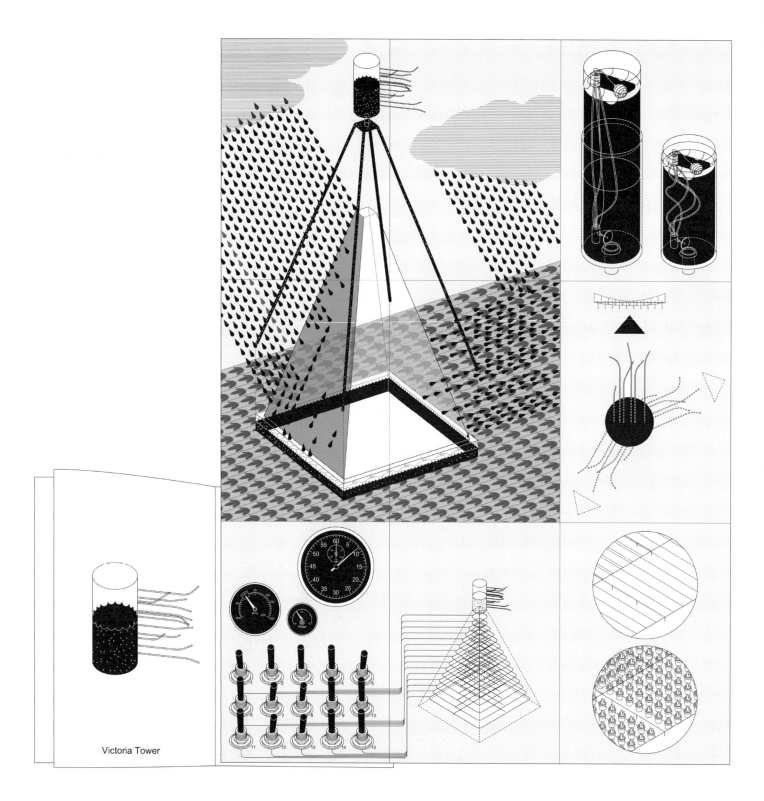

Victoria Tower

The Victoria Towers

'The Victoria Tower is the tallest tower of the Palace of Westminster. Named after Queen Victoria, it reigned as the tallest stone tower in the world for many years at 98.5m high.'[4]

The Victoria Towers are the highest fixed points of Parliament atop each glasshouse pyramid of Westminster Hall. Each cylindrical tank stores and recycles the rainwater collected on the surface of Westminster Hall. The collected water is used to irrigate plants propagated in the glasshouse laboratories. The Victoria Towers are equipped with apparatus to fill and flush rainwater from the cylindrical tanks. A series of flush levers allow a laboratory assistant to selectively irrigate individual storeys of vegetables in a single glasshouse. When a flush lever is plunged, the irrigation valve is pulled up, exposing an opening at the base of the Victoria Tower. Water is immediately discharged with gravitational force to irrigate growing vegetables. The weight of the water lowers a float arm that in turn opens a fill valve. Rainwater collected on the surface of Westminster Hall is temporarily stored in a gutter-like reservoir that follows the perimeter of each pyramid. Thus, the Victoria Towers are refilled ready to provide the plants with more water when needed.

227

facing page: The Components Manual of the Victoria Towers.

left: The rainwater irrigation system uses natural water to feed crops at little cost. By using rainwater, energy-expensive potable water is retained for more appropriate uses. Each of the pyramidal greenhouses collects rainwater runoff from its pitched glass surfaces. The water is pumped into the Victoria Tower where it will be used for irrigation. Electronically timed valves control the watering of the crops.

4. 'The Victoria Tower' [http://www.Parliament.uk/about/living-heritage/building/palace/architecture/palacestructure/victoria-tower/], retrieved 1 August 2013

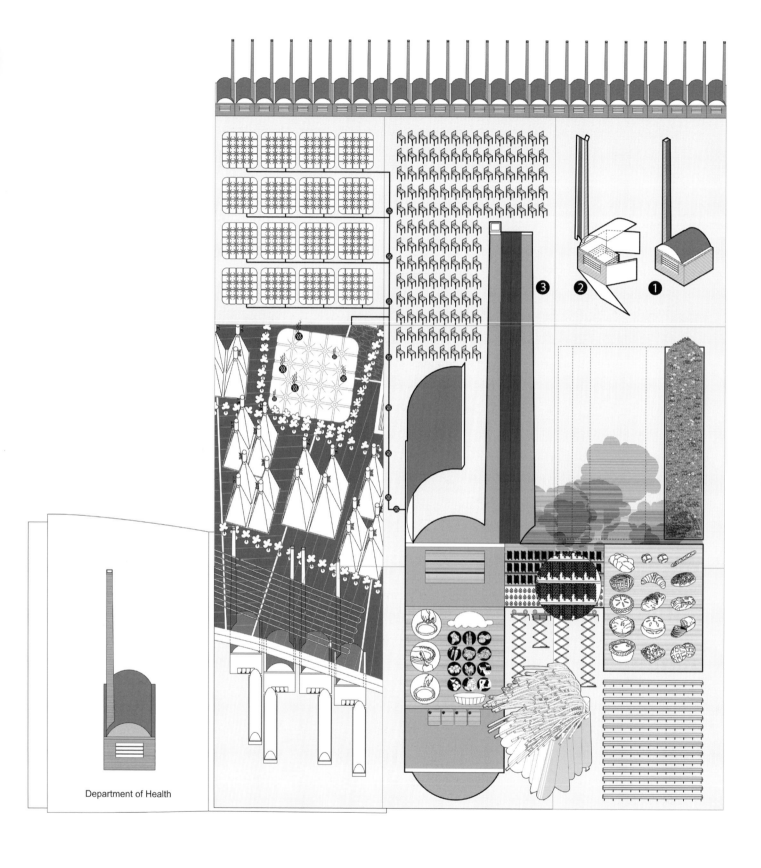

Department of Health

The Department of Health

'The Department of Health is responsible for funding, shaping and ensuring the functioning of the health care system. The Department is tasked with ensuring the health, wellbeing and longevity of each citizen.'[5]

The Department of Health's 'Nutritional Health Service', the urban bakeries, line the bank of the river Thames, along the southern perimeter of Westminster Hall. The bakeries produce and bake the hot and nutritious 'Victory Pies' shortly before election rallies. Each bakery is a rectilinear, masonry structure, 15m high x 35m deep x 25m wide. One-and-half red brick walls in English bond support a vaulted brick roof. An internal arrangement of timber preparation tables and benches are manned by Parliament's dieticians. The bakeries benefit from timber's natural properties of a surface of microcavities and roughness that are not conducive to the growth of bacteria. Each table and bench is spaced to allow two pie trolleys to pass side by side. Once a trolley is fully laden with pies, the dieticians ferry it to the oven at the far end of the bakery. The pies are transferred to the pie rack and baked to perfection. The bakery oven acts as a chimneybreast and gathers at the ceiling vault. The flue, constructed from a red brick chimneystack, is stacked 105m high and protrudes above the glass floor of Westminster Hall through designated openings. As the pies bake, smoke billows from the tapered pots to signal the coming of an election rally, and simultaneously inflates the Woolsack, providing a thermally comfortable environment for meetings.

231

facing page: The Components Manual of the Department of Health.

left: Heated Air Transfer System. A network of insulated pipes integrated within the Food Parliament's structural glazing grid links the Woolsacks to the collection of bakeries. Heated air generated within the billowing chimneys is channelled into the goose-feather-insulated Woolsack where several outlets disperse the warm air. This mechanism is only employed during the winter.

Warming Winter Woolsacks

5. 'The Department of Health' [https://www.gov.uk/government/organisations/department-of-health/about], retrieved 1 August 2013

facing page top: MPs coordinate the daily fresh pies from the Department of Health.

facing page bottom: Constituents contribute their time to prepare local produce delivered from the laboratories of Westminster Hall to the Department of Health on a conveyor belt.

left: The Department of Health's Nutritional Health Service baking for a healthier London.

facing page: The heat from baking keeps the Woolsacks nice and warm throughout winter.

left: Pies are carefully hung on the underside of the MPs' white coats, before they travel out to their nutritional campaigns in public parks.

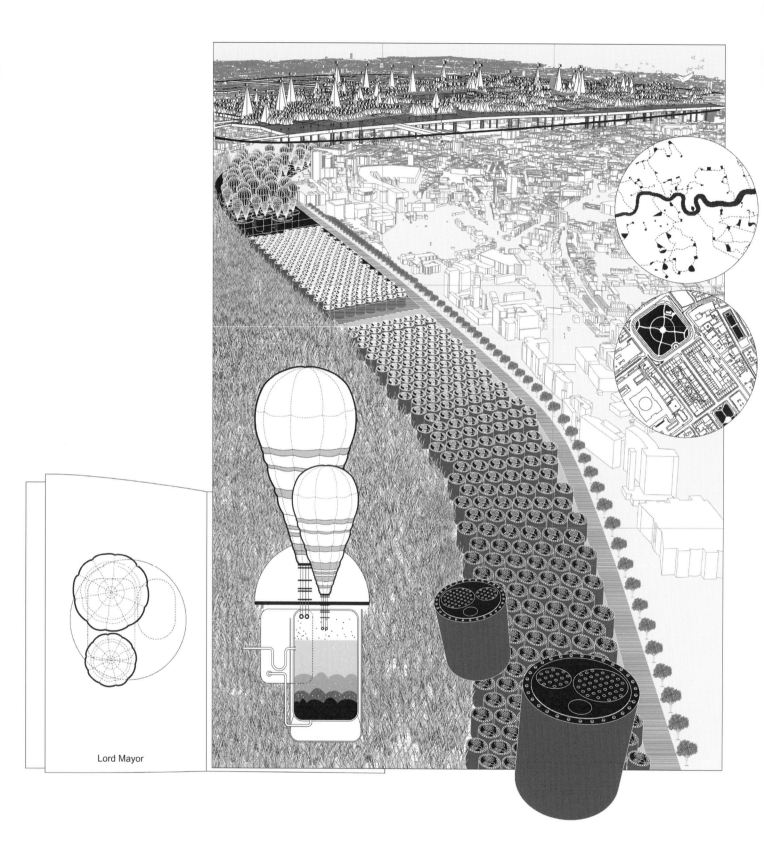

Lord Mayor

The Lord Mayor

'The Lord Mayor is the highest authority within the City of London, overseeing local, policing and other services. In the Square Mile, only the Queen takes precedence.'[6]

London's Lord Mayor assumes the role of the Right Honourable Champion of green energy and commerce development. The Lord Mayor is manifest in the city as a white 'pixel' river of anaerobic digesters. From above, each digester appears as a white-pixel; a trading floor of green energy along the River Thames. The trading floor exchanges organic waste for biogas, compost and water that supply Parliament's green national grid. Constituents freely trade their own organic waste for compost on the trading floor to fertilize their vegetable plots. Below each white-pixel lid is a composting container. Aerobic digestion ferments organic food waste, yielding biogas to meet Parliament's energy demands. Methane is directed to Big Ben and the local Woolsacks to maintain their buoyancy. Excess contaminated water discharge from composting is directed to the squares of London – the reed beds of Parliament. Contaminated water is filtered to be recycled for sanitary distribution.

237

facing page: The Components Manual of the Lord Mayor.

left: Biogas Production and Usage. Fuel: Urban kitchens at the base perimeter of the pyramidal greenhouses source their gas from the methane balloons. Stoves and ovens are piped through from a pressurized methane distributer to ensure a steady supply.

Light: Within the pyramidal greenhouses, a secondary pipe system is laid alongside the irrigation network. These pipes feed methane to lamps which burn at a low rate, providing localized lighting and warmth for plants during winter months. As the greenhouses are situated above the glass plate of Westminster Hall, the city beneath benefits from the extra lighting. The methane powered lamps provide a longer day in winter to encourage a larger crop yield.

Buoyancy: As a lighter-than-air gas, methane can assist in keeping Big Ben afloat. Through each of Big Ben's hour arms, the gas is piped into air-tight ballonets which surround the Food Parliament. From these ballonets, flowers overflow their hanging baskets, their colours indicating a month. Methane's buoyancy is affected by local temperatures, causing Big Ben to lower when it is cold, and rise when warmer – this serves as a secondary visual environmental indicator.

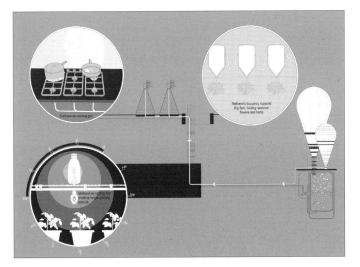

6. 'The Lord Mayor' [http://www.cityoflondon.gov.uk/about-the-city/who-we-are/key-members/the-lord-mayor-of-the-city-of-london/Pages/default.aspx], retrieved 1 August 2013

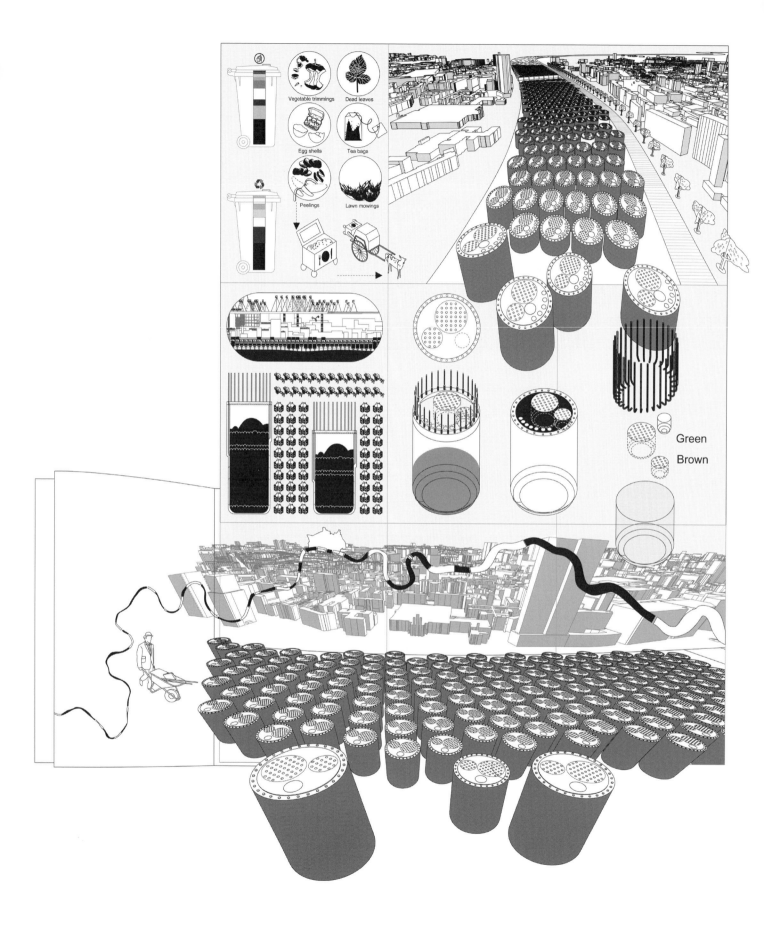

Vegetable trimmings   Dead leaves

Egg shells   Tea bags

Peelings   Lawn mowings

Green

Brown

Interseasonal Heat Storage: Thermal Collectors

Interseasonal Heat Storage: Thermal Bank

facing page: The Components Manual of the Composter.

left top + bottom: Inter-seasonal Heating Systems – ICAX. Heat accumulated in the pyramidal greenhouses (thermal collectors) is pumped through insulated pipes into the thermal banks system located at the river bed of the Lord Mayor. Developed by ICAX, the thermal banks, made of large volumes of earth, are used to store collected heat over many months; unlike a traditional heat store which maintains a high temperature for a short time. The system exploits the thermal inertia to input surplus heat into the ground over the summer and extract that heat in the winter months for the heating of buildings.

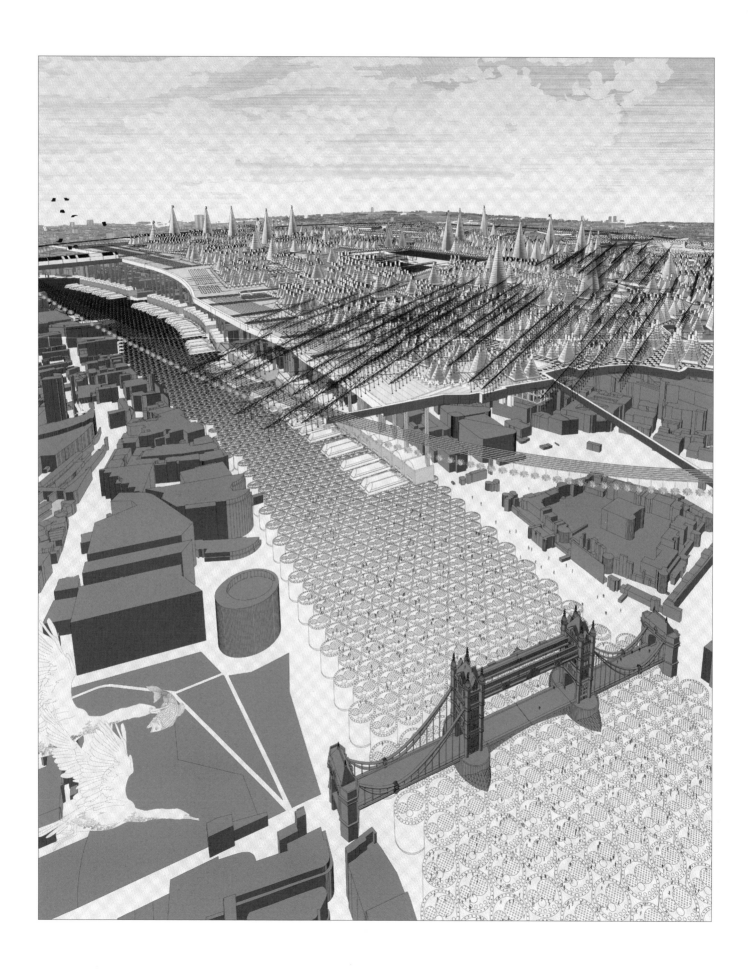

Pipes transport summer
greenhouse warmth to thermal
banks

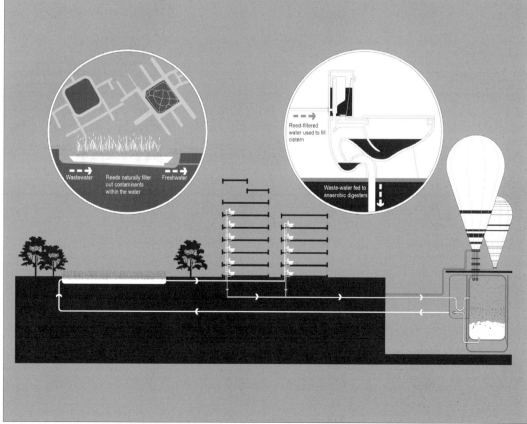

Reed-filtered
water used to fill
cistern

Wastewater Reeds naturally filter Freshwater
out contaminants
within the water

Waste-water fed to
anaerobic digesters

facing page: Anaerobic digesters and composters flood the River Thames, stitching north and south London together, while providing easy access and energy transparency for London.

left top: Inter-seasonal Heating Systems – ICAX. At the base of the Thames River, approximately 7m below ground, the temperature will be close to 10°C, varying very little between summer and winter. Combined with the slow transfer of heat through the earth, these stable conditions make heat storage ideal. The greenhouses transfer their heat through an array of pipes filled with fluid to the Lord Mayor.

left bottom: Greywater System. The combined technologies of rainwater harvesting and reed bed filtered water offers a low long-term cost of delivering greywater. With inputs such as sewage and household waste, part of the anaerobic digestion has a sludge-like output known as digestate. The pumpable material is separated into liquid and fibrous states, each producing products of different qualities. The liquid digestate is pumped to London squares; the waste water moving slowly through the mass of reed roots can be successfully treated.

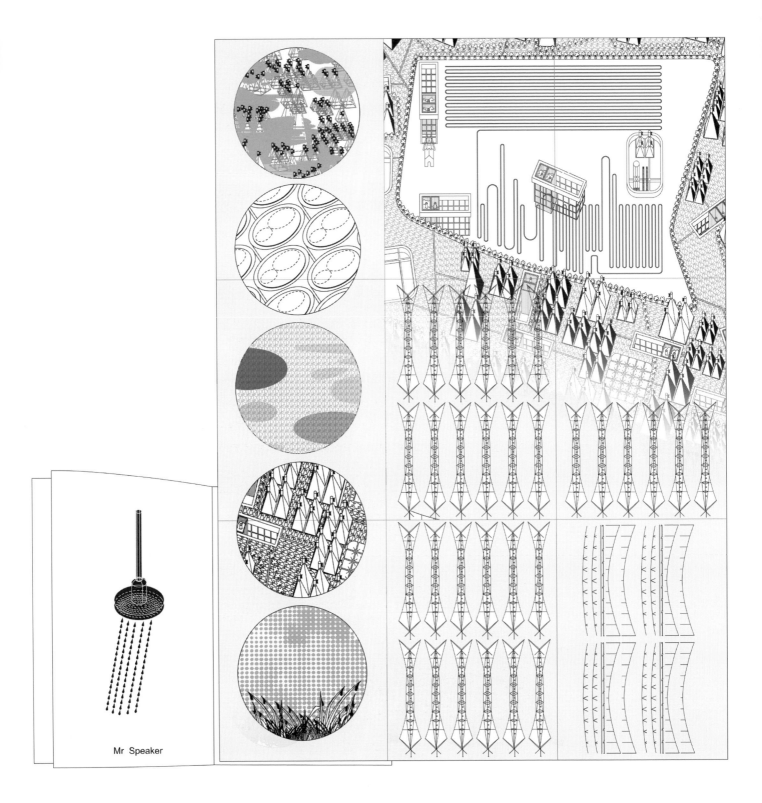

Mr Speaker

Mr Speaker

'The Speaker is the chief officer and highest authority of the House of Commons and must remain politically impartial at all times. During debates, the Speaker keeps order and calls MPs to speak.'[7]

The Speaker is manifest in the form of a 'temperamental cloud'. The cloud is constructed from a modular system of irrigation pipes and sprinkler heads. At dawn, Mr Speaker drifts to the green parks of his surrounding constituencies harvesting the morning dew, buoyed by the harvested methane. Atmospheric water extractors draw water from the surroundings by cooling air below its dew point and pressurizing the collected gas. Air is passed through the cloud to a cooled coil which condenses atmospheric water molecules causing them to condense. A compressor circulates refrigerant around the coil to keep it cool. Mr Speaker returns to Parliament with a store of water in multiple holding tanks. Order is restored over any unscrupulous dealings in the form of inclement weather. A series of sprinkler heads in the cloud wash away any sight of filth and maintain the uncompromisingly 'purer than pure' appearance of Westminster Hall.

243

facing page: The Components Manual of Mr Speaker.

left: Mr Speaker drifting calmly, keeping order over Parliament and the city.

following page left: In the early hours every morning, Mr Speaker visits parks and gardens to harvest morning dew.

following page right: On a hot summer day, one may find London completely submerged in a giant cloud of fine water droplets. Mr Speaker aims to provide all the necessary moisture required by the plants in the Parliament.

7. 'Mr Speaker' [http://www.parliament.uk/about/living-heritage/evolutionofparliament/parliamentwork/offices-and-ceremonies/overview/the-speaker/], retrieved 1 August 2013

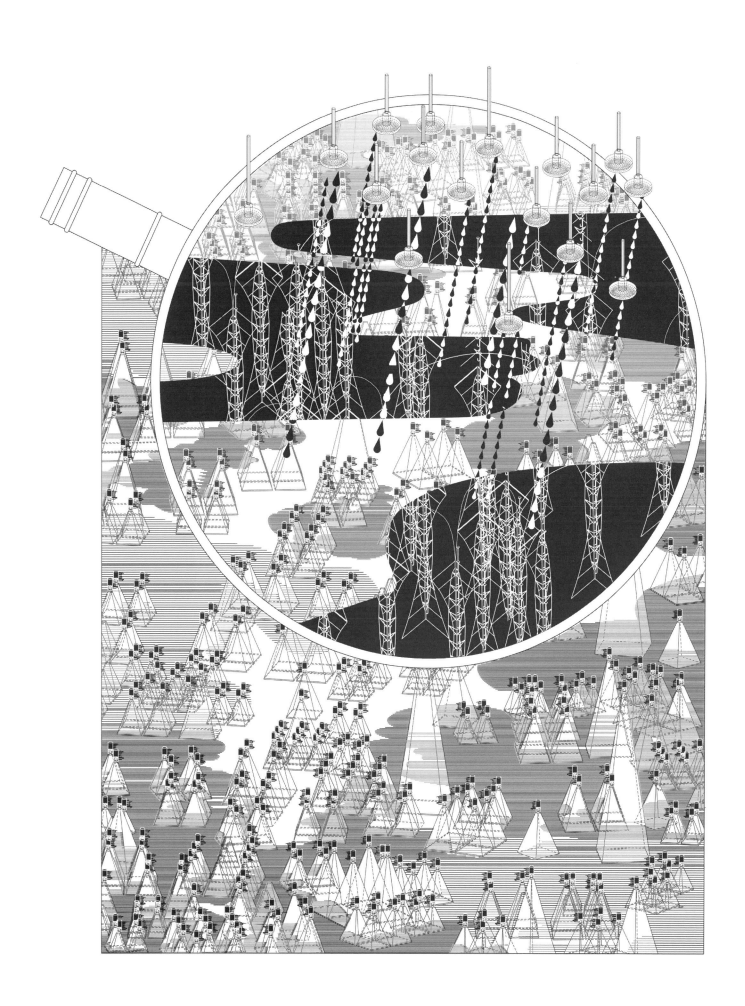

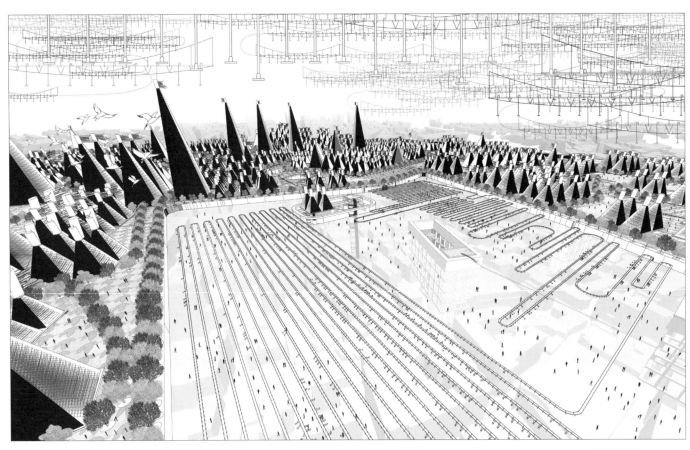
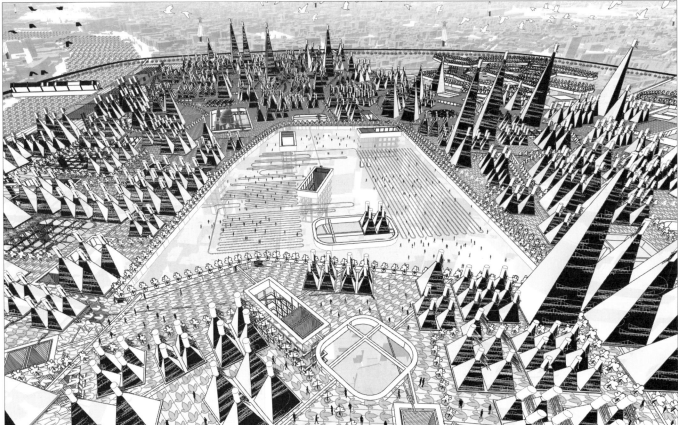

The Table of the House

'In each of the legislative chambers, a table sits between the front benches of the Government and the Opposition. The table is an administrative platform used by the Clerks to organise proceedings in the House.'[8]

The Table of the House acts as an altar for the city. The Table, an urban scale conveyor belt, simultaneously invites the hungry to dinner and Parliamentary debate. The conveyor belt navigates the House of Commons. Each politician is duty bound to arrive at the table equipped with a briefcase containing a dinner plate and cutlery, ready to deliberate matters of gastronomic importance. Whilst the conveyor is in motion, meals are distributed to the gathered mouths, delivered fresh from the House of Lords. The Table operates on a 'have your fill and have your say' policy and politicians are thus embedded in a position of active engagement with the core matter of the Parliament.

249

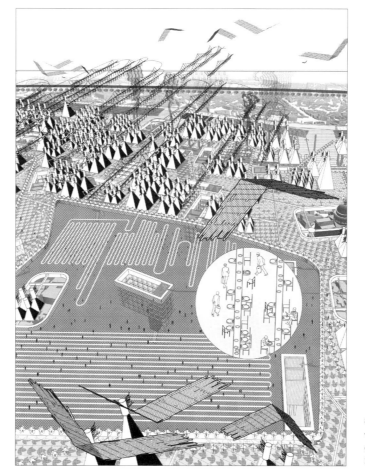

facing page top: Eat, drink and debate for Parliamentary members and citizens.

facing page bottom: The Table of the House holds court at Parliament.

left: The Speaker of the House of Commons chairs debates in the Commons chamber.

8. 'The Table of the House' [http://www.Parliament.uk/site-information/glossary/table/], retrieved 1 August 2013

MPs

Members of Parliament (MPs)

'In the United Kingdom, eligible voters elect Members of Parliament (MPs) as representatives of their views and interests in the House of Commons. MPs are responsible for upholding the concerns of their constituents in the formation and tabling of legislation and debate on current issues.'[9]

The MPs are crusaders of the Food Parliament in the form of travelling banquets that accompany the pre election rallies in local constituencies. The MP's take the form of towers that stand 100m tall. The MPs bare all as volunteers mount platform lifts to reach inside their giant Thermawrap cloaks and maintain a suspended stock of fresh, hot 'Victory Pies' from the Department of Health; each pie packed with the wealth of Parliament and its nutritional goodness. A 'toupee' of giant rubber 'hairs' is fitted atop each MP. The 'toupee' buffs against the glazed underside of Westminster Hall as the MP circulates, cleaning and polishing the semi opaque glass to maximize daylight penetration. Stocked with 'Victory Pies', MPs are towed out to the corner of each constituency's green park by a drove of wild deer on loan from the Ministry of Transport. A wheel fitted beneath each timber leg permits steady manoeuvres. At the park corner, the MP's timber legs, fixed by an apex hinge under the toupee, roll outward, cascading the structure towards the ground. The Thermawrap cloak drapes over the structure, constructing a temporary marquee that acts as a 'community house' for the local and accountable provision of democracy. Hot 'Victory Pies' dangle from the canopy for local constituents to pluck within arms reach. Chairs are dispensed from the central stack and demarcate a permeable territory. Local constituents are invited to join their MP and have their say at these gastronomic pre-election rallies. Each MP thus acts as a deployable site for instant consultation and deliberation directly with constituents. Each 'Victory Pie' thus acts as a vehicle facilitating the education, nutrition, food sovereignty and social wellbeing of the city's constituents.

left: The Components Manual of the MPs.

9. 'MPs' [http://www.Parliament. uk/mps-lords-and-offices/mps/], retrieved 1 August 2013

facing page: On Sundays, MPs join the
public at Speaker's Corner.

left: As the MPs circulate, their
'toupees' buff the underside of
Westminster Hall, cleaning and
ensuring complete 'transparency'
within Parliament.

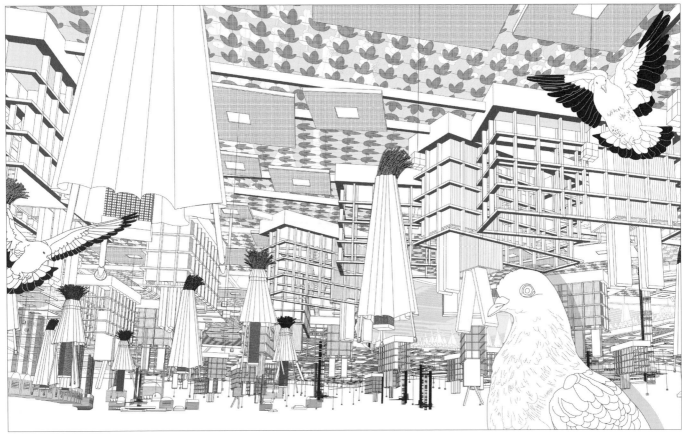

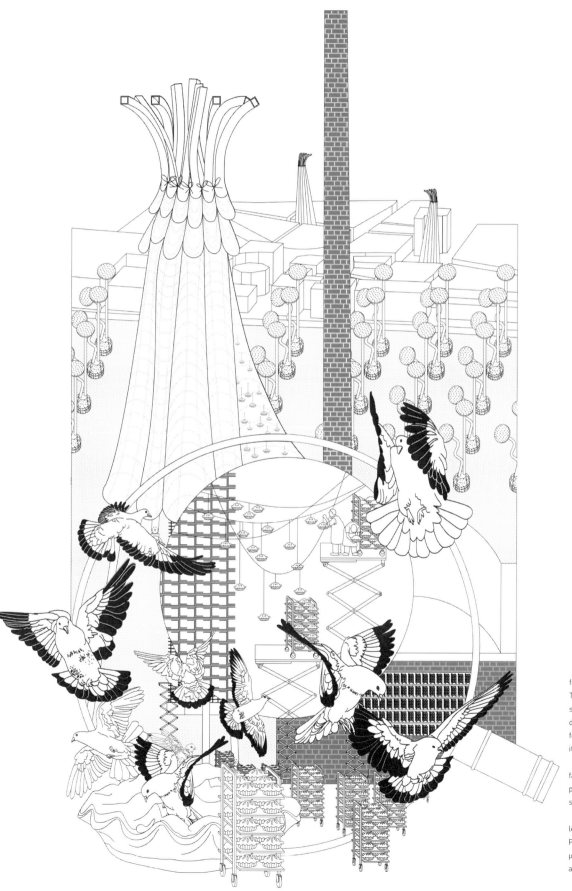

facing page top: Similar to the Trojan Horse, each MP conceals the structure of a pigeon tower. Pigeon droppings are valuable organic fertilizer for the Food Parliament and its constituents.

facing page bottom: The London pigeons are getting curious about the sudden abundance of food.

left: MPs disseminate hot 'Victory Pies' from the Department of Health, packed with the wealth of Parliament and its nutritional goodness.

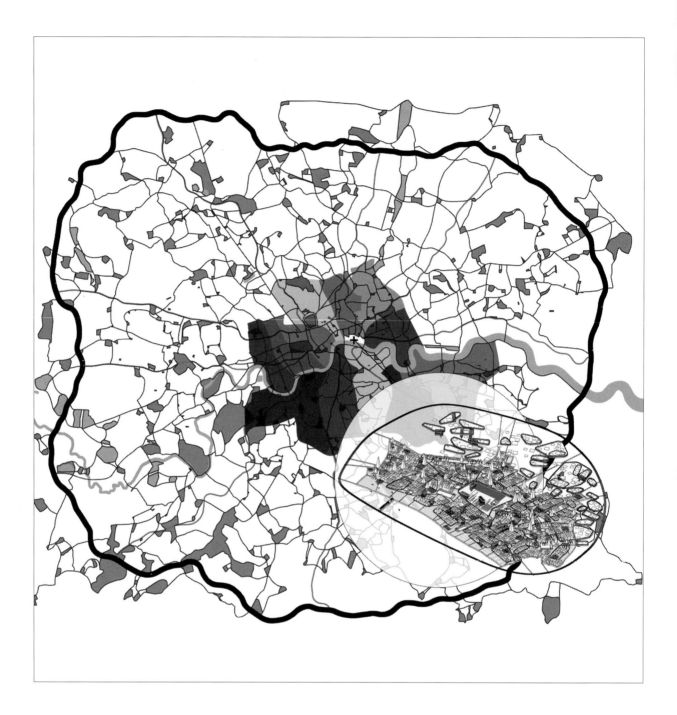

The Regal Canopy

'Each November when the Queen opens Parliament, she sits under a canopy in the House of Lords known as the Regal Canopy. From this position, she outlines "Her Government's" plans for the coming parliamentary year.'[10]

The Queen's opening of Parliament marks the beginning of harvest season at the onset of autumn in the city. Orchard avenues that overgrow the routes of a bygone transportation network, the M25, turn golden yellow in November, forming a temporary regal canopy. Each avenue welcomes the Parliamentary procession and becomes host to harvest festivities. Within the network of the Regal Canopy, the main roads in London are divided into lanes for droving, cycling, deer carriages and Parliamentary vegetable allotments. This provides the Food Parliament with greater growing area. The deer pastures, droving routes and docks are maintained by the existing Greater London Authorities.

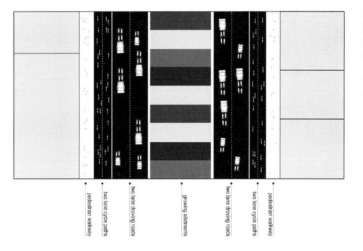

pedestrian walkway | two lane cycle paths | two lane droving roads | growing allotments | two lane droving roads | two lane cycle paths | pedestrian walkway

facing page: A new food network for London, utilizing all the existing parks and decommissioned roads for cultivation of fruits and vegetables.

left: Main roads in London reallocated usage.

10. 'Houses of Parliament' [http://127.0.0.1/HousesofParliament. html], retrieved 1 August 2013

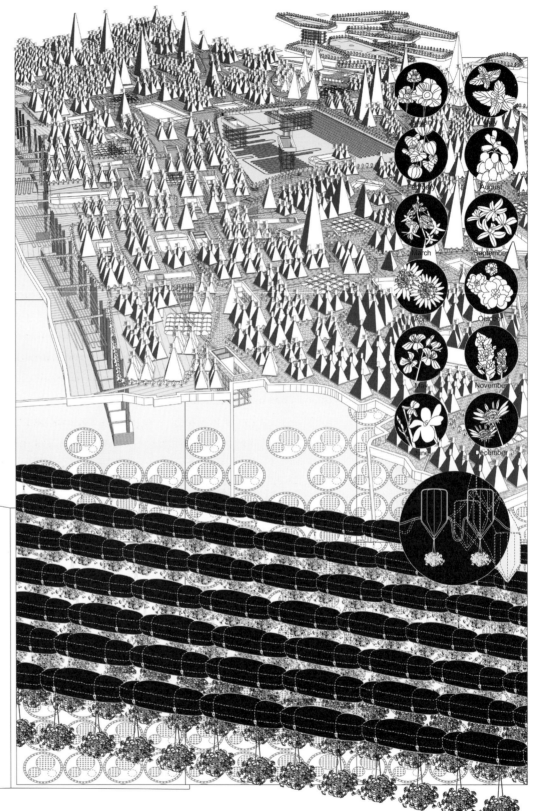

Big Ben

Big Ben

'A clock tower has stood on the site of Parliament since the 13th century and was the position of the first chiming clock in the United Kingdom. Today's Elizabeth Tower signals the passing of time in Westminster and is home to the Great Bell that Londoners have affectionately come to know as "Big Ben".'[11]

261

Parliament has acted as a timekeeper of London for centuries. The new Parliament border, just inside Goose-Guard-Parade, is densely planted. Big Ben assumes the form of a series of inflatable metalized nylon sacks which encircle Westminster Hall supported by a lightweight steel frame. The sacks are inflated with methane gas garnered from the Lord Mayor's anaerobic digesters. Air inflators electronically control and maintain the exact amount of methane gas required for buoyancy. Although methane provides only half the lift of helium it is less prone to leak due to its composition of larger molecules of gas. The buoyant structure is adorned with seasonal flowers. A diverse range of native plants provides a succession of flowers, pollen and nectar throughout the growing season to boost bee populations. Native pollinating bees forage amongst the inviting habitat – vital for varied fruits and vegetables in Parliament. Amongst the varieties Big Ben declares the exact time of year and growing season demonstrated to the city by its alternating colour blooms. Each bloom is picked, pulped and dispensed along London's canals. Seasonally, sequential hues bleed through London, a peal of silent church bells. The canal's changing hues inform the entire city about sowing, growing and harvest seasons. The construction of Big Ben acts as an example of the symbiosis between citizen and the seasonal ecology of the city; each reliant on the workings of the other to construct the phenomena of the 'silent bells' changing the hues of the canal.

facing page: The Components Manual of Big Ben.

11. 'Parliament's Clock Towers' [http://www.Parliament.uk/about/living-heritage/building/palace/big-ben/building-clock-tower/Parliaments-clock-towers/], retrieved 1 August 2013

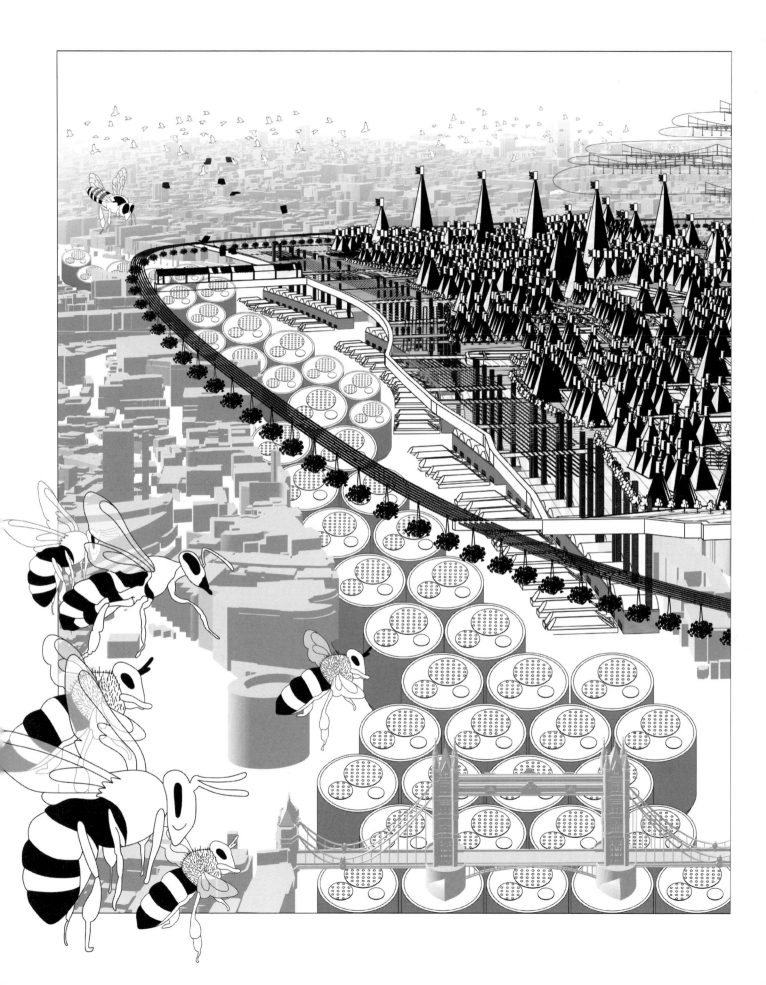

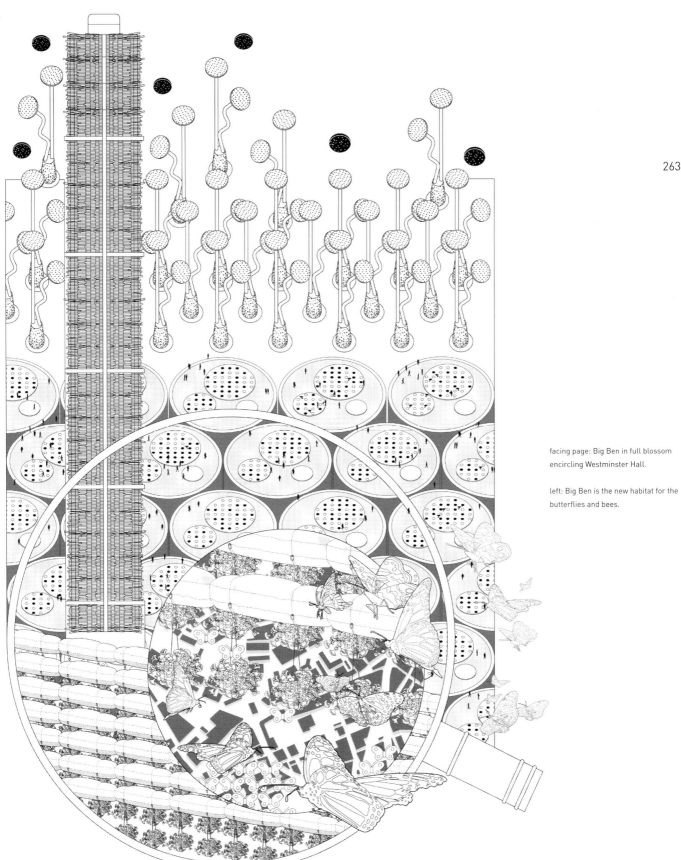

facing page: Big Ben in full blossom
encircling Westminster Hall.

left: Big Ben is the new habitat for the
butterflies and bees.

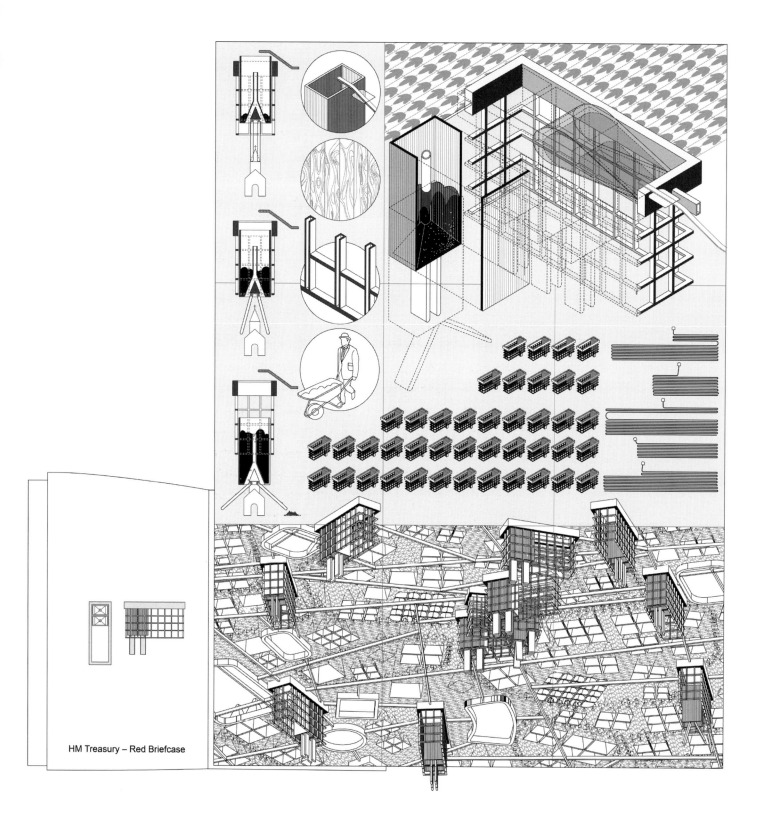

HM Treasury – Red Briefcase

The Red Briefcase

'Whilst all ministers are given a red briefcase, without doubt the Chancellor of the Exchequer's red box is the most famous. The Chancellor's tradition of brandishing the budget in the box has become so famous that today a special scaffold has to be constructed on the steps of Number 11 to enable the hundreds of gathered photographers to capture the iconic scene.'[12]

265

The Red Briefcase takes the form of a series of giant, timber barns (70 x 20 x 50m). Constituent members contribute their time and sort produce delivered from the laboratories of Westminster Hall on an 8km long conveyor belt, located along the southern edge of Parliament. The conveyor belt distributes food to each Red Briefcase situated above every church below Westminster Hall. As each Red Briefcase banks Parliament's new food currency, the timber barns descend toward the church below by overcoming a counterweight balance. The bigger the harvest, the bigger the budget; in the good years the briefcases descend to maximum capacity and surplus food is discharged via an overflow valve to ground level. Food is publicly available at the City's church. During leaner months, the Red Briefcase ascends. Each Briefcase is a physical urban manifestation of food availability. There is no hiding place for a budget deficit or seasonal bonus; all is visible.

facing page: The Components Manual of the Red Briefcase.

12. 'Chancellors Boxing Clever', BBC News [http://news.bbc.co.uk/1/hi/events/budget_98/budget_briefcase/did_you_know/61409.stm], retrieved 1 August 2013

facing page: Anticipating the arrival of the Food Budget. All the crops are harvested, prepared and delivered into the Red Briefcase.

left: A community of cat officers try to keep the rats away from the food filled Red Briefcases.

The Woolsack

'The Lord Speaker in the House of Lords sits on a large square cushion, stuffed with wool and encased in red cloth known as the Woolsack. Dating back from the reign of Edward III, when wool was a precious commodity, the seat is a symbol of the wealth of the United Kingdom.'[13]

269

The Woolsack is an urban scale silver foil cushion for constituents to sit on and debate issues of food legislation. Each cushion is an urban park maintained by an upholsterer. The metalized nylon foil upholstery is inflated with methane gas collected from the Lord Mayor's anaerobic digesters. Multiple film and foil layers are applied with flame retardant coatings, protecting the Woolsack from damage. The multi-layer high strength film integrates UV (ultra violet) light inhibitors and is patched and sealed to make the Woolsack gas tight. Each Woolsack is subject to regular safety inspections enforced by the upholsterer. Constituents can enjoy a picnic and converse about current affairs on the warm cushions all year round.

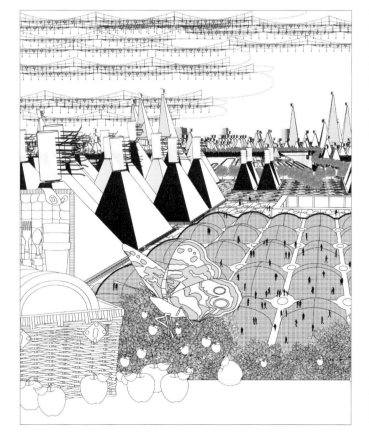

facing page: The temperature regulated Woolsack provides a comforting environment for rest and contemplation. The thermal comfort is supplied by the Department of Health's bakeries and the Lord Mayor.

left: Constituents enjoy picnics and discuss parliamentary matters on the urban scaled Woolsack.

13. 'The Woolsack' [http://www.parliament.uk/site-information/glossary/woolsack/], retrieved 1 August 2013

The Red Lines

'Two red lines are stitched into the carpet between the front benches of the Government and Her Majesty's Opposition in the House of Commons. The lines demarcate a distance two swords length apart, a historical boundary which speaking members are duty bound not to cross in order to maintain order and peace in the notoriously confrontational chamber.'[14]

Party differences are demarcated between rows of apple trees that bear red fruits during the autumn harvest. Each row marks an urban boundary, set out according to the Food Parliament planning guidelines and Smart Standards:

SS 1001: 2010

001 DISTANCE BETWEEN STRUCTURES

01.1   Apple tree and cherry tree rows shall mark a distance between structures in order not to obstruct sunlight and precipitation.

The Red Lines are publicly accessible and local constituents are encouraged to harvest the apples and enjoy the nutritious fruits at their leisure upon the urban Woolsacks.

facing page top: Beekeepers providing a pollination service for maximum levels of apple production.

facing page bottom: Apples are harvested for the making of cider and pies, contributing to the Treasury – the Red Briefcase.

14. 'Churchill and the Commons Chamber' [http://www.Parliament. uk/about/living-heritage/building/ palace/architecture/palacestructure/ churchill/], retrieved 1 August 2013

Ministry of Defense

The Ministry of Defence

'The Ministry of Defence oversees the security, independence and interests of the United Kingdom and its territories abroad. The MoD finances and directs the armed forces.'[15]

The Goose-Guard-Parade is the city's defender of the Food Parliament. Hairpin structures stand approximately 50m tall when stationary on guard along the edge of Westminster Hall. Each hairpin is fabricated from low-density polyurethane memory foam. The polyurethane foam absorbs organic pesticide from a ground level cradle pool, 10m in diameter. Each cradle pool is filled with organic pesticides by a dedicated team of pesticide controllers. The sensory hairpins spin into combat when approached by hostile pests. The revolving motion applies a centrifugal force to the hairpins that quickly mould into whirling armatures, spraying pesticide from their lotus heads. After combat, centripetal force draws each guard under control and the polyurethane memory foam returns to its original hairpin state and absorption capacity.

facing page: The Components Manual of the Ministry of Defence.

left: The Goose Guards resting upright but always on the alert.

following page left: In the line of defence – protecting Queen, Parliament and London's food security.

following page right: The Goose Guards propel themselves up through centrifugal force as they squirt out the pesticides.

15. 'The Ministry of Defence' [https://www.gov.uk/government/ organisations/ministry-of-defence/ about], retrieved 1 August 2013

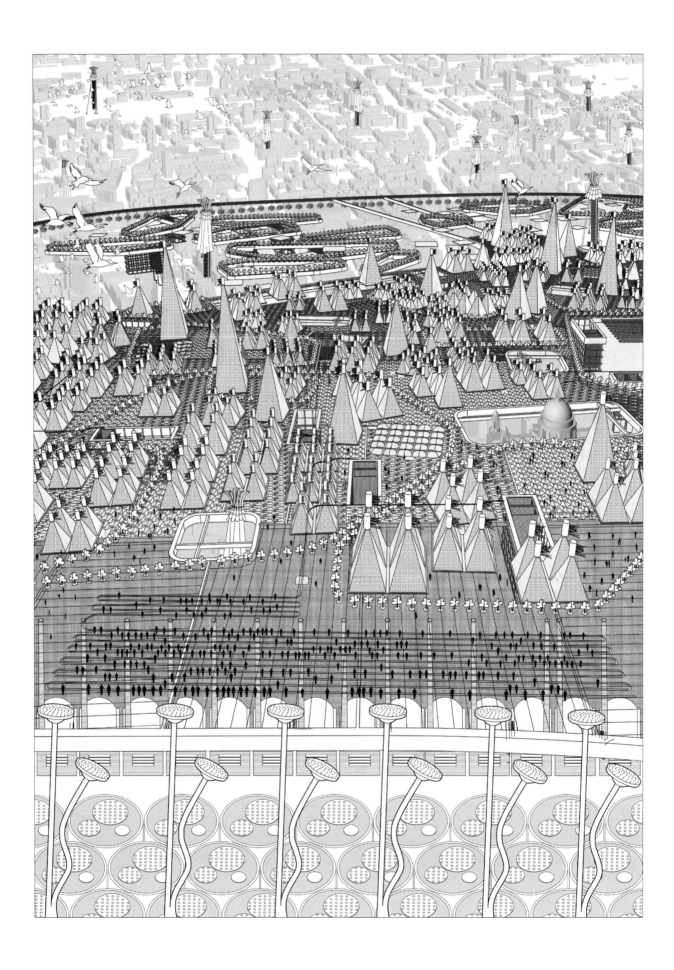

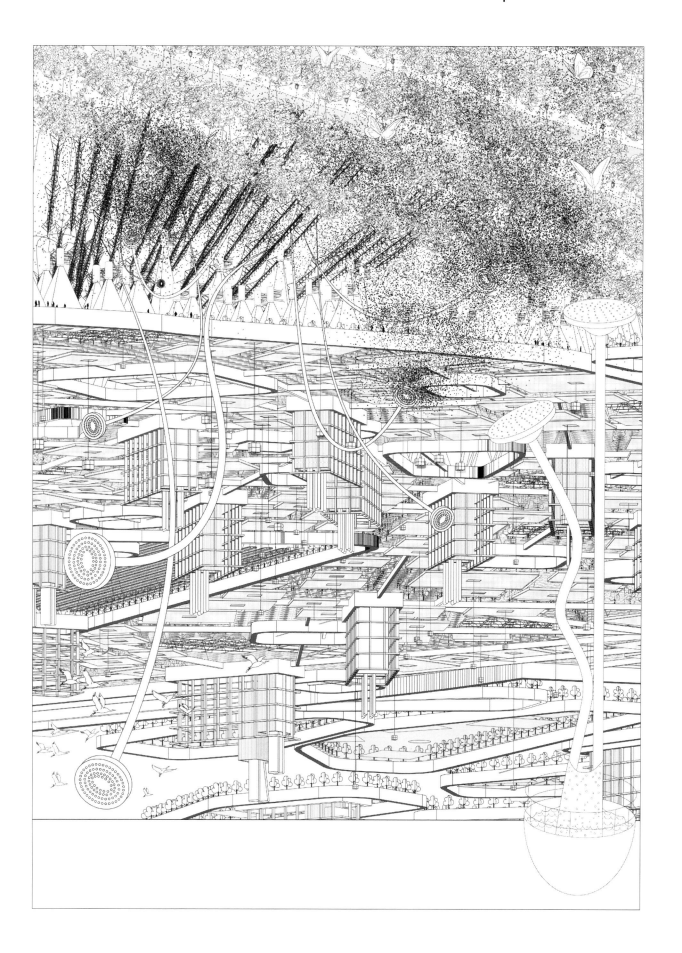

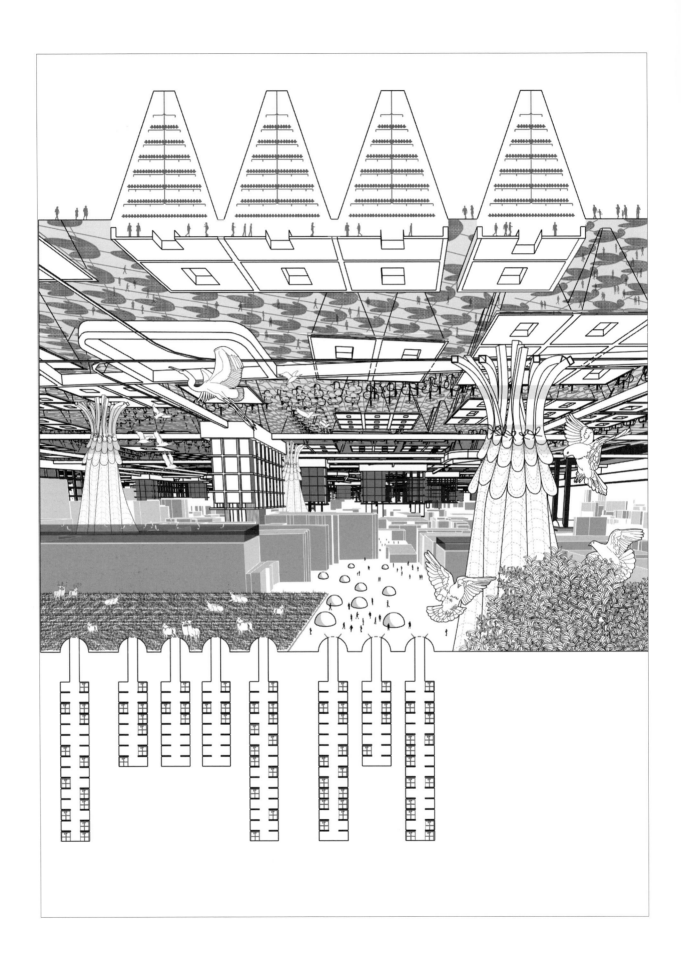

The Parliament Library

'The House of Commons Library provides impartial, non-partisan support and information to Members of Parliament enabling them to make informed decisions which best represent their constituents.'[16]

The Parliament Library is the archive of national security. Buried deep underground, these archives are gargantuan urban refrigerators and freezers, securing the nation's wealth. The dimensions of the stores vary in depth from 20 to 40m in accordance with local ground conditions. Basements of vacant, local building stock are adapted where appropriate. Excavations are reinforced with high-density concrete to reduce water permeability. An application of mastic asphalt is given to the internal surfaces, ensuring a sound waterproofing membrane. An additional protective layer of cement and screed is applied to complete the internal tanking. The entrance to each library is located directly beneath the glasshouse laboratories of Westminster Hall. A librarian, a crane that automatically hauls food between the laboratory and library, is capable of removing and re-shelving the Parliamentary stock and services each library. The stock includes a wealth of recipes, seeds, food and preservation techniques.

277

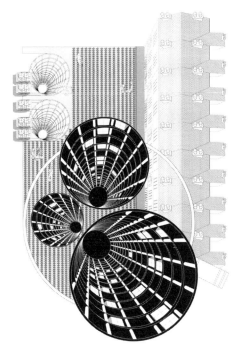

facing page: The Parliament Library archives all the species of plant grown across London.

left: Looking down into the urban food wells.

16. 'The House of Commons Library' [http://www.Parliament.uk/mps-lords-and-offices/offices/commons/commonslibrary/], retrieved 1 August 2013

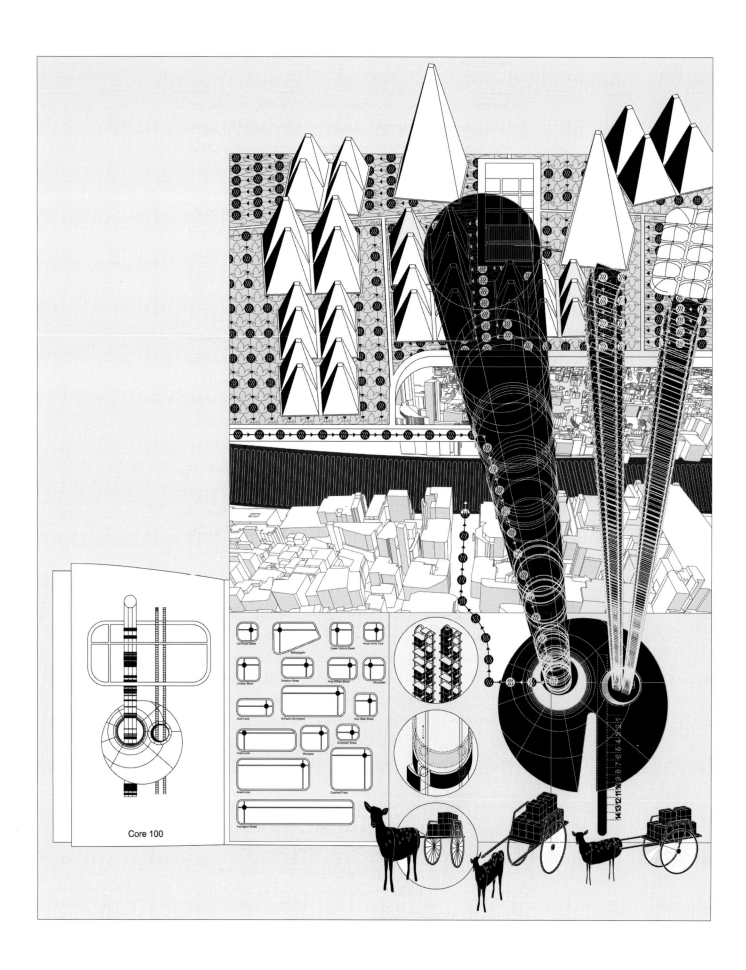

Core 100

The Ministry of Transport

'The Ministry of Transport is responsible for ensuring the smooth passage of people and goods travelling around the United Kingdom. The Ministry plans and funds the upgrading of the country's transport infrastructure.'[17]

The Ministry of Transport has established the Deer Commission for England and Wales (DCEW) to govern the sustainable management of deer and the production of high quality venison. The Commission works together with existing charity-run organizations such as the Deer Initiative (DI) and the British Deer Society (BDS). Stags and yearlings are used as the primary form of transportation, for the public and the provision of services. Transport for London (London's integrated body responsible for the Capital's transport system, TfL) implements a new sustainable policy that replaces all London buses and taxis with deer pulled carriages; zero carbon porters of Parliament and her constituents.

Vehicles are prohibited from using the main droving routes that are solely used by deer carriages, cyclists and pedestrians. Portions of the routes are also used as Parliament allotments. Deer Docking Stations are scattered around greater London. Each Docking Station is a point of pick-up and drop-off as well as a watering hole for the deer.

TfL is responsible for the welfare and the maintenance of the stag and yearling herds that are on carriage duties. All droving routes are maintained and regulated by the governing body to ensure public and deer safety. The efficient management plan for the new droving routes reduces the amount of vehicle traffic and minimizes the amount of Deer Vehicle Collisions (DVCs) in urban areas. Stags and yearlings are exercised regularly, with a typical herd fulfilling carriage duties for a month at a time on a rotational basis.

The Vehicle Restriction Traffic Order (2014) considers vehicular transport an undesirable reality in London. With motor vehicles abolished, land formerly used by cars is re-appropriated for growing food. The Ministry of Transport reduces London's carbon footprint, encouraging the use of eco-friendly forms of transportation – deer carriages, cycling and walking.

279

facing page: The Components Manual of the Ministry of Transport.

following page: The Cores loyally transport continuous food, energy and people between the existing city and the Food Parliament. Deer Docking Stations are located at the base of each Core.

17. 'The Department for Transport' [https://www.gov.uk/government/organisations/department-for-transport], retrieved 1 August 2013

CURRENT UK VENISON INDUSTRY
(Numbers quoted from Ed Dyson, Policy officer of the Deer Initiative 2010 unless otherwise stated)

- The UK produces an estimated 6,500 tonnes of venison (wild & farmed) every year, equivalent to 246,920 deer.

- 95% of this is obtained from wild deer and 5% is farmed.

- With wild deer, around 2/3 is sold to game dealers, 1/3 kept by hunters (either sold or consumed)

- 88.5% of production is Red deer venison and 11.5% Fallow deer.

- An average carcass weight of 54kg and realistic venison yield of 25kg. *(BDFA)*

- The UK exports 70% of their own venison abroad and imports roughly 1000 tonnes of venison from New Zealand every year.

- 8% of the UK currently eat venison. *(link report on venison 2009)*

- UK Dealer price (2010) average £3.55/kg *(taken from 3 wholesale sites)*

- UK Retail price (2010) average £13.00/kg *(taken from 3 major supermarkets)*

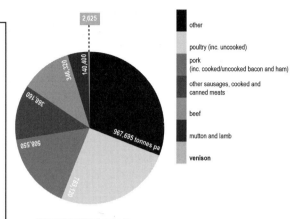

Estimated total UK meat consumption
(DEFRA 2008)

Estimated annual wild deer venison production
(95% of Total UK production of venison)
(95/100) x 6,500 tonnes	= 6173 tonnes
6,173,000/25kg	= 246,920 deer

Estimated annual farmed deer venison production
(5% of Total UK production of venison)
(5/100) x 6,500 tonnes	= 325 tonnes
325,000/25kg	= 13,000 deer

Total maximum UK consumption of venison (inc. imports)
(Total UK venison produced - Maximum venison exported (up to 70%)) + (Total venison imported)
(6500 – 4875 (70/100 x 6500)) + 1000	= 2,625 tonnes
2,625,000/25kg	= 105,000 deer

Total UK consumption of UK produced venison
(Total maximum UK consumption of venison (inc.imports) - imports)
2,635 - 1000	= 1,625 tonnes
1,625,000/25kg	= 65,000 deer

Estimated annual UK consumption of venison per person
(Total UK consumption of venison / 8% of population consume venison)
2,625,000/4,800,000	= 500 grams

Estimated annual London consumption of venison
London accounts for 12.5% of the Total Population
(12.5% of Total maximum UK consumption)
(0.125 x 2,625,000)	= 328 tonnes
328,000/25kg	= 4,934 deer

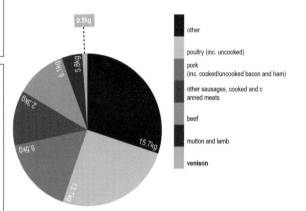

Estimated annual meat consumption per person
(Office for National Statistics 2008)

Total maximum UK Red Deer consumption (inc. imports)
(88.5% of Total Maximum number of deer consumed)
(88.5/100) x 105,000	= 92,925 deer
92,925 x 25kg	= 2,323 tonnes

Total maximum UK Fallow consumption (inc. imports)
(11.5% of Total Maximum number of deer consumed)
(11.5/100) x 105,000	= 12,075 deer
12,075 x 25kg	= 302 tonnes

Total maximum UK Red Deer consumption by UK consumers
(88.5% of Total Maximum number of deer consumed)
(88.5/100) x 65,000	= 57,525 deer
57,525 x 25kg	= 1,438 tonnes

Total maximum UK Fallow consumption by UK consumers
(11.5% of Total Maximum number of deer consumed)
(11.5/100) x 65,000	= 7,475 deer
7,475 x 25	= 187 tonnes

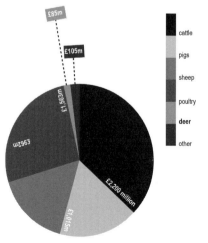

Total UK livestock production income at 2009 prices
(Office for National Statistics 2009)

Roast	Protein	Fat	Calories
Venison	33.5	6.4	207
Beef	26.8	21.3	225
Lamb	20.1	17.9	273
Pork	26.9	26.9	284
Chicken (skinless)	22.6	14.0	216

Nutritional information per 100g for venison compared to other meats
(data obtained from BDFA)

PROPOSED UK VENISON INDUSTRY

- Sustainable Development Committee (SDC) advises cutting weekly current meat consumption of 1kg by at least half to 500g, for healthier and sustainability reasons. The Food Parliament implements a production cap on all meat production.

- It also suggests we cut out all processed meats and meats in high fat (such as pork and beef) by a further half.

- The Parliament promotes eating venison, a healthier and more sustainable alternative. With under 8% of the population currently eating venison, it sets a new target of 50% to achieve by the year 2050.

- Consumers are encouraged to double their yearly intake of venison and only buy UK produce.

- Production increases five times in order to supply new demand.

- Recommended yearly venison consumption, 1.2kg.

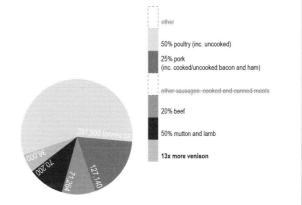

Proposed annual meat consumption per person
(Food Parliament target by 2050)

283

	Current yearly consumption 2008 (kg)	Minimum yearly consumption by 2050 (kg)	Proposed yearly consumption by 2050 (kg)
Other Meat Products	15.7	7.9	-
Poultry (inc. uncooked)	13.1	6.6	6.6
Pork (inc. cooked/uncooked bacon and ham)	8.5	4.3	2.2
Other sausages/cooked and canned meats	6.1	3.1	-
Beef	5.8	2.9	1.2
Mutton and Lamb	2.3	1.2	1.2
VENISON	0.5	0.25	1.2
TOTAL	52	26	12

Table comparing current and proposed annual consumption of venison per person
(data obtained and estimated from the National Food Survey, Office for National Statistics 2010)

Estimated annual UK consumption of venison
((total UK population/2) x Average consumption of venison per person)
30,000,000 x 1.2kg   = **36 million kg**
                        = **36,000 tonnes**
36,000,000/25kg   = **1,440,000 deer**

Estimated annual London consumption of venison
((total London population/2) x Average consumption of venison per person)
3,750,000 x 1.2kg   = **4.5 million kg**
                        = **4,500 tonnes**
4,500,000/25kg   = **180,000 deer**

Greater London herd
1 stag:30 Hinds:28 (93%) yearlings (23 (77%) of which are for venison) and 5 (23%) kept for breeding)

Hinds   = **233,766 hinds**
Stags (number of hinds/30)   = **7,792 stags**
Number of herds   = **7,792 herds**
Calves/Yearlings for breeding (23%)   = **53,766 calves**
Calves/Yearlings for venison (77%)   = **180,000 yearlings**

Max number of deer in Greater London at any time
(number of hinds + number of stags + number of yearlings + number of calves)
233,766 + 7,792 + 180,000 + 53,766   = **475,324 deer**

Inner Borough Herd
Total yearlings/2   = **90,000 yearlings**
Total Stags/2   = **3,896 stags**
Number of herds   = **313 herds**
Total   = **93,896 deer**

Outer Borough Herd
Hinds   = **233,766 hinds**
Total Stags/2   = **3,896 stags**
Number of herds   = **1,271 herds**
Number of outer borough herds   = **5 outer borough herds**
Total yearlings/2   = **90,000 yearlings**
Calves/Yearlings for breeding (23%) = **53,766 calves**
Total   = **381,428 deer**

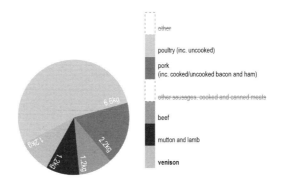

Proposed annual meat consumption per person
(Food Parliament target by 2050)

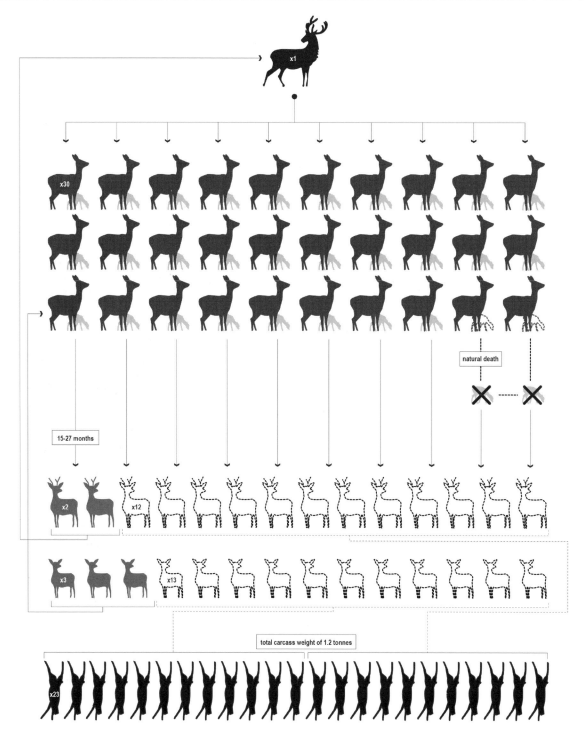

Red Deer Reproduction and Returns Programme
All data quoted from the British Deer Farmers Association (BDFA)

A mature stag (3yrs +) can rut a herd of 30 mature hinds (2.5yrs +) who can give birth to 1 calf per season after a gestation period of 8 months. After 15-17 months, the yearling stags reach their prime stock age for venison. A grass finished yearling stag should weigh about 100-110kg live and provide a carcass weight between 48-60kg. Yearling hinds reach their prime a little later with the maximum age of slaughter at 27 months. From a group of 28 yearlings, the best 2 yearling stags and 3 yearling hinds are retained for breeding herd replacements. The rest of the herd are culled for venison. 23 yearlings produce an estimated total carcass weight of roughly 1.2 tonnes, with an average carcass weighing at 54kg.

Receipts assume pregnancy rate of 100%, death loss of 2 calves out of 30 and 1 stag:1 hind birth ratio
Model based on a study by Penn State College of Agricultural Sciences (2005)

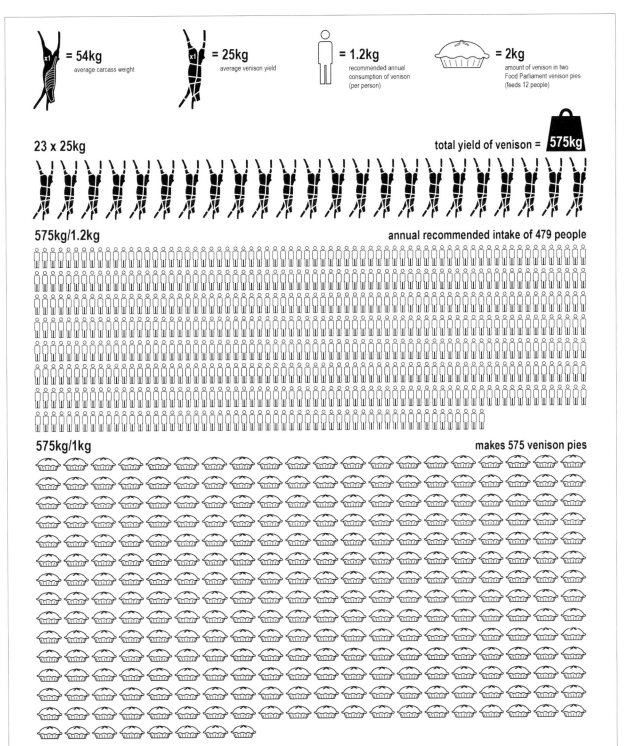

= 54kg
average carcass weight

= 25kg
average venison yield

= 1.2kg
recommended annual
consumption of venison
(per person)

= 2kg
amount of venison in two
Food Parliament venison pies
(feeds 12 people)

23 x 25kg

total yield of venison = 575kg

575kg/1.2kg

annual recommended intake of 479 people

575kg/1kg

makes 575 venison pies

Carcass Returns and Venison Yields
All data quoted from the British Deer Farmers Association (BDFA)

The average sized stag/hind provides an average cold carcass weight of of 54kg. After the carcass is dressed, de-boned and divided into cuts, the average yield of venison from 1 carcass is 25kg. Therefore, 23 yearlings from a herd of 1 stag and 30 hinds produces roughly 525kg of venison. This is equivalent to the annual total recommended intake of venison (recommended by the Food Parliament) for 479 people. It also makes 579 venison pies.

All numbers are estimates

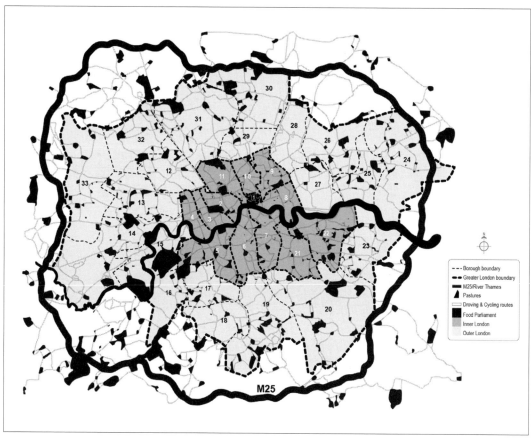

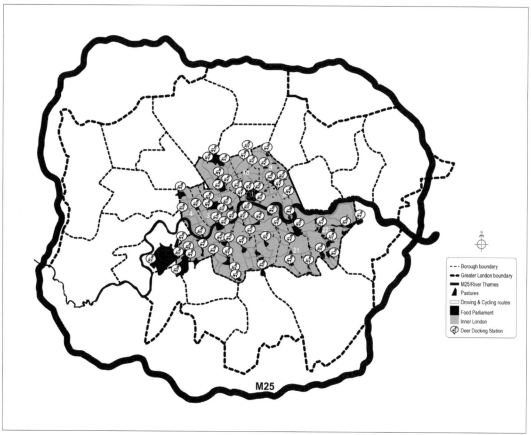

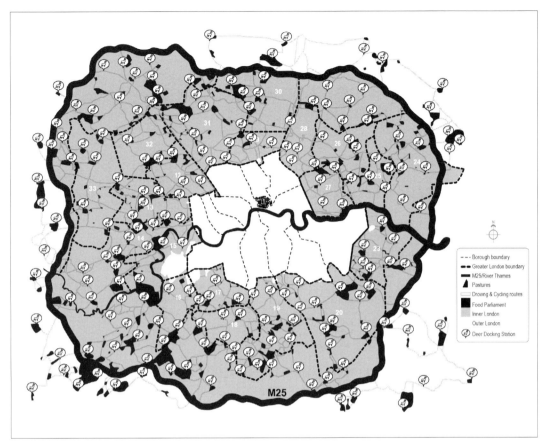

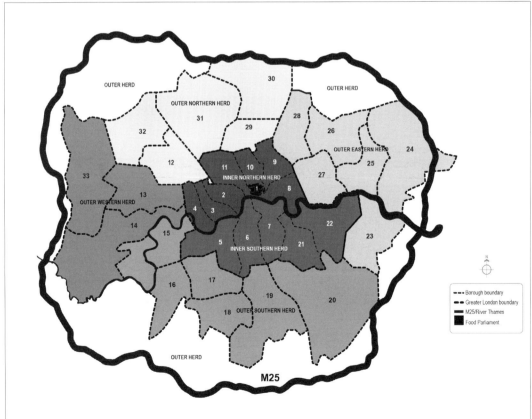

facing page top: Greater London Authorities Deer Parks and Routes. Deer graze in urban pastures and selected existing roads are allocated as droving routes. The droving routes are solely for deer, cyclists and pedestrians. A portion of the route is used as Parliament allotments. Vehicles are prohibited on these roads, reducing vehicle traffic in Greater London.

facing page bottom: Inner London Authorities Deer Parks, Docks and Routes. The inner London herd consists of stags and yearlings. Stags rotationally graze inner London pastures and are permanently used as transportation in and around the Food Parliament along designated deer and cycle routes. Yearlings graze inner pastures for supplementary feeding and are temporarily used as transportation until the culling season. Deer docks are scattered around inner London for pick-up and drop-off purposes.

left top: Outer London Authorities Deer Parks, Docks and Routes. The Outer London herd consists of hinds and their calves that rotationally permanently graze the outer pastures. Half of the stag herd are moved from their Inner London location during the rut season for breeding purposes. Calves remain in Outer London until they reach yearling age, they are then moved into Inner London pastures for supplementary grazing before the culling season.

left bottom: Greater London Herds are divided into two (Inner and Outer London) that are subdivided according to their geographic location for management purposes. Boroughs are allocated a specific number of deer that is proportional to their grazing capacities. Deer graze pastures within their allocated boroughs.

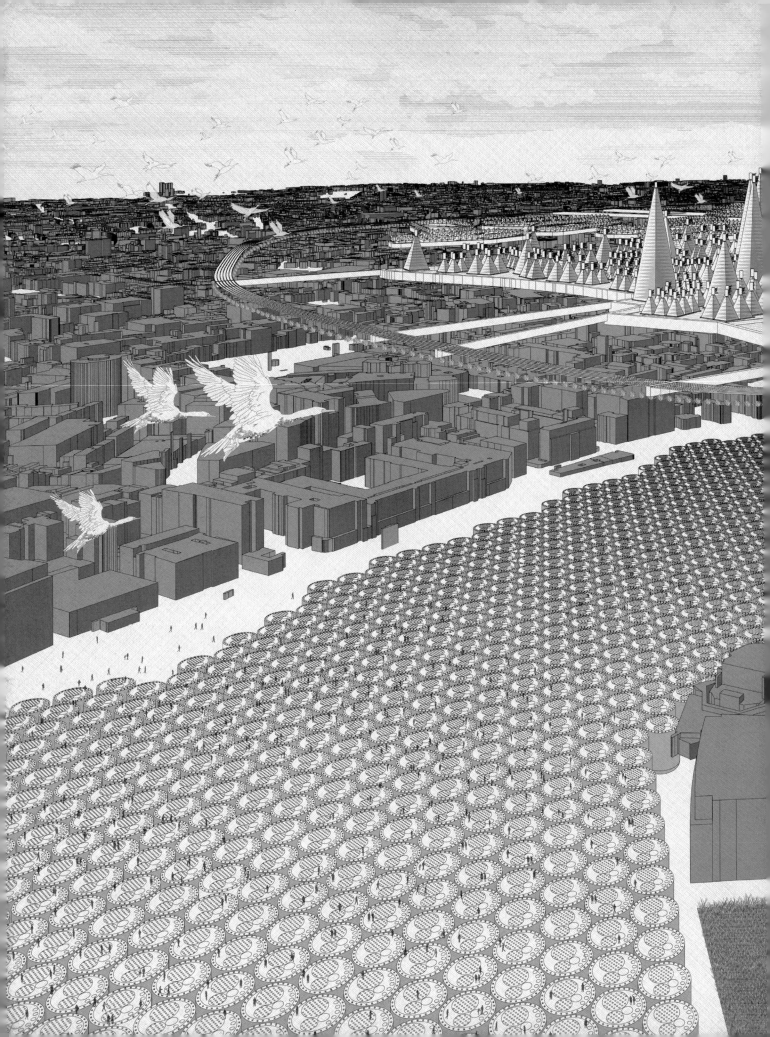

'Sadder than destitution, sadder than a beggar is the man who eats alone in public. Nothing more contradicts the laws of man or beast, for animals always do each other the honor of sharing or disputing each other's food.'

– Jean Baudrillard, French philosopher (1929–2007)

Fertility

Urbanization and agricultural development have evolved together in a symbiotic relationship for over 12,000 years.[1] Before the dawn of agricultural cultivation, it can be argued that there was no such thing as the city. Prior to the Neolithic revolution some ten thousand years ago, hunting and gathering was employed as the only method of food acquisition. Due to the dependence on the natural landscape, societies frequently moved in order to make use of the varied availability of the natural resources that sustained them. To be far from dependable sources of food was to risk malnutrition and starvation and as human beings tracked the animals that formed the basis of their diet, permanent settlements were not a necessary feature of life. Instead, humans had an intimate, nomadic connection to land.

The first urban societies arose in Mesopotamia and Egypt in the Middle East, in the Indus Valley region of modern Pakistan, in the Huang He (Yellow River) Valley of China, on the island of Crete in the Aegean Sea, and parts of Mexico in Central America.[2] Agriculture and urbanism came together for the first time during the ninth century in the ancient Middle East area known as the Fertile Crescent (present day Iran, Turkey, Syria). Major climatic conditions shifted the last Ice Age northwards leaving behind a fertile land rich in new species of digestible plants and vegetables, such as chickpeas, lentils and beans, onions, garlic and leeks, cress, dates, figs and grapes. Climatic change forced the usual diet of large, wild animals northwards and the growing pressures of an expanding population forced people to adopt a new method of obtaining food in the form of agriculture. It was the discovery of grain that produced a food source large enough and sustainable enough to support the first permanent, scattered settlements. Dispersed settlement was an efficient organizational strategy that provided space for food production in the midst of other activities.

Early Sumerian settlements characterized the first period of transition from rural to urban life in ancient Mesopotamia. Jericho is one of the oldest cities in the world, with evidence of human inhabitation dating back to the ninth century BC. Derived from the Hebrew word 'yerah', meaning month or new moon, early inhabitants of the area worshiped the moon god, whom they believed controlled the cycles of the moon and consequently the agricultural seasons. Situated on a narrow plain on the western side of the

facing page: One of the reasons for the ancient Egyptian's success was that they were able to farm the fertile soil around the Nile River to produce their own food. Society did not live in fear of hunger and food security gave the inhabitants power.

1. C Steel, 'Hungry City: How Food Shapes Our Lives', Vintage, 2008, p.11

2. R Guisepi, 'Ancient Civilizations; The Ancient City of Jericho', 2007 [http://history-world.org/ancient_civilization.htm], retrieved 10 December 2010

Jordan Valley, a perennial spring supplied the city with abundant water, making Jericho a productive tropical oasis in ancient times. The city was referred to in the Hebrew Bible as 'The City of Palm Trees', an indication of the extraordinary production of dates the city harvested. Located adjacent to the River Jordan, Jericho was able to feed its inhabitants through both hunting and rigorous foraging of plant life. This gave the settlement and its urban environment a seasonal cycle and access to a fertile rural fringe. The success of this agriculturally hinged approach to food production allowed the community, a mix of urban and rural settlements, to survive for 65,000 years.[3]

Similarly in Uruk, located on the alluvial plain area near the confluence of the unpredictable Tigris and Euphrates Rivers, agriculture led the settlement to establish itself as a large urban agglomeration by the second century BC. At its height, Uruk was estimated to have contained 50,000–80,000 residents living in 6km2 of walled area. It was the largest city in the world at the time and ruled by a semi-mythical king, 'Gilgamesh'. The city lost its prime importance around the third century BC in the context of the struggle for control between the Babylonian and Elam cultures, but remained inhabited throughout the Seleucid and Parthian periods until it was finally abandoned during the Sassanid period shortly before the Islamic conquest of Mesopotamia.[4] By utilizing extensive irrigation techniques to protect a vast area of edible vegetation, the city was able to grow into a large urban centre and build a bureaucratic society. Sumerian cities established the basic ground rules of urban civilization through shaping their natural surroundings.

Food played an important role in controlling how early settlements were governed. Agricultural cultivation became linked with religion and together they controlled the order of early settlements. Cities such as Lagash, Eridu, Kish and Ur located in ancient Mesopotamia around the third century BC were constructed around productive farmland governed by large temples. These cities differed from primitive farming settlements, as they were not composed of family-owned farms, but were encircled by large belts of land. It was believed that the green belts were 'owned' by a local god.[5] Cities organized in this way acted as central food distribution centres defined by religious beliefs. Priests organized clusters of labourers to work the land and provide food for the community around the temple of the local god. The temples, known as 'ziggurats', were large monumental buildings commonly constructed in receding tiers upon a rectangular, oval or square platform. Sun-baked bricks made up the core of the ziggurat with facings of fired bricks addressing the exterior, often glazed in distinctive colours thought to have had astrological significance.[6]

The Mesopotamian ziggurats such as the 'Great Ziggurat of Ur' constructed by 'Ur-Nammu' in the twenty-first century BC were not places for public worship or ceremonies. The pyramidal structures were believed to be dwelling places for the gods, strictly controlled by the priests who were the only members of the society permitted to enter the ziggurats or the rooms at their base. One practical function of the ziggurat was that it provided a high place on which priests could escape rising water that annually inundated the lowlands which, occasionally, flooded for hundreds of miles.[7] The ziggurat also functioned as a place of security. The priest's responsibility to care and attend to the needs of the gods who governed the city made them very powerful members of the Sumerian society.

The seasonal production of crops and grain defined the spiritual and ritual life in these early cities, and the monuments built to accommodate these practices are the lasting remnants of this early urbanization. Numerous temples controlling the commodity of food addressed the needs of early societies and drove the advancement of settlements during the third century BC.

For centuries, religion has reflected the human desire for order as the populace believed it to have its origins in the divine. Food has often featured prominently in the functional interpretations of religion and been used as a type of language that has helped human beings express their basic perceptions of reality.[8] In some cultures, sacred stories have determined rules for the consumption of raw and cooked foods. These rules were intended to reflect underlying notions about the differences between nature and culture, but can also be interpreted as codes for class distinctions. The ancient Hindu 'caste system' is an arrangement of social stratification, communicated primarily through eating. New members are only brought into the caste by birth. Religious purity is attached to the maintenance of social boundaries. 'Brahmans', the highest caste, maintain their purity by avoiding food touched by those of lower castes. In an ancient sacred myth, Brahman created the world by cooking it in sacrifice, thus performing a priestly act.[9] A Brahman's privileged status in society is still enforced by his role as priest, representing where he stands between the gods and rest of the world.

Spiritual space often manifests through the rituals of food. The most holy point in Christian churches is the altar or pulpit where the sacred meal of Christ's body takes place and it is from there that Christians are fed God's word. In Hindu temples, advocators are often separated from images of the deities by a rail from which food is offered to the gods who then also deliver it in return. Domestic eating spaces have also become sacred spaces. Some Hindu and Buddhist homes have shrines that are miniature temples for gods who are fed daily. Many Chinese kitchens contain a shrine to the stove god. These sacred spaces provide a platform through which the human and divine communicate through the medium of food.[10]

Throughout history, dietary laws have sustained spiritual identity in the face of invasion and forced conversions by foreign tribes and religions. Ancient Hebrew laws professed that to be holy in this context was to be completely separated. Israelites were 'clean' because they remained within the bounds of God's order by not mixing with outsiders, their gods or their ways. The Jewish laws defining clean and unclean foods, or 'Kashrut' in Hebrew, more commonly referred to as 'Kosher', regulate which foods may be eaten and how they must be raised, slaughtered and prepared. Jewish food laws specifically regulate eating the meat of four-legged animals. According to the Talmud, Animals that both 'chew the cud' and 'have split hoofs' are clean and fit for consumption. Cattle, sheep, goats, deer and bison are all kosher meats and ritually clean.[11] Animals must be slaughtered according to a specific procedure in order to be considered kosher. Pigs are 'dirty' because their physical characteristics are abnormal according to the way in which the ancient Israelites understood types of animals. Animals that die of natural causes, are found to be diseased at the time of slaughter, or are killed by other animals are all considered unclean. Purity of food and body were used to strengthen the boundaries of Israelite society and religion.[12]

Food customs and dietary laws are found at all stages of community development and vary according to culture or to religious tradition. Societies have always attached symbolic value to different foods. Forced to follow the rhythm of the seasons, the actions of our ancient ancestors whose judgements and characteristics structured civilization itself are repeated through every communal meal we eat together today. Life, death, sacrifice and rebirth have always been the ageless subjects of every religion and lie at

293

3. 'Walking In Their Sandals; Jericho: Location Profile' [http://www. ancientsandals.com/overviews/ jericho.html], retrieved 10 December 2010

4. S Bertman, 'Handbook to Life in Ancient Mesopotamia', Oxford University Press, New York, 2005

5. R Guisepi, 'Ancient Civilizations; The Ancient City of Jericho', 2007 [http:// history-world.org/ancient_civilization. html], retrieved 10 December 2010

6+7. K Kuiper, 'Mesopotamia: The World's Earliest Civilization', Britannica Educational Publishing, New York, 2011, p.143

8–10, 12. CE Norman, 'Food and Religion', 2010 [http://www.enotes. com/food-encyclopedia/religion-food], retrieved 10 December 2011

11. JM Lebeau, 'The Jewish Dietary Laws: Sanctify Life', United Synagogue of America, Department of Youth Activities, New York, 1983

the heart of all ritual feasting. Whether or not we believe in a god or gods, the history of human spiritual belief is inherent in almost every meal we eat.[13]

By the late sixth millennium BC, fully agricultural based cities proliferated as highly productive systems and infrastructures supported expanding populations. Tribes migrated to the Nile River where they developed an agribusiness and a more centralized society. Ancient Egypt was blessed with annual flooding from the Nile and its inhabitants used irrigation techniques to take advantage of the floodwater that delivered nutrients from the Nile riverbed to the flood plains. Power was concentrated in a sacred headman who was believed to be able to control the Nile flooding. The headman's power rested on his reputation as a 'rainmaker king'. The headman, and associated sacred beasts, were held responsible for the course of nature and would also be blamed if there was crop failure.[14] The flooding of the Nile produced surplus grain that was stored and kept to feed the labourers of irrigation schemes and pyramid tombs, prolonging their ability to stay settled. One of the reasons for the ancient Egyptian's success was that they were able to farm the fertile soil around the Nile to produce their own food and cloth. Society did not live in fear of hunger or starvation and they were able to produce materials for shelter. The food security that the city controlled gave its inhabitants power. Food also gave them a vehicle for trade.

The strength of animals was harnessed to wheeled transport and to the plough in ancient Egypt. Simple hand-held digging sticks and hoes had been used in the highly fertile banks of the Nile where the annual flood rejuvenated the soil, creating small ditches where seeds could be sown.[15] An increase in food production became possible as the animal drawn plough enabled an individual to cultivate considerably larger areas of land than before. Wheeled transport, provided by animal husbandry, also meant that the surplus produce could be moved around more conveniently. The introduction of agricultural tools and the use of animal labour led to an increased production in cultivated food and therefore to an increase in population. These changes also led to socio-economic differentiation. The intelligent use of tools and animals in farming led to an efficient use of land. There was no need to employ as many people to work the land as previously, except under conditions of slavery. The majority of small families had an equal supply of food in which the sharing of edible provisions was methodically regulated. The introduction of the plough caused the equality of the ancient agricultural community to transform. The ability of a single labourer to cultivate a much larger area of farmland led to the acquisition of additional land and became a way of creating higher standards of living.[16] Farmers were able to pay additional labourers to work on their land and use the surplus harvest generated to exchange goods from traders.

Governance and Trade
The Inuit are the descendants of the 'Thule' culture, who emerged from western Alaska around the first century AD and spread eastwards across the Arctic region. The unpredictable and unforgiving northern environment forced the Inuit to adapt rapidly to unexpected changes in climatic conditions or face starvation and death. The Inuit developed a practice of food sharing, a form of food distribution where one person caught food and shared it with their entire community. Once hunters brought meat to a camp or village, it was usually delivered in person part or in full to close family in other households, as a sign of respect. Furthermore, Inuit hunters would offer meat to their neighbours, elders, the sick, namesake partners and ritual midwives in the village. Inuit in need of food would often visit a successful hunter to obtain a portion of meat. Food sharing was not only a tradition, but also a way for families to make bonds with one another, which helped to strengthen their communities.

The sea provided a stable diet of food for the Inuit civilization, commonly hunting animals from single-passenger, covered sealskin boats called 'Qajaq' (Kayak), such as walrus, ringed seal, bearded seal, beluga whales, muskoxen, birds (including their eggs) and fish.[17] During the eighteenth century Dutch and French whalers and fisherman groups that had been regular visitors to Strait of Belle Isle and Southern Labrador succeeded in establishing a trade in blubber and furs. Contacts became so frequent that an Inuit-French pidgin language soon developed to strengthen trade links.[18]

295

Cities that had access to the sea grew, as it was possible to import and export from distant shores around the world. In ancient times cities were governed by grain and the harvest that sustained them. It was cheaper and easier to send grain by sea rather than by land in ancient times. Food was difficult to transport over roads that were commonly undeveloped and the food went off very quickly. Small ports such as Lentini in Sicily were in the proximity of grain growing areas that acted as chief markets to larger cities and allowed them to prosper. Grain-laden ships from Italy preferred crossing to Spain from Sicily than from Tuscany owing to the shorter distance, encouraging cities with direct sea links to grow.[19]

The location of mainland ancient Greece and the necessity of importing grain pressured the Greek world to engage in maritime trade. The areas that provisioned Greece with a sustained food supply were Cyrenaica in present day Libya, Egypt, the coastal areas of Southern Italy on the Tarentine Gulf, and regions surrounding the Black Sea. The cities of Athens in the Attica periphery, and Corinth in the Peloponnese region of Greece served as posts of trade and exchange for the isles of the Aegean Sea. Aside from the imported foodstuffs such as grain, products included metals, fabrics, spices, papyrus and shipbuilding materials such as wood and linen. Greek cities exported wine, pottery and olive oil.[20] The Athenians sold marble extracted from the Penteli Mountains surrounding the capital city together with silver coins, known for their acute artisanship and high content of precious silver. The exported coins served not only as a means of exchange, but also as a source of metal, allowing them to still be used as a medium of currency in cities that did not use money as they could be melted back into silver.[21]

Cities shaped their surroundings through their desire for food. Athens and Rome were expanding capitals during the seventh century BC and conquests of territory became paramount in order to secure a food reserve and sustain their civilizations. A growing population required an augmented food supply that the people could depend on. Political allegiances were made with strategic neighbouring states such as Cyprus and Egypt by the ancient Greeks to not only bring political protection but access to their natural grain assets. Vital trade supply routes were defended and strategically secured even in times of peace to protect their food supplies. Athens exerted its influence to protect the narrow straits of the Bosphorus, part of the boundary between Europe and Asia, in times of war with a specific military force.[22] Elsewhere, the Roman conquest of Carthage gave the Empire its third most important city in the first century BC. Healthy grain cultivation in the nearby Tunisian mountains gave Carthage a secure food supply that the Romans demanded.

Land has always been a possession that everyone has valued. The ability to own and control a commodity capable of producing food was of great importance and needed protecting. The feudal system offered

13. C Steel, 'Hungry City: How Food Shapes Our Lives', Vintage, London, 2008, p.211

14. JG Frazer, 'The Golden Bough: A Study in Magic and Religion', Wordsworth Editions, Ware, 1998, p.48

15. BR Johnston et al., 'Water, Cultural Diversity, and Global Environmental Change: Emerging trends, sustainable futures?', UNESCO, Springer, 2011, p.13

16. J Goody, 'Civilization and Food', 2010 [http://www.answers.com/topic/civilization-and-food], retrieved 10 December 2010

17. N Kishigami, 'Contemporary Inuit Food Sharing: A Case Study from Akulivik, PQ. Canada', 2004 [http://www.minpaku.ac.jp/staff/kishigami/040522.pdf], retrieved 10 December 2010

18. PR Magocsi, 'Encyclopedia of Canada's Peoples', University of Toronto Press, 1999, p.49

19. CR Wright, 'Grain Trade in the Mediterranean', 1999 [http://www.cliffordawright.com/caw/food/entries/display.php/topic_id/25/id/8/], retrieved 10 December 2010,

20. MD Coogan, 'The Oxford History of the Biblical World', Oxford University Press, New York, 1998, p.122

21. MD Coogan, 'The Oxford History of the Biblical World', Oxford University Press, New York, 1998, p.327

22. C Steel, 'Hungry City: How Food Shapes Our Lives', Vintage, London, 2008, p.72

the safeguarding of land for lords in medieval Western Europe during the tenth century. The land management system typically gave control to large areas of farmland around villages of towns to the noblemen while peasants were forced to cultivate all year long. Local peasants farmed the land to provide food to a person higher up on the feudal pyramid who in turn commonly rewarded them with protection in times of conflict. Land ownership became a prerequisite of power.

With the passage of time the feudal system became complex and open to abuse. An alternative currency began to replace the original simple obligation of providing food, and eventually the system in Medieval Europe dissolved, unable to cope with the growing demands of providing for an expanding population. People needing physical protection from lawless nobles began to gravitate together from isolated and dispersed villages toward walled population centres. Throughout Europe, rural communes started to emerge offering a new sanctuary in an agriculturally based, Christian configuration. Communes were self-sufficient communities that had an intimate involvement with their rural hinterlands.[23] The gravitation of communities frequently arose more from a need to collaborate and manage the agricultural land than purely out of defensive needs. Rural communes such as Siena and San Gimignano in Tuscany grew large and developed into fully fledged city-states.

Agriculture has played a defining role in the historical cause of much conflict and dispute over land ownership throughout the centuries. Land reform programmes designed to redistribute possession and the use of geographic land is one characteristic of the strategic role agricultural potential has on the development of our communities.

Evidence of land reform began in ancient Greece during the second century BC. A governing tribe or clan owned land in ancient Greece. Small agricultural plots were allocated according to family size and soil fertility intended for individualized sustainable food production that were purposely too small for any monetary prosperity. The programme of land reform was aimed at creating a social class of free peasants.[24] Land reform signalled the ambition of a society in which Greeks were equals that could individually support themselves as opposed to working for the affluent. Land reform in Greece developed many strong city communities as a result of agricultural value.

A feudal period existed during the first century BC in ancient China. Evidence of a strong political system with a genuine feudal order occurred in the eastern Zhou Dynasty. Formal oaths of allegiance to Chinese rulers were exchanged for land and permission to obtain revenues and service from farmers. In return, farmers pledged a loyalty to the monarch and sent tribute to the capital. In a similar situation to European feudalism all the land of the dynasty was owned by a king who in turn gave further divisions to heads of state in a hierarchical pyramid. Titles of governance were even adopted in a virtually identical manner to their European counterparts.

Feudalism in China commonly adopted the well-field system, a land distribution method that divided a plot of land into a grid of nine squares that shared produce between the individual and the government. Eight surrounding outer segments were allocated for private consumption whilst the central segment was reserved for communal or public assignment, which was usually paid to the king as tribute. Private ownership was repeatedly abolished in China, perceived as an individualistic, exploitative mode of production. However, redistribution of land into multiple segments or 'Noodle-strip farms' saw a loss to the Chinese economy due to land degeneration, despite an initial increase in productivity.[25]

Historically, the ambitions of land reform have been to reduce poverty by expanding agrarian development or to return land to a previous owner. The outcomes of land reform can be a consequence of social and economic requirements. History has shown that ethnic or racial division can also drive agrarian reform, manipulated by political inclination, rather than by any desire to allocate land fairly. Land continue to be a contentious issue, and will always be a store of value and wealth for individuals and cities.

Agriculture in England went through a period of change to cater for an increased demand for food caused by a rapidly growing population in the eighteenth century. The Napoleonic Wars caused unrest through Europe. Napoleon's Continental System prevented all trade, consequently forcing England to increase its food production or face a threat of starvation. The price of food rose rapidly throughout the country, increasing profitability and encouraging an expansion of agricultural production. Small villages that had previously been self-sufficient began to look at producing food for a wider market. Changes ensued and a new capitalist business ethic encouraged farmers throughout England to grow new crops such as potatoes, red clover and turnips for the first time. Food production encouraged farmers and communities to become more confident in self-sufficiency. Settlements and the hinterlands of local population areas thus extended, allowing more farmers to produce for the market.

Garden Cities

The 'Little Ice Age' was a period between the thirteenth and sixteenth centuries during which Europe and North America were subjected to cold winters.[26] Around this time communities of farmers began to experiment with new agricultural methods in order to adapt to increasingly unpredictable climate changes. Large flooded areas of the Netherlands, England and other countries around the North Sea were reclaimed from subsequently raised sea levels. The Dutch possessed sufficient technological expertise and a competent degree of organization to diffuse the worst effects of short-term climatic variations. Significant land area was gained through land reclamation and preservation through an elaborate system of 'polders' and 'dikes', constructed throughout the country to hold back and regulate water levels. 'Wind-pumping' windmills were used to reclaim areas of low-lying land in the Zuiderzee Bay area, north of Amsterdam. Huge areas were drained and reclaimed primarily for agricultural use in the form of 'polders'. These rescued, man-made 'gardens' were commonly rectilinear in aspect and connected via an efficient network of canals that hastily delivered food from vast fields to the cities. The floods might have imposed more benefits than costs on Dutch society. Extensive land reclamation for farming and horticulture with the use of new mechanical technology, as well as the intensive exploitation of agricultural resources such as peat turned liabilities into assets so powerful that they helped to forge the first modern agronomy in Europe.

Agriculture and reclamation technologies as well as other mechanical techniques were introduced in Britain, notably in East Anglia, allowing new cities to emerge during the seventeenth century. Villages, such as Whittlesey and March, thrived after draining excavations allowed land surrounding them to be cultivated for prosperous trade. The Fen reclamations created a uniquely organic land that became dedicated to pastoral farming, such as that of cattle and sheep, as well as fishing, fowling and the harvesting of reeds and sedge for thatch. Through the farming of food, the Fens stood as a productive 'garden' and flourished as a sustainable community, in contrast to the rest of southern England which

297

23. C Steel, 'Hungry City: How Food Shapes Our Lives', Vintage, London, 2008, p.22

24. MD Coogan, 'The Oxford History of the Biblical World', Oxford University Press, New York, 1998, p.92

25. L Beehner, 'Land Reform Revisited', 2005 [http://www.cfr.org/forests-and-land-management/land-reform-revisited/p9475], retrieved 10 December 2010

26. J Oosthoek, 'Environmental History Resources', 2010 [http://www.ehresources.org/timeline/timeline_lia.html], retrieved 10 December 2010

was primarily an arable agricultural region. This legacy continues today and an estimated 4,000 farms involved in agriculture and horticulture in the Fens produce 37% of all vegetables grown in the open, and 24% of all the potatoes grown in the UK.[27] The Fens are the only place that English Mustard is still grown for 'Colman's of Norwich'.

During the nineteenth century, English industrial cities such as Birmingham, Leeds, Liverpool, Manchester and Sheffield had come to simultaneously represent both the accomplishment of the economic progress in the country and the tangible reflection of the social and environmental consequences. Already by 1801, 20% of the population of England and Wales lived in towns with more than five thousand inhabitants, and by 1851 the proportion had grown to 54%, rising to 72% by 1891.[28] The population was growing rapidly and the largest cities and towns were attracting a great proportion of the increase, both by immigration and natural increase. Local government structure was ill equipped and unwilling to regulate a massive urban expansion. National concern for public health arose following the widespread cholera epidemics of 1831–1834, which had claimed 114,000 victims.[29] The relationship between disease and polluted water supplies, arising from the lack of sewage and waste disposal facilities and burial practices, particularly due to overcrowding called for a comprehensive social and political reform.

Robert Owen, amongst other socialist reformers such as Karl Marx and William Morris, helped to provide an inspiration for a utopian approach to urban planning in the late nineteenth century as a reaction to Victorian industrialization. Ebenezer Howard's concept of the 'Garden City' offered a comprehensive vision of social and political reform involving the gradual transformation of existing concentrated cities into a decentralized but closely interrelated network of garden cities.[30] The 'Garden City' was proposed to address the problems of the contemporary metropolis with such coherence that its appeal won the financial backing of supporters such as Lord Leverhulme, Joseph Rowntree and the Cadbury family. Once the Garden City grew to a specific size, development was to stop and a new Garden City was to be established that linked to other cities via canals and tramways. Together they would form a cluster of self-sufficient, ecologically concerned settlements, collectively termed the 'social city'.

The fundamental elements in Howard's city manifesto were a careful balance in jobs and housing to avoid local unemployment and inward or outward commuting. Cities were required to be of a defined proportion that meant they would be self-contained, capable of hosting all the functions needed for a city without being dependent on a larger municipality for their survival.[31] The Garden City was formulated as a self-sufficient system in terms of food supply and energy production, inherently standing as a significant precursor to the idea of environmental self-sufficiency that had come to emerge later in the nineteenth century. Howard wanted to achieve a balance between an urban way of life and a rural setting, which led to an approach towards town planning designed to give an impression of being in the countryside whilst still being inside a town.[32]

The first Garden City was designed by the architects Barry Parker and Raymond Unwin on 3,818 acres of land at Letchworth, Hertfordshire, in England at the beginning of the twentieth century. Letchworth gave architectural expression to Ebenezer Howard's concept. The project was financed through a system that Howard called 'Rate-Rent', which combined financing for community services (rates) with a return for those who had invested in the development of the city (rent).[33] Appropriate to the rural ideals, only one tree was felled during the entire initial construction phase of the city, and an area devoted to agriculture surrounding the city was included in the plan; the first 'Green Belt'.

By the early twentieth century the cost of building houses for farm workers was high in England, as low wages made it uneconomical to build. The problem was derived from the restrictive byelaws that allowed only expensive materials such as brick and stone to be used in the construction of homesteads in the provincial districts of the realm. This was one of the factors leading to a mass exodus of farm workers from the country to the urbanized city, resulting in a subsequent lack of labour in the rural hinterlands of the country.

In an attempt to find a solution, John Strachey, editor of 'The Spectator' and owner of 'Country Gentleman Land & Water Magazine', wrote an article, starting a campaign for 'a £150 Cottage' which would use cheaper building materials and could be let to a rural labourer for an affordable £8 a year.[34] He proposed a competition where entrants could display examples of cottages free from the restrictions of the byelaws, which could utilize innovative new building methods and materials. In 1905 the 'Cheap Cottages Exhibition' was held in Letchworth Garden City. The event attracted some 60,000 visitors and later had a significant effect on planning and urban design in the UK, pioneering and popularizing such concepts as pre-fabrication, the use of new building materials, and front and back gardens.[35]

The Modern Movement of the early twentieth century was positive about new technology and encouraged buildings and cities to be designed and constructed in ways that embraced industrial design, mass production and high-speed transport. The Garden Cities Movement took a reactionary position against industrialization.[36] The success of Letchworth Garden City inspired a style of housing and residential street layout that influenced the design of Britain's vast interwar suburbs in the 1920s and 30s. 'Hampstead Garden Suburb', founded in 1907 by Henrietta Barnett in North London, became the first of countless similar developments that steadily receded from Ebenezer Howard's original vision.

The many separate elements of the Garden City idea are still embodied in the emerging environmental and social agendas of Western society in the early twenty-first century. The desire for small town living and working and a devotion to a new 'green' lifestyle coupled with the progressive rejection of the current way of life in the city, represent widely shared social values.

27. V Gerrard, 'The Story of the Fens', Robert Hale Ltd., London, 2003, p.167

28. M Miller, 'Letchworth: The First Garden City', Phillimore & Co. Ltd., 2002, p.1

29. M Miller, 'Letchworth: The First Garden City', Phillimore & Co. Ltd., 2002, p.2

30. S Ward, 'The Garden City: Past, Present, and Future', Routledge, London, 1992, p.2

31+32. A Alexander, 'British New Towns', Routledge, London, 2009, p.22

33. E Howard, 'To-morrow: A Peaceful Path to Real Reform', Cambridge University Press, 2010, p.29

34. F Dean, ' Postcard of the Cheap Cottages Exhibition', 2010 [http://www.gardencitymuseum.org/node/958/lightbox2], retrieved 10 December,

35. M Miller, 'Letchworth: The First Garden City', Phillimore & Co. Ltd., 2002, p.16

36. A Alexander, 'British New Towns', Routledge, London, 2009, p.22

Research and Reproduction Credits

Research Credits

Food and the City (2010–2013)
research team: CJ Lim with Thandi Loewenson, Alex Gazetas, Ned Scott, Dean Walker

The Food Parliament (London, 2011–2013)
research design team: CJ Lim with Martin Tang, Pascal Bronner, Jen Wang, Geraldine Ng, Barry Cho
consultant: Techniker (structural engineers); Fulcrum Consulting (environmental + sustainability engineers) Andy Ford; Centre for Advance Spatial Analysis (CASA,The Bartlett, UCL)
Total Area: 3.15km2 (2,319.43km2 including the Regal Canopy)

The research is supported by ADAPTr, Marie Curie Research Fellowship and the Architecture Research Fund, The Bartlett, UCL.

Reproduction Credits

Index

Note: Page numbers in bold denote an image

301

302

304